ARCHAEOLOGY IN
BRITAIN
SINCE 1945
NEW DIRECTIONS

EDITED BY IAN LONGWORTH AND JOHN CHERRY

with contributions by
NICK ASHTON, JOHN CHERRY, JOHN HURST,
IAN LONGWORTH, TIMOTHY POTTER,
VALERY RIGBY, LESLIE WEBSTER

with line illustrations by
SIMON JAMES

Published for the Trustees of the British Museum by
British Museum Publications

© 1986 The Trustees of the British Museum

2nd impression 1988

Published by British Museum Publications
46 Bloomsbury Street, London WC1B 3QQ

Designed by Harry Green

Set in Monophoto Photina
Printed and bound in Great Britain by
Biddles Ltd, Guildford and King's Lynn

Frontispiece
Lindow Man, found in 1984 in a Cheshire
bog by a peat-cutting machine, which
sliced him through the waist and destroyed
much of the lower half of his body. Naked
but for a fur arm-band, he had been felled
by blows on the head, garrotted and had
had his throat cut before being dumped in
a shallow pool in the bog. This was no
ordinary death, and the bog was not a
normal burial ground: it seems likely that
Lindow Man was the victim of a ritual
sacrifice, *c.* 300 BC.

Contents

Photographic acknowledgements

The photographs were acquired from the individuals and institutions listed below. The authors and publishers would like to thank the copyright holders for permission to reproduce them.

Ashmolean Museum, Oxford 107
Grenville Astill 85
H. Atkinson FRPS 88
R.N.E. Barton 3
British Library, London 105 (Cotton MS Augustus 1.20,21)
British Museum 4 (courtesy of R.N.E. Barton, who provided the material), 11, 15–17, 23, 24, 34, 37–39, 42, 43, 45, 48, 50, 58, 59, 63
Buckinghamshire Record Office 126
Cambridge University Collection of Air Photographs (Copyright reserved) 46, 54, 93, 117, 130, 133
Carlisle Archaeological Unit 47
Professor J.M. Coles 7
Crown copyright reserved 70 (photo J.K. St Joseph), 100, 111
Professor Barry Cunliffe 62
Durham University, Department of Archaeology 82
English Heritage 40
A. Fleming 26
Giraudon 96 (by permission of the town of Bayeux)

Hunterian Museum, University of Glasgow 51
Medieval Village Research Group 118, 119, 122, 129
R.G. Mercer 6
John Mills Photography Ltd 102
National Monuments Record 70
Norfolk Archaeological Unit 66 (photo D. Wicks), 97 (photo D.A. Edwards)
Pilkington Bros Ltd 81
Dr F. Pryor 12, 13
P.A. Rahtz 68
Dr A. Ritchie 20
Royal Archaeological Institute 71–3 (drawings by Simon James)
Society of Antiquaries of London 109
Sutton Hoo Research Trust 69 (photo Nigel Macbeth)
University of Southampton, Department of Archaeology 114
Wakefield Metropolitan District Council 99a
York Archaeological Trust 76

The front cover illustration is reproduced by courtesy of Colin and Janet Bord.

The line drawings are by Simon James, with the exception of 87, 112a and b (by Jim Farrant) and 79 (by Karen Hughes).

Foreword

Towards the end of the Second World War an *ad hoc* meeting of some 280 archaeologists held at the Institute of Archaeology drew up a plan for the future of the subject in Britain. Many of the scholars were young, all were enthusiastic and in many ways far-seeing, but their greatest aspirations have been far exceeded by the energy and opportunities which have transformed our knowledge of Britain's past since the end of the War. Technical innovations, particularly in co-operation with natural scientists, have introduced methods of dating and analysis – of which the most dramatic is undoubtedly the radiocarbon technique. These methods allow the dating of prehistoric periods within narrow margins and have revolutionised, not only our knowledge, but also our understanding of the past. Improved techniques of prospecting and excavation have enabled scholars to reveal the past with greater confidence and greater clarity. Town excavation, the examination of vast areas by total excavation, a willingness to use archaeological techniques on historical sites, a responsible attitude to publication and a greater public awareness of the potential of the past have widened and illuminated our vision of this country's history.

Resources – although never enough – have been made more freely available, particularly as the result of the crusading zeal of the founders of the Rescue movement. There has been an explosion in the number of students and in the production of trained archaeologists. There were three – perhaps four – university departments concerned with British archaeology in 1950. Only two (Cambridge and Edinburgh) produced first degree graduates in the subject; now there are over twenty departments. Government money for rescue archaeology has increased by leaps and bounds from £400,000 in 1970 to £5.7m in 1986–7. Research excavation is more selective and better funded and co-operation with natural scientists is now a *sine qua non* of any archaeological project, from initial survey to final analysis of finds and of soils.

This book portrays some of the developments of the last forty years. It is based on the work of scholars throughout the country and, although published by the British Museum, is a celebration of a national achievement in the understanding of the past. Its contents draw on the work, knowledge and expertise of a large number of scholars from universities and museums, from the private sector and official bodies. The Museum is grateful for their co-operation, not least that of John Hurst, who has contributed to the text itself. In 1932 two members of the staff of the British Museum wrote a similar survey, *Archaeology in England and Wales 1914–1931*; to measure the achievement of archaeologists over the last half century compare Tom Kendrick's and Christopher Hawkes's work of 1932 with that presented here.

We show here only a segment of British archaeological endeavour. British archaeologists are active throughout the world, from Thailand to Belize. Archaeologists trained in Britain are to be met with in many countries at all levels of seniority. There influence is, however, based almost in its entirety on training in excavation and museum activity at home. This book is not then merely a chauvinistic celebration of past achievements, it is a portrait of one aspect of the work of the archaeological community of this country.

D.M. WILSON
April 1986

The Contributors

NICK ASHTON is a Research Assistant in the Department of Prehistoric and Romano-British Antiquities in the British Museum. His current research is on the Middle Palaeolithic industries of France.

JOHN CHERRY is Deputy Keeper of Medieval and Later Antiquities in the British Museum. He has excavated the site of the Longton Hall porcelain factory and is particularly interested in the archaeological evidence for medieval crafts and industries.

JOHN G. HURST is Assistant Chief Inspector of Ancient Monuments in English Heritage. In 1952 he was a founder member of the Medieval Village Research Group and the Wharram Research Project. His main interests are medieval and rural settlement and pottery.

DR IAN LONGWORTH is Keeper of Prehistoric and Romano-British Antiquities in the British Museum and a Vice President of the Society of Antiquaries of London.

DR TIMOTHY POTTER is Assistant Keeper in charge of Roman Britain in the British Museum. He has excavated extensively in Britain, Italy and North Africa and is the author of six books on the Roman archaeology of these countries.

VALERIE RIGBY is a Research Assistant in the Iron Age Section of the Department of Prehistoric and Romano-British Antiquities in the British Museum. She has excavated at numerous Prehistoric and Roman sites. Her primary specialist interest is the Early Roman Gallo-Belgic pottery industry.

LESLIE WEBSTER is Deputy Keeper of Medieval and Later Antiquities in the British Museum. Mrs Webster excavated in the Anglo-Saxon cemetery at Broadstairs and has written on various aspects of Anglo-Saxon art and archaeology.

Acknowledgements

The authors are grateful to all those who have helped in the preparation of this book. In particular they would like to thank Grenville Astill, Guy Beresford, Maurice Beresford, Martin Biddle and Birthe Kjølbye-Biddle, Victor Bowley, Martin Carver, Jenny Chattington, Marjorie Caygill, Henry Cleere, Jonathan Coad, Brian Davison, Derek Edwards, James Graham-Campbell, Patrick Greene, Catherine Hills, Susan Hirst, Ralph Jackson, Simon James, Catherine Johns, Pamela Judkins, Derek Keene, Tony King, Ian Kinnes, Judy Medrington, David Miles, Sarah Muldoon, Hilary Murray, Dennis Mynard, Ken Penn, Richard Porter, Jenny Price, Philip Rahtz, Warwick Rodwell, Kenneth St Joseph, Peter Salway, Ron Shoesmith, Ian Stead, Gillian Varndell, Susan Youngs and Robert Zeepfat.

Introduction

This book has been written for the general reader who may wish to go beyond the rich but haphazard diet of archaeology on television and understand something of the intellectual background to today's profession. Its purpose is to review, albeit in summary form, some of the major contributions to our understanding of man's long social history which have been made since the Second World War. In so doing the book will provide a useful introduction for students of the subject and, with these in mind, a select but comprehensive bibliography has been added. The work is concerned primarily with the archaeology of England, Scotland and Wales and ranges over a time-span from earliest prehistory through to around AD 1700.

In Britain the last forty years have witnessed an explosive expansion in archaeological interest. Spurred on by the realisation that much of our common past was being actively destroyed by a combination of urban renewal, motorway construction, deep ploughing and the extraction of stone and mineral resources, this period has seen a major injection of funding in support of active fieldwork and research at all levels. This has led to a massive increase both in the number of sites discovered and in the information recovered from them, but the very speed of this advance has created new problems, and the sheer quantity of new techniques and new forms of analysis, often borrowed from other disciplines, has tended to promote a highly fragmented view of the past. The interpretation and synthesis of these disparate strands become ever more difficult and laborious and in many areas remain still to be achieved.

In all periods the enhanced recovery of environmental data has provided an opportunity for the archaeologist as never before to recreate the living landscape and assess the effects of man upon that landscape. Techniques of open area excavation and a new-found ability to recover and interpret the often exiguous traces of timber and lightly built stone structures have transformed our knowledge of dwellings from the simplest huts to the greatest of halls. The scale on which these can now be recognised owes much to aerial photography and with this has gone a greater appreciation of sites in their natural settings. As Beresford and St Joseph have aptly put it, 'distance lends elucidation as well as enchantment to the view', and in the later periods landscape studies have stimulated archaeologists to look for documents and maps to help explain many of the features which still survive. Dating has become more precise with the introduction of many new forms of assessment – radiocarbon, dendrochronology, thermoluminescence – allowing, in many periods, a more accurate perception of the time scale against which change and continuity can be seen to operate.

Inevitably every aspect cannot be encompassed in a survey of this nature and two areas in particular, underwater and industrial archaeology, have had to be omitted. For the rest, the authors have made a personal selection of what to them seem the most important achievements within the periods they cover. Throughout stress has been laid upon results rather than the methods used to achieve them and considerable effort has been made, with the assistance of Simon James, to convey by way of reconstructed drawing a visual impression of situations and structures as disparate as the Boxgrove Palaeolithic site and the Anglo-Saxon watermill at Tamworth.

The authors would like to take this opportunity to offer their warmest thanks to all their colleagues, too numerous to mention by name, whose work and expertise they have drawn upon in the making of the book. Without their help this work would not have been possible.

KEY

68	Aston
104	Balbridie
69	Baldock
37	Balksbury
112	Ballyglass
113	Ballynagilly
52	Blackpatch
25	Bowls Barrow
50	Boxgrove
47	Bramdean
70	Braughing
123	Brenig
83	Brigstock
94	Burton Fleming
26	Bush Barrow
49	Butser
54	Canterbury
1	Carn Brea
74	Clacton

N.Yorkshire Moors

Fens

Preseli Mts

Somerset Levels

Dartmoor

land over 250 metres

0   200 kms

0   200 miles

1 Prehistoric Britain

New perceptions

The past forty years have witnessed dramatic changes both in our appreciation of the later prehistoric periods and in the way the study of prehistory has been pursued. In the period immediately following the Second World War prehistoric archaeology in Britain had lain firmly within the conceptual framework of the culture-historical school established by V. G. Childe. Geographical determinism, as propounded first by Crawford and developed by C. Fox, had also exerted a strong influence. But by the 1950s archaeological thought was again on the move. The economic–ecological approach developed by J.G.D. Clark laid stress upon the recovery of the total range of evidence in order to assess man's response to his environment and the economic exploitation of the resources which lay within his grasp. The publication of Clark's *Prehistoric Europe: the Economic Basis* in 1952 mapped the achievements of this approach, while the excavation of Star Carr (N. Yorkshire) became the yardstick against which other information retrieved in the field could be judged, demonstrating the wealth of knowledge to be gained from close analysis both of the environmental evidence and of the surviving material culture which could be recovered. Detailed study and observation leading to the accumulation of precise data now became the prerequisites for writing prehistory. New precision was demanded in excavation, and the profession felt sufficiently confident to tackle the greatest monuments in the land: Stonehenge and Silbury Hill. As the amount and quality of the data grew, the need for quantification was seen to be an essential ingredient for a better understanding of the past.

The culture-historical school had been based upon the belief expressed by Childe that when certain types of remains consistently recurred together these could be termed a 'culture' and formed 'the material expression of what today would be called a people'. Given a chronological framework, it was possible to stand back and observe how these cultures influenced, changed and superseded each other. A basic tenet of this school had been the belief that major technological discoveries were made but once, and it was assumed that knowledge of these innovations was spread by the movement of people. It was also believed that most of these innovations occurred first in the Near East ('the cradle of Civilisation') and that they had gradually diffused outwards from that source through folk migration. The appearance of radiocarbon as a viable dating method in the late 1950s was to challenge these beliefs.

Radiocarbon dating offered for the first time a new approach to the ordering of events hitherto achieved by extrapolation or intuition from historically recorded chronology. Not only was the very framework of contemporaneity and succession to be radically altered, but the time scale itself within which these events were known to have occurred was considerably extended. Yet not all was challenged. The diffusion of farming from its inception in the Near East could still be traced using the new radiocarbon dates, gradually moving across the map of Europe, though now reaching the north-west very much earlier than had previously been supposed. Further proof of the mechanism by which farming knowledge spread came from excavation of Linear Bandkeramik settlements across Central Europe and into the Low Countries. To bring farming to Britain required a leap across the Channel, but, given the stark realities of the Second World War, such a crossing seemed all too possible. The cumulative effect, however, of the new date lists which were now becoming available for events in prehistoric Europe, coupled with the sheer weight of new archaeological data being actively compiled, prompted many to challenge the simple diffusionist explanation for other developments. For one thing radiocarbon dates had shown that some events which should have been successive had occurred either at the same time or in reverse order. Copper-working, for example, seemed more likely to have been independently developed in south-eastern Europe than to have been derived from the Near East, while dates for many of the chambered tombs of Western Europe showed these to have been in existence long before their projected ancestors in the eastern Mediterranean. Perhaps major innovations did not require large-scale movements of people after all. For British archaeology such questions were crucial, since hitherto the interpretation of most major events in Britain had been explained in terms of new colonists from abroad. Now independent development became a concept to be taken seriously, while the accumulation of new data began to reveal numbers of an order which seemed to throw new doubt on the credibility of wholesale movements of population to explain all forms of culture change. For Britain the outcome was to be the rejection of the invasion hypothesis as a universal explanation. Continuity was the process thenceforth to be demonstrated.

The 'new archaeology' of the 1960s was to demand more than just the quantification of accurately observed data. At a time of increasing doubt about the direction and values of contemporary society itself, the demise of the diffusionist approach now made way for an array of new questions and refutations. Batteries of new analytical techniques were deployed by archaeological scientists working in both the environmental and the physical sciences. The time was ripe to ask whether archaeology itself was not a science, or at least a discipline in its own right. But if it was, where was its underlying body of general theory? In this climate the culture-historical school was not simply to be rejected, it was to be denigrated as the purveyor of a 'steady flow of counterfeit history books'.[1] What was now required was 'the development of increasingly comprehensive and informative general models and hypotheses'. Not to agree to this was to run the danger of being labelled a '3rd class archaeologist', likely 'to cultivate the popular and lucrative fields of vulgarization and blinker themselves to narrow aspects of narrow problems without the comfort of knowing the value of their activities'.[2] The tone of the new archaeology was confident, intemperate and eminently divisive. The publication of D.L. Clarke's *Analytical Archaeology* in 1968 was to expose British archaeology, and more particularly prehistoric archaeology, to a body of theory grounded, as its author was at pains to point out,[3] in mathematics rather than pure science. While much of this was stimulating it brought with it, and called for, a new vocabulary which many were to find difficult to comprehend. Amongst these would be numbered in particular, as Clarke accurately predicted,[4] three major groups: amateurs, historical archaeologists and practical excavators.

Initially at least the new archaeology was to have little overt effect on fieldwork in the prehistoric periods. The massive programmes of post-War development and road-building which had been gaining momentum in the 1960s had created an unprecedented threat to the surviving traces of man's prehistoric past. This threat was more obviously acute in the cities than in the countryside, but road development, gravel extraction, and agricultural improvement in the form of deep-ploughing, drainage and removal of man-made obstructions posed equally telling threats in many a rural area. The growth of what was to be termed 'rescue archaeology' was the response. Though it was only in the later 1970s that national funds were to be deployed on a scale remotely commensurate with the problem, the scale and number of excavations undertaken had already risen markedly by the 1960s. To some the apparent orgy of indiscriminate recovery of often partial data seemed unacceptably wasteful. The mid-1970s emerged as a period of recrimination in which 'research' and 'rescue' became polarised and opposing philosophies. While the Council for British Archaeology Rescue pamphlet *Archaeology and Government* was to declare (para 2.2) that 'All active archaeology is research. What has come to be known as rescue archaeology forms part of this general research effort. Every rescue excavation provides further valuable information', others disagreed, arguing that the 'simple gathering of archaeological data, however professionally conducted, is something less than [research].[5] This charge of waste was perhaps less justified in the prehistoric field, and the prompt publication of the rescue excavations undertaken at Durrington Walls (Wiltshire) together with the subsequent programme of exploration of comparable structures within Wessex, demonstrated for many that rescue and research could on occasion be ably reconciled. As an attempt to bring a semblance of order to this scene and, perhaps consciously at a time of increasing financial constraint, to reduce the task to something approaching the human dimension, problem-orientated excavation was to emerge as the new philosophy for the fieldworker of the 1980s.

In the 1970s and 1980s the interests of theoretical archaeology were to move on yet again into social archaeology, the search for general theory leading to the adoption of concepts developed within the spheres of social anthropology, sociology and the behavioural sciences. It is perhaps too soon to assess how much of this will survive the winnowing of time, but the ecological approach, coupled with the critical testing of received wisdom which had formed the backdrop to the new archaeology of the 1960s and all that followed, has already left an indelible mark on British prehistory. That 'loss of innocence' which was proclaimed[6] is real enough, if not quite in the specific terms originally framed. Every dogma, every label has come under scrutiny. The limitations of much of the recovered data and of the assumptions made in their interpretation have been all too clearly revealed. The subject is now pursued with a greater rigour than ever before. What is at present uncertain is whether the end product will prove to be social prehistory or merely in turn, a form of counterfeit sociology.

Palaeolithic

Unlike the later prehistoric periods, Palaeolithic archaeology has seen no dramatic increase in new data. Aerial photography and field survey have made little impact. The vast majority of sites have long been known, and, though some new excavation has taken place at such classic sites as Clacton (Essex) and Swanscombe (Kent), these have tended merely to confirm the results of previous workers rather than alter our appreciation of the period. Current excavations now under-way at Boxgrove, a Lower Palaeolithic open site in W. Sussex (2), promise to be the first to make a major contribution to our knowledge, offering a glimpse of flint-working *in situ* and the opportunity to recover a near-complete picture of the environment of the time. The main thrust of post-War studies has been seen in methodology and the reassessment of finds already in museum collections.

Many of the difficulties of interpretation which have persisted in Palaeolithic fieldwork have stemmed from the state of Quaternary research. Historically, the study of glacial moraines and river terraces had led to the adoption of a scheme which saw four major glacial and interglacial phases. This sequence seemed confirmed by the pollen analytical and faunal studies used to characterise each phase. Attempts had been made to tie individual sites into this sequence and some refinement could even be claimed. At Hoxne (Suffolk), for example, it had been possible to recognise four vegetational phases for the Hoxnian interglacial, from birch and pine to the warmer species of oak, horn-beam, elm and lime and then back to the cooler species. But problems met in trying to correlate archaeological discoveries with the broadly similar Northern European and Alpine schemes pointed to the need for a better framework, and the difficulties and theoretical weakness of the

2 Boxgrove (W.Sussex) Reconstruction drawing to convey an impression of some of the activities likely to have been carried out on the site.

existing approach were to be highlighted by the early geological dating of a typologically advanced industry at High Lodge, Mildenhall (Suffolk).

The study of deep-sea cores was to provide a new perspective. These sample cores of sediment taken from the ocean floor offered an opportunity to measure ocean temperature through time, providing a much clearer and more detailed picture of the climatic fluctuations which had taken place. It soon became clear that over the past 700,000 years a far more complex pattern of oscillations had occurred. These, however, reflected broad changes in world climate, and their correlation with local sequences was to remain a problem. For this reason the need for an independent range of absolute dates for archaeological events persists, and while radiocarbon has proved useful in the later phases, thermoluminescence remains the most promising technique for establishing the age range of the earlier periods. A recent successful application of this technique has been the dating of a sample from the cave site of Pont Newydd (Clwyd) in North Wales, where a date of 200,000 ± 25,000 bc is in broad agreement with uranium series dating of calcite above the main occupation deposit. The new chronology to emerge would see the earliest flint industries in Britain dating some time prior to 250,000 bc. The last glacial period would be dated between 75,000 and 8,300 bc,* with the first Upper Palaeolithic people arriving during a short amelioration in the climate around 40,000 bc.

In the study of stone artefacts the emphasis has moved from typology to technology. Typological analysis, which had provided a useful means of characterising and differentiating individual assemblages, was seen to have only limited further application in an age increasingly more interested in the behaviour of man and his day-to-day existence than simply in his material possessions. By studying the complete cycle from selection of raw material, through the creation, use and ultimate discarding of an implement, it was hoped that new insights could be achieved into how Palaeolithic man thought and behaved. Two lines of approach in particular were to prove fruitful: the re-fitting of flakes back onto the parent core and experimental tool production.

By fitting together (3) the actual flakes struck off during the making of a flint implement, it has been possible to show how the raw material was progressively reduced to the required shape. Coupled with experimental work aimed at replicating Palaeolithic tool forms, considerable advances have been made towards understanding the problems and techniques of tool manufacture. This in turn has led to a study of the type and quantities of waste flakes produced at each stage of the shaping process. Typical handaxe 'thinning' flakes, for example, can now be recognised and their presence sought on archaeological sites as positive evidence of handaxe manufacture. Other experimental work has revealed that the position adopted by the flint-knapper produces different types of flake scatter, and these too can be recovered by careful excavation.

Different raw materials have also been shown to affect production. Obviously the size and shape of the raw material will impose some limitations on the size and form of the final product, but the composition of the material itself can be a decisive factor. At Pont Newydd experimental work has pointed to the difficulty of producing thin or twisted handaxes from the igneous rocks actually utilised on site. Not the least disturbing feature of this work has been the realisation that only 14 per cent (by weight) of the waste produced could be recognised as knapping debris. It is perhaps fortunate, therefore, that, for the Palaeolithic at least, the majority of sites in Britain lie in the south and east of the country, where flint was abundant and formed the principal material exploited.

Re-fitting has also been shown to provide a simple but highly effective way of demonstrating that what could have been taken to represent two distinct assemblages from the same site were in fact contemporary. The earlier excavators at Hengistbury Head (Dorset) had concluded on the basis of the flints recovered that in one area of the site two periods were represented. More recent excavations have shown that vertical disturbance had sorted the material by size and that at least some of the supposed 'Mesolithic' flints re-fit onto those from the 'Upper Palaeolithic' assemblage.

Other techniques to be developed include those designed to analyse the different types of wear that implements received during use. Much of the pioneering work for this study had already taken place in the Soviet Union during the 1950s, but it is only during the last ten years or so that similar research has been taken up on any scale in Britain. The basis of such research is the belief that certain tasks performed by the implement, such as scraping, chopping or sawing, over a range of

3   Flint core with blades re-fitted, from the Upper Palaeolithic site at Hengistbury Head (Dorset). Length of core 13.5 cm (5.35 in.).

different materials – for example, hide, meat, wood and bone – produce characteristic traces of wear which can be identified under high magnification. Initial experimental work appeared at first to confirm these beliefs, but more recent research has revealed a number of limitations and doubts. The vast majority of implements have proved unsuitable for study due to edge abrasion, rolling or patination. A more fundamental problem has proved to be the highly subjective nature of the results claimed, leading to an inability to reproduce similar results by different research workers or to reach universally agreed terms of reference.

Mesolithic

Whereas Palaeolithic archaeology had been dominated by the study of how implements were made, with relatively few sites seeing recent excavation, Mesolithic archaeology became geared towards the study of man in his environment with an excavation programme actively pursued. Prior to the excavations in the early 1950s at Star Carr interest had largely centred around the study of flint artefacts, principally microliths, but with the publication of this excavation the importance of organic materials, such as bone and antler, wood and hide, were to be thrust into the foreground. Ethnographic research into the behaviour of modern primitive societies had also promoted a general awareness of the economics of hunter–gatherer existence. The result was an upsurge of interest into the various types of activity which could be deduced from the site evidence and an increasing awareness of the mobility of the groups involved.

The Star Carr site had consisted of a platform made of birch wood, set along the margin of a lake. Abundant evidence for antler-working had been recovered, principally for the production of projectile points. A probable wooden paddle pointed to some form of water transport, while other organic remains ranged from antler mattocks, modified stag frontlets (used perhaps in stalking deer) to birch bark rolls. A mass of other faunal and floral evidence fleshed out a picture of the immediate surroundings and supplied further insights into the products of hunting and gathering forays. No sites examined since have equalled Star Carr for its wealth of data.

Star Carr was to focus particular attention upon the relationship between man and the animals on which he preyed and to inspire study of how man chose to exploit that relationship. At Star Carr red deer, roe deer and elk had been the prime target of the hunt, elk and red deer providing the bulk of the meat consumed. But the need to conserve the strength of the herds may already have been appreciated. Analysis of the age and sex of the roe deer remains suggests some degree of selective hunting, not dissimilar to levels reached in modern culling. Other sites provided further evidence of the importance of deer to Mesolithic subsistence and the annual cycle of deer-hunting has been used to explain the apparent seasonal occupation of many sites. Thus many of the upland sites in the Pennines have been assumed to have been for summer occupation on the grounds that the herds of red deer, after congregating in the warmer lowlands over winter, would have dispersed as smaller groups in the summer into the hills, to be followed by their human predators.

Some support for this seasonal use of sites has also come from study of the antlers themselves. Different deer exhibit different annual cycles of antler growth, but all shed their antlers at a particular time of year, depending on age. By studying the state of the antler, the month of the year in which the deer was killed or the antler shed can often be estimated. The significance of such studies for archaeological interpretation depends, however, on the assumption that the antlers reached the site soon after deposition. Unfortunately, differing approaches have often been in conflict. At Star Carr initial study favoured winter occupation, while subsequent analysis suggested year-round settlement. More recently a study based on the tooth-eruption of the roe deer recovered has implied a probable summer occupation. Supporting evidence is clearly still required.

Population levels have also remained difficult to assess. The bulk of the evidence comprises scatters of flint – representing both the manu-facturing of implements and their domestic use – retrieved as surface collections or by limited excavation. Comparative studies have shown that a considerable number of such scatters can be produced by relatively small groups over short periods, and occasional finds of hearths or small stake-supported structures, such as those at Oronsay ((Strathclyde), Downton (Wiltshire) or Morton (Fife) offer little clue as to the actual numbers of human groups involved. The likelihood of seasonal move-ment creates further problems of interpretation, and as few sites have been closely dated by radiocarbon or pollen analysis – even broad estimates of population size seem premature.

In terms of information yield, detailed investigation of riverine, coastal and marine areas offers perhaps the greatest archaeological potential. Sites in these localities can call upon a range of local resources, some always to hand, others available for only part of the year allowing settlement – perhaps fluctuating seasonally – to be near permanent. Here, too, conditions of preservation are often above average. Recent work on Oronsay, a small island less than six hectares (15 acres) in extent off the west coast of Scotland, has produced a particularly useful picture of how a single group of late Mesolithic hunter–gatherers living around 3500 bc exploited the resources of the sea, strand and hinter-land. A number of lines of research, including a detailed analysis of the ear-bones (otoliths) of saithe, the principal fish caught, have provided evidence for the seasonal use of a string of sites located around the southern coast. Elsewhere such coastal midden sites as Morton (Fife) have added useful information. Unfortunately, this type of evidence is confined largely to the north of Britain, for sea-level changes over the past few millennia are likely to have destroyed or concealed all such coastal sites in southern England. For example, Westward Ho (Devon), a site yielding quantities of artefacts and economic data can now be examined only at low tide.

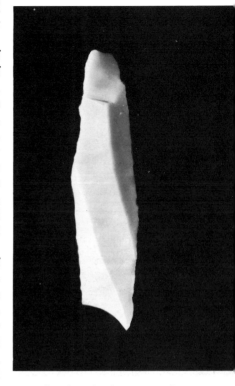

4 Archaeological and experimental flint points from the Mesolithic site at Hengistbury Head (Dorset), showing similar impact fractures. Point on left 7.5 cm (2.9 in.) long.

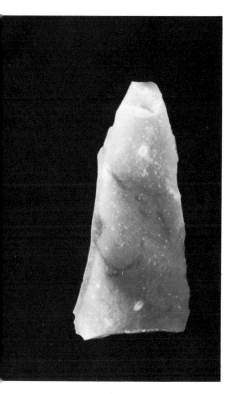

Interest in artefacts has become concerned less with cultural preferences and more with likely use. Flint arrowheads replicated in connection with the Hengistbury Head excavations showed that a small spall was removed from the tip on impact when shot into a modern deer carcass. A subsequent search of the arrowheads recovered from the excavation showed similar damage to be present (4). The relative scarcity or abundance of particular forms has also been seen as offering a guide to the type of activity being performed. The high proportion of microliths on many of the Pennine sites, for example, could suggest their use as short-lived camps occupied during deer-hunting expeditions, while the high proportion of scrapers recovered at Star Carr would underline the importance of hide-processing on that site. Other studies have sought to show how differing raw materials influence the type of implements produced and the distance over which choice materials, like Portland chert, could travel by exchange.

One of the more interesting products of our growing knowledge of the environmental background has been an increased awareness of man's own impact on the landscape at this phase. At Iping Common (W. Sussex) the change from a hazel scrub vegetation to a more open habitat may have been due to man's use of fire, as indicated by charcoal and burnt flints from the site. Similar evidence of burning has been found on other sites particularly on Dartmoor and on the North Yorkshire Moors. Deforestation could have played a major role in Mesolithic man's hunting strategies. The removal of woodland by fire would certainly have led to the regeneration of ground vegetation, resulting in an increase in the carrying capacity of the land for herbivores and greater mobility for the hunter. But whether systematic clearance and control were practised, anticipating the type of economy which was to follow, has yet to be convincingly demonstrated. At present what evidence there is would suggest that a real contrast still exists between a formal Mesolithic economy with its attendant technology and those of the succeeding Neolithic.

Neolithic

One of the major products of the 'loss of innocence' has been a willingness to consider the complexities of both the evidence and the inferences to be drawn from it. In that light it is perhaps hardly surprising that the first appearance of subsistence farming should remain an area of continuing debate. The accepted view of the immediate post-War years had been that expressed by S. Piggott in his classic review of the period:[7] farming was introduced by an immigrant population, the Windmill Hill Culture, which around 2000 BC first colonised 'the chalk massif of Wessex and its Sussex prolongation', thence expanding onto the equally farmer-friendly lands of the Cotswold oolite to the north-west and the chalk Wolds of Lincolnshire and Yorkshire via the line of the Icknield Way to the north-east. This picture was to be made untenable by the first radiocarbon determinations of the late 1950s and early 1960s, which forced a review of both the chronology and the pattern of introduction. Under the cumulative impact of a lengthening date list, coupled with excavation, a new picture was to emerge of early farming communities already widely spread and well established by 3000 bc. For those convinced by the absence in the British Isles of suitable domesticates, both animal and cereal, into believing that immigrants were still the key factor in the appearance of farming, two features of the new evidence seemed distinctly puzzling. Given the likely mode of introduction, by skin boat, it seemed reasonable to suppose that the shortest sea-crossings would be attempted, yet the new evidence showed a dispersed population from an early date. Worrying too was the fact that many of the early dates came from sites, such as chambered tombs, which manifestly called for considerable outlay of time and resource unrelated to food production. Surely an immigrant community of subsistence farmers would be unlikely to undertake such work until sufficiently established and confident of the necessary surpluses. A period of consolidation had therefore to be assumed prior to the appearance of these sites. Very early dates for the migration would in turn create problems, not least of which is an absence of plausible parent communities along the Atlantic seaboard of the European continent from which the immigrants could be derived. These difficulties have led others in recent years to adopt a different view. Accepting the negative evidence at face value, they have argued that no sites of the colonising phase survive because there were no colonists. The indigenous Mesolithic population, by whatever means, simply acquired the necessary farming skills. This, they claim, would account for the widespread nature of the early farming phase when this can first be perceived. Both views are finely balanced at present in their lack of supporting evidence, but with the advantage still with those seeking actual immigrants, for no sites have yet yielded evidence of a transition from Mesolithic to early farming, while the making, not simply adoption, of pottery of a technical competence far superior to what was later to be in common use implies again the arrival of new people with new skills. What appears beyond doubt is that the ability to practise successful subsistence farming created the necessary conditions for a widespread food surplus and through it a steady rise in population which was to continue well into the Bronze Age before receiving its first major check.

The complexity of society at this phase is only now beginning to come into focus. Until recently, for example, causewayed enclosures had generally been assumed to have had only a limited distribution and, despite obvious variations in form, to have served some specific need in the community, as cattle kraals perhaps, or more likely, as the setting for a range of communal activities of the type seen at medieval fairs. The cumulative evidence of aerial photographic and ground survey has now revealed a distribution stretching well beyond the English Southern Uplands out to East Anglia, the Fens and into the Midlands, covering a diversity of location from hilltop to valley bottom. More dramatic has been the demonstration that this type of enclosure can itself form just one component of more complex sites and that enclosures which at a

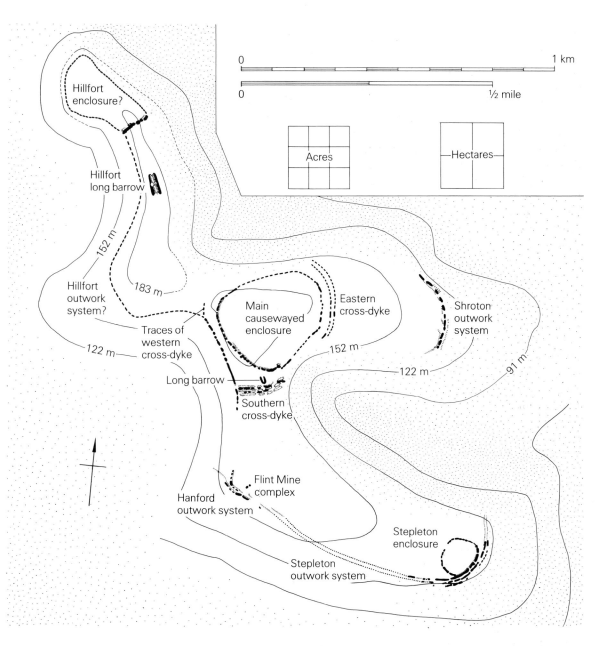

5 Plan of Hambledon Hill (Dorset) with the Neolithic enclosures and defences marked. After Mercer

superficial level may appear morphologically similar could have served a variety of distinct functions. At Hambledon Hill (Dorset) three such enclosures have been discovered set along the crest of the same hill and its attendant spurs (5). Two have been examined by excavation, revealing that the one on the Stepleton spur had been occupied by the living, but the second had marked an area reserved for the exposure of the dead.

Exposure of the dead to allow the flesh to decay from the bones was probably widely practised by the early farming communities, and

Hambledon Hill has provided further insight into how certain bones were later selected to serve in further ritual use. The placing of skulls along the bottom of the enclosure ditch and the careful burial of bone residues in this and in the ditches of the neighbouring long barrow show how the dead were manipulated, perhaps by appealing to the power of the ancestors, reinforcing an interpretation already reached from the more sporadic presence of human bones in the ditch fills of a number of excavated enclosures. Such evidence complements information recovered from many of the funerary monuments of the period, where the absence of certain parts of the skeleton has been noted more than once. Excavations of earthen long barrows like Fussell's Lodge (Wiltshire) and Wayland's Smithy (Berkshire) have shown that bodies brought to a mortuary area defined by walls, but not necessarily roofed, were already in skeletal form, the bodies having been exposed elsewhere. Not all the bones of the skeletons are present, few remain in articulation, and some have been stacked. Stacking and sorting of certain bones is also a feature noted in the stone chambered tombs. Recent excavations at Hazleton North (Gloucestershire), a Cotswold long cairn, have shown that only the latest burials placed in the passage were in articulation, but whether these had been interred as bodies or already partly defleshed is not clear.

Evidence is also growing for the burial of the dead in simple pits rather than in elaborate monuments. At Fengate (Cambridgeshire) a large unmarked oval pit contained the remains of four individuals, an adult male and female together with two children aged 8–12 and 3–4. Only the body of the male lay certainly in articulation, while those of the female and elder child were clearly not. A flint leaf-shaped arrowhead lodged between the eighth and ninth ribs of the man may have been the cause of death. The excavator noted that the pit had been filled in shortly after being dug. The occasion for burial was, therefore, the death of the man, the remains of the woman and at least that of the elder child being brought from elsewhere. It is possible that this pit, too, simply marks a further step in a process which would see the gathering up of this and other 'temporary' burials for final burial elsewhere, but the absence of monumental funerary sites in the near vicinity makes this perhaps less likely. Such discoveries must at least make for caution in trying to deduce population size from burials placed only within the major standing monuments. The Fengate burial is also suggestive of kinship ties strong enough to warrant the reburial of the female and at least one of the children on the death of the male. Such ties are perhaps also explicit in the very nature of the digging of the ditches of the causewayed enclosures, where small individual lengths of ditch are quarried and left separated from the next by undug ground (6). Excavation of the cairn at Hazleton North showed that here, too, the cairn had been constructed in separate cells. Both work-patterns imply the desire to mark individual (perhaps family) contributions within a task calling for communal effort.

Prominent amongst the surviving monuments of the period are the

6   Aerial photograph of Hambledon Hill (Dorset) under excavation. The photograph shows the triple ditches of the Stepleton Outwork System swinging away from the causewayed ditch of the Stepleton Enclosure (see 5).

stone chambered tombs of the north and west. By the early 1960s the majority of these had been listed in some detail, and interest turned from cataloguing to excavation and interpretation. The diffusionist approach had been supplanted by the view that differing forms of tomb were simply the product of local elaboration, sometimes through repetition, of a basic common tradition of burial within a stone or wooden box. Support for this view came from excavations. At Dyffryn Ardudwy (Gwynedd, North Wales) a simple dolmen was shown to be a primary and chronologically early feature in a cairn later to see extension.

Excavations at Mid Gleniron (Dumfries and Galloway) and Wayland's Smithy, further confirmed the likely complex history of many of the cairns. The catalogues were seen to have recorded only the final state of monuments, many of which had a history of modification and development. The very complexity of these monuments also gave rise to doubts about their true function. Many appeared to be more than just tombs, and their siting often along the margins of possible land divisions suggested use as territorial markers. Attempts to define possible territories have been based largely upon an appraisal of these 'natural' land divisions and have often been coupled with an appeal to 'central place theory'. This theory, however, was developed in relation to more advanced societies practising a free market economy and its relevance and applicability at this period remain doubtful. In practice little is known of the structure of society at this time, or of the actual deployment of population, for surprisingly little progress has been made towards recovery of actual settlements dating to this period.

What little is known appears to support the view that the early farming population was living in small family units in dispersed farmsteads. Certainly no timber-built villages have yet come to light, and some of the individual structures claimed – for example, at Crickley Hill (Gloucestershire), Balbridie (Grampian) and elsewhere – are not without problems of interpretation. Amongst the most convincing house-plans are two from Ireland. At Ballynagilly (Co. Tyrone) a rectangular structure measuring some 6×6.5m (19.5×21ft), was traced, with side walls formed by radially split oak planks set within continuous bedding trenches, and with two internal hearths placed near the centre of the structure. A second, somewhat larger house with internal divisions at Ballyglass (Co. Mayo), measured 13×6m (42.5×19.5ft). Yet the size and paucity of surviving traces of settlement are in many ways out of step with the evidence accumulating for the extensive use of timberwork in other contexts and with our understanding of the size of some of the communal tasks now undertaken. The timber trackways painstakingly traced over thousands of metres in the Somerset Levels (7), the revetments and façades of long barrows and cairns like Fussell's Lodge (8) and Street House (Cleveland), and the timber-faced ramparts slung round the most vulnerable spurs of Hambledon Hill leave no doubt about the woodworking skills of the farmers at this period, nor about their appreciation of the properties of the different woods they chose to use. Timber was in use, and on a grand scale. It would be remarkable if such skills had not also been deployed in domestic housing. Too great a dispersion of population is also problematic when faced by the scale of the Hambledon defences, for these must surely imply an immediate population of some considerable size, and the very fact that defence was necessary here, and at sites like Crickley Hill and Carn Brea (Cornwall), suggests that in some areas at least a growing population had already led to competition for resources, whether in the form of land, stock or human, before the close of the first half of the third millennium bc. Whatever else remains uncertain, there can be no doubt that the

7 A length of the Sweet Track (Somerset Levels) exposed. The track was made by first setting up a row of vertical posts about every 3 m (9 ft). Rails, about the size of telegraph poles, were next laid end to end along the line of the posts. These were held in place by pegs driven obliquely into the peat. Turves were then heaped over the rails. Finally, hewn planks were laid along the top of the rails and packing and secured by long pegs driven through prepared holes or notches cut in the planks.

8 Reconstruction drawing of the final appearance of the Neolithic earthen long barrow at Fussell's Lodge (Wiltshire). The height of the retaining timbers of the mound would have averaged about 4m (12 ft) of which more than half would have been visible above ground. In all, some 630m (2,070 ft) of timber would have been required for its construction.

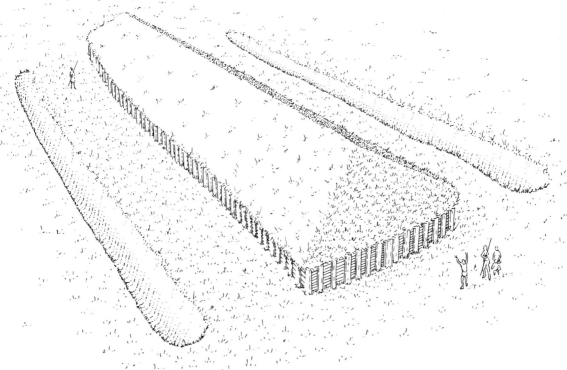

NEGATIVE LYNCHET

0   5 m

0   20 ft

9   Traces of cross-ploughing preserved beneath the earthen long barrow at South Street, Wiltshire. After Evans

farming economy was by now clearly capable of creating those surpluses required to underwrite communal tasks conceived on a gigantic scale, while the farmers were themselves sufficiently organised to carry these through to successful completion.

In fact, it is only in recent years that the extent and impact of this early farming phase has begun to be fully appreciated. The evidence of cross-ploughing beneath the earthen long barrow at South Street in Wiltshire (9) and the recovery of surviving traces of actual fields beneath blanket peat in the west of Ireland have given new substance to our knowledge of early farming methods, showing agriculture by no means confined to hoe and plot, with the ard certainly in use by 2600 bc. The resulting picture of a much more widespread and effective agricultural exploitation of the countryside now offers a more credible backdrop to the diversity of monumental evidence surviving from the period.

Detailed study of the procurement and exploitation of many of the basic raw materials in use such as flint, stone, wood and antler, has already begun to yield significant new information. Flint is relatively abundant, occurring as a surface material over a wide arc of southern and eastern England. Early settlement was often located in areas where a ready supply in serviceable quantity could be easily obtained. Better-quality flint lay buried within the parent chalk, sheltered from the effects of periglacial frosts, and for this the farmers had to mine. A clear chronological separation has now emerged between the flint mines of Sussex, which were already being exploited before the close of the fourth millennium, and those of East Anglia, principally at Grimes Graves, where the main mining phase has been dated between 2100 and 1800 bc. Initial results of flint analysis have been promising, offering the hope that in future it will be possible to assign products made from mined flint to specific regional deposits. Considerable success has already been achieved in the complementary search for the different sources of fine-grained metamorphic rocks favoured for stone axe manufacture (10). Much of this has been published by the Implement Petrology Committee of the Council for British Archaeology, and this in turn has provided the basis for studies of the dispersion patterns of axes made from specific rock sources. Some, like the products of the Craig Llwyd (Group VII) factory in Gwynedd, North Wales, show a predictable falling-away in quantity with distance, but others, most notably axes made from rocks whose source is attributed to Langdale (Cumbria) (Group VI) and south-west Cornwall (Group I), suggest dispersion also from secondary centres at some remove. Further work is required both to identify specific quarry sites and to establish that specific types of rock are indeed unique to a particular locality. Until such work has been completed more detailed analysis of possible trade and exchange networks will remain problematic. The distance over which certain prized materials could pass has, however, been ably demonstrated by study of jadeite axes (11). These were undoubtedly imported into the British Isles from an early date and are likely to have possessed a high symbolic value for the early farming communities. Their source is now shown to lie, not in Brittany as was once believed, but in Central Europe somewhere in the area of the Swiss and Italian Alps.

The imbalance in the archaeological record due to the absence from most dryland sites of many of the main organic components – wood, leather, rope and basketry – has long been a source of concern. In recent years a positive attempt has been made to explore the potential of the wetlands in the knowledge that these are a fast diminishing resource. Major programmes of exploration have been mounted in the Somerset Levels and the Fens, building on the pre-War work of the Fenland Research Committee. The result has been a growing insight, not only into carpentry skills and the use and selection of timber, but also into the way prehistoric man managed the woodlands as a useful resource. The local farming community, for example, which had begun to exploit the potential of the Somerset Levels well before 3000 bc, improved access by throwing elaborate timber trackways across the swampy ground. Many of these remain well preserved, the earliest constructed of hewn planks secured by peg and rail. In the Fens excavation of the causewayed enclosure at Etton (Cambridgeshire) has shown just how much evidence has been lost where organic materials no longer survive. Many of the activities here preserved in the ditch would have left no trace (12). Such projects have also begun to flesh out the artefact record in a way not seen since the classic discoveries at Ehenside Tarn (Cumbria)

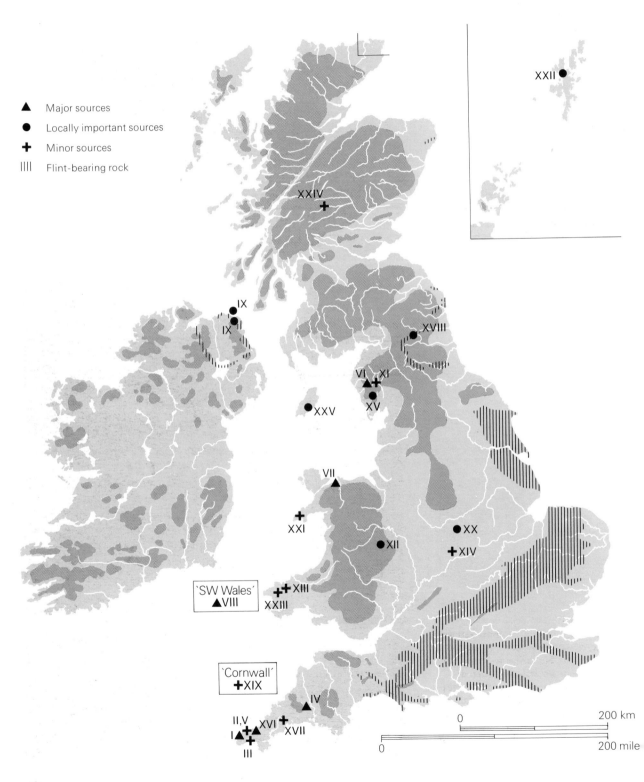

▲ Major sources

● Locally important sources

✚ Minor sources

|||| Flint-bearing rock

XXII ●

XXIV ✚

IX ●
IX ●

XVIII ●

VI ▲ XI ✚

XXV ●

XV ●

VII ▲

XXI ✚

XII ●

XX ●

XIV ✚

'SW Wales'
▲ VIII

XIII ✚✚
XXIII

'Cornwall'
✚ XIX

IV ▲

II,V ✚ XVI ▲ ✚
I ▲ ✚ XVII
III

0   200 km

0   200 mile

10 Map showing main sources of rock exploited for axe manufacture during the Neolithic period.

11 Neolithic jadeite axehead probably found near Canterbury (Kent). Length 21.9cm (8.5in.). Much time and work went into the preparation of these carefully shaped and polished blades, none of which appears to have been intended for normal functional use.

12 A general view of the waterlogged deposits at the bottom of the ditch of the Etton (Cambridgeshire) enclosure. Clearly visible are discarded wooden rods, probably from a coppiced tree, large pot sherds, numerous animal bones and many wood chips, the result of nearby woodworking. On a dryland site only the pottery and perhaps the bone would have survived.

13 Wooden axehaft lying in the ditch of the Etton (Cambridgeshire) enclosure.

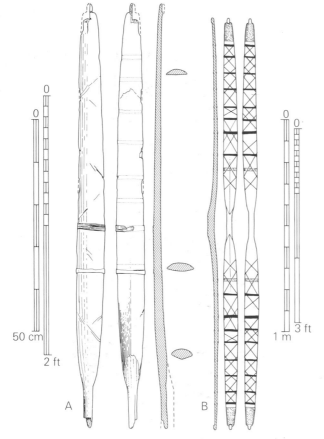

14 Surviving portion and reconstruction (after Clark) of a Neolithic bow made of yew from Meare Heath (Somerset). When complete the bow would have measured almost 2m (6ft) in length. Impressions surviving in the wood show that the bow had once been bound round with a web of fine thread as well as strips of hide, fragments of which survived. The bow has been dated to 2690 bc.

in the nineteenth century. The axehaft of ash from Etton (13), the magnificent long bow of yew from Meare in Somerset (14), the mattock and wooden dish from near the Sweet Track (Somerset), steadily extend our knowledge of tool, weapon and utensil otherwise unrepresented in our museum collections. With these have also come objects which cast light on areas of belief otherwise unsuspected, like the remarkable god-dolly recovered from the Bell Track (15). Backed by extensive detailed research into the contemporary environment, such work has increased immeasurably our understanding of how the early farmers lived and utilised the natural resources about them.

Signs of increased tension, as witnessed by hostilities at sites like Hambledon Hill and Crickley Hill, herald changes in society which became marked by the middle of the third millennium bc. The earthen long barrows and many of the stone chambered long cairns pass out of use. It is a time of increased ceremonial activity, as new forms of monument testify, with the erection of passage graves in the west and north, stone circles, henge and cursus monuments, avenues and alignments. New and more elaborate forms of pottery and artefact are manufactured, many embodying an outlay in skill and time not required to meet a mere functional need. Skilled use of wood and stone, a

15 Wooden 'god-dolly' recovered from the Bell Track (Somerset Levels). Height 15.5 cm (6.1 in.).

16 Peterborough Ware bowl from the River Thames at Hedsor (Buckinghamshire). The bowl carries a typical impressed decoration, both inside the mouth and over much of the external surface, made with short lengths of twisted cord. Height 12.5 cm (5 in.).

flourishing of symbolic art and an interest in solar and lunar observations all mark this phase.

One tangible sign of a growing diversification in society can be seen in the new forms of pottery which now emerge. The new traditions are characterised by the use of prolific decoration, in contrast to the restrained, largely plain wares of the earlier period. Of these, Peterborough Ware and Grooved Ware have the most extensive distribution. The origins of Peterborough Ware (16) can be traced back to the round-based bowls of the earlier farmers, transformed by the introduction of extensive impressed, often corded, decoration, but Grooved Ware (17) with its flat-based bucket or splay-sided bowl forms carrying grooved or applied ornament, has no obvious ceramic ancestry either within Britain or on the Continent. The two traditions differ somewhat in distribution, Peterborough Ware (19) being confined to England and Wales with only minor penetration of Scotland, and Grooved Ware (20) being more widely spread, extending out to Orkney in the north, and west to Ireland. But in southern and eastern England the two are found over much the same territory, sometimes occurring on the same site though rarely in direct association. While largely contemporary, the two traditions share little in form, method of manufacture or range of decoration. It is tempting to see in these contrasting pottery styles reflections of divisions within society itself in which specific forms of pottery were in use by elements who saw themselves distinct.

The two pottery traditions occur on similar but often contrasting types of site, both ceremonial and domestic, though the nature of actual settlement at this period remains little known. True, the only Neolithic villages with surviving structures belong to this phase, but these lie in

17 Grooved Ware Bowl (detail) found in one of the deep mines at Grimes Graves (Norfolk). The bowl is only decorated on the inside and carries a complex incised geometric pattern. Diameter 25.8 cm (10.2 in.).

the far north on Orkney. To Skara Brae and Rinyo, explored before the Second World War can now be added Links of Noltland on Westray. All show the same type of cellular stone-built house construction set within a midden, and all three were built by Grooved Ware users. Recent excavations at Knap of Howar on the adjoining island of Papa Westray have added a new dimension to this picture. Here a farmstead, perhaps of earlier foundation but certainly overlapping in date the Grooved Ware villages, has produced houses of markedly different construction (18), pottery of local Unstan style and artefacts of a different range. Differences extend, too, to the funerary monuments in use. Whereas Grooved Ware occurs in passage graves of Maes Howe type, the inhabitants of Knap of Howar buried their dead in stalled cairns whose

18   Interior of House 2 at Knap of Howar (Orkney) as revealed by excavation. The house, which measured 7.5 by 2.6–3.6m (24.5 by 8.5–11.8ft), was divided into three compartments by upright stone slabs. The outer walls were formed by midden material faced with dry-stone. At the far end can be seen five storage cupboards created within the thickness of the wall.

construction closely mirrors the plan of their houses. There can be no doubt that here archaeologically distinct elements in society co-existed in close proximity to each other. Unfortunately, elsewhere in the British Isles such detailed information is lacking. With rare exceptions – the stake-built house with Grooved Ware beneath the barrow at Trelystan (Powys) and the stock enclosure similarly associated at Hunstanton (Norfolk) are two – sites yielding evidence of domestic use of either Peterborough or Grooved Ware present little more than residual fragments. Pit and remnant occupation layers are frequently all that now survive, too little to offer grounds for serious interpretation.

19   Distribution map of Later Neolithic
Peterborough Ware.

20   Distribution map of Later Neolithic
Grooved Ware.

0   200 km

0   200 miles

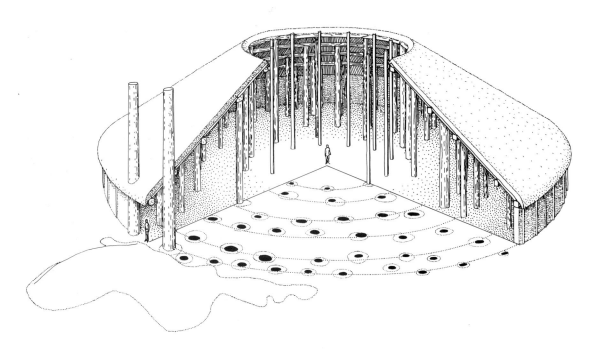

By the close of the third millennium those who used Grooved Ware are clearly amongst the most prominent members of society, at least in southern Britain. The programme of excavations carried out at three of the major Wessex enclosures – Durrington Walls and Marden (Wiltshire), and Mount Pleasant outside Dorchester (Dorset) – have shown that at all three Grooved Ware was associated with both the construction of the earthworks and the erection of the large wooden structures which lay within their circuits. Some debate has ensued as to whether these were free-standing settings of posts or roofed structures (21) with, on balance, the latter preferred, but whether roofed or not their massive scale leaves no doubt about the engineering skills, planning and communal effort which went into their construction. Exploration of the flint mine complex at Grimes Graves (Norfolk) has similarly revealed that both the deep mining of flint and its subsequent processing at the surface are again the work of Grooved Ware users. The scale of these undertakings is no less impressive. Shafts up to 15m (49ft) deep and 5m (16.5ft) wide were sunk through the solid chalk to reach the 'floorstone' layer (22). This contained flint of the highest quality lying in large tabular lumps. The floorstone was first extracted from the base of the shaft, then further quarried by means of radial galleries (23). A rough calculation suggests that just one of these galleried mines might have yielded as much as 40 tonnes of floorstone. The entire site could therefore have produced in excess of 14,000 tonnes, enough to make some 28,000,000 flint axes.

Grooved Ware users were by no means the only archaeologically identifiable groups to indulge in major undertakings. Excavations in the Boyne Valley, Ireland, at New Grange and Knowth (Co. Meath) have

21 Reconstruction drawings of the timber buildings found within the Neolithic enclosure at Durrington Walls (Wiltshire): (*below*) the northern circle; (*above*) the southern circle.

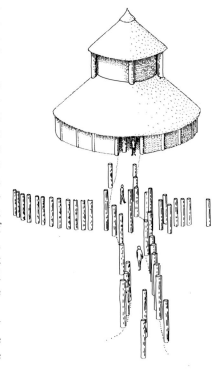

22 Section through one of the deep flint mines at Grimes Graves (Norfolk). The main flint layers are shown on the right. Once the flint had been extracted from the base of the shaft, radial galleries were dug. As each gallery was excavated, the spoil was thrown into the gallery previously exhausted. When the final gallery was worked, the chalk extracted was heaped at the base of the shaft.

revealed not only the majesty of the great passage graves built during the latter half of the third millennium, but also the complexity of their construction and the continued ritual use of the areas around. At Knowth the remains of no less than seventeen attendant passage graves have been found set around the main mound, itself 80×90m (262.5×295ft) in diameter and up to 11m (36ft) high. At the neighbouring site of New Grange the monument had been so orientated that for a few days either side of the winter solstice the sun's light could shine through a slot left above the entrance along the length of the passage to illuminate the chamber. Such a refinement speaks not only of engineering ability but also of careful solar observation, apparently unaided by written record. Similar skills are to be seen again in the use of stone in the construction of the tomb of Maes Howe on Orkney, with its near perfect corbelled roof. But for sheer size nothing can compare

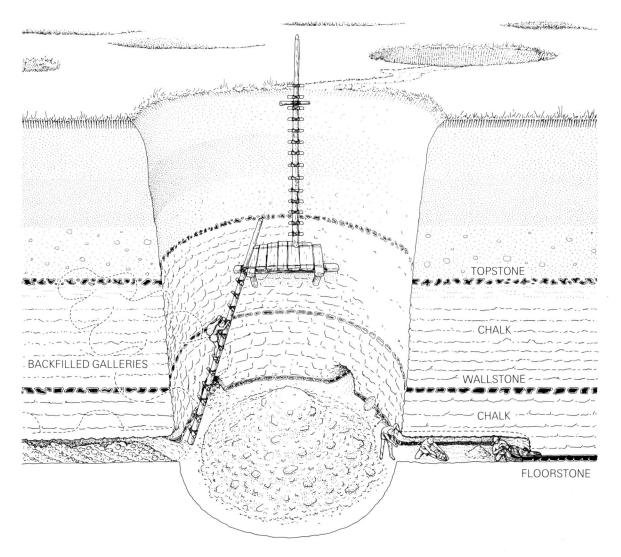

TOPSTONE

CHALK

BACKFILLED GALLERIES

WALLSTONE

CHALK

FLOORSTONE

with Silbury Hill (Wiltshire), the largest man-made mound in Europe, 40m (131ft) high and 165m (541ft) across. A quarter of a million cubic metres of quarried chalk went into its construction calling for the organisation and expenditure of some 18,000,000 days. It is ironic that despite careful investigation such a colossal monument has left few clues as to the ideas and beliefs which impelled its construction.

Elsewhere lesser but more numerous henges and stone circles were erected, sometimes obviously aligned, as with the first monument at Stonehenge, on solar, less frequently lunar, sightings. At Stonehenge that event was the mid-summer sunrise. Less obviously explained are the cursus monuments, yet these strange linear monuments comprising roughly parallel banks with external ditches must also have been an impressive feature of the now partially cleared landscape. The Dorset Cursus in its final form traversed almost ten kilometres (six miles) of southern downland and may already have been started in the early farming phase, but others, like the Springfield Cursus in Essex, have been shown on excavation to be the work of those who used Peterborough Ware.

If the impression has been given of a period strongly weighted towards a vast expenditure of human effort on the construction of monuments related to ceremony rather than to the housing of the living or the veneration of the dead, little has been encountered in post-War years to redress that picture. Even the great passage graves appear to have served more as shrines than as simple burial chambers, and no doubt the great wealth of megalithic art now revealed at both New Grange and Knowth underpinned a ritual which we have but little chance of comprehending.

Certainly some of the symbols used had wide currency, and one must presume significance, for they appear again in Grooved Ware decoration and on objects of the highest craftsmanship, like the magnificent carved flint macehead recently found in Knowth or the carved chalk cylinders discovered in the last century at Folkton (N. Yorkshire). By the second

23 View looking into the cleared galleries of pit 15 of the Grimes Graves flint mines in Norfolk, near Brandon. The flint seam known as the 'floor stone' can be clearly seen at the base of the chalk pillar.

half of the third millennium, however, new forms of burial are beginning to appear, single interments accompanied by a range of objects set beneath a large round or oval mound, harbingers of a more profound change in society which saw the status of the individual increased at the expense of the community and the communal dead.

The Beaker problem

An outstanding feature of post-War archaeology has been the reassessment of the significance and role of Beaker pottery.[24] For much of the 1950s and 1960s that role had seemed clear enough. Beaker pottery had been brought to Britain by Beaker folk, and their power and influence could be traced by studying the contexts in which that pottery occurred. Since some of the first metal objects to be found in Britain were deposited in their graves, the Beaker folk were judged also to have introduced metallurgy, and the reason for their apparently explosive migration the length and breadth of Europe was thought to be at least in part due to their evident need to prospect for new metal ores. The Beaker folk, equipped with knife and bow, were seen as warriors, pastoralists, traders and, in contrast to the farmers who had gone before, individualists, for the burial rite which they practised was one of interment of a single crouched or contracted inhumation, often set beneath a small round mound of earth. In their graves could be found occasionally, along with the Beaker, other objects of prestige, including gold, amber and jet. The Beaker folk clearly possessed personal wealth and included among their kind men of power who soon exerted influence over the (apparently supine) peasant population. They were credited with most undertakings of imagination, most notably organisation of the transportation of the blue stones from the Preseli Mountains (Dyfed) in Wales to Stonehenge (Wiltshire) and their erection to form the first stone-built monument on that site.

Much of this picture was still current when Clarke published his major corpus of Beaker pottery from the British Isles in 1970.[8] Clarke retained the view that Beaker pottery was introduced by folk migration but saw this less as an invasion and more of a gradual colonisation, waves of settlers arriving over time bringing with them different styles of pottery, which he argued could be traced to different areas of Continental Europe, principally in the north-west. This colonising phase was followed by a prolonged spell of insular development. The Dutch were less sure of much of the Continental derivation and criticised the work for placing too much emphasis on this and too little on insular regional development. By the later 1970s the anti-diffusionist school was to offer a more fundamental review. Following the post-War dislike of 'ethnic' solutions, the concept of a Beaker folk was abandoned as such, the Beaker and the principal objects associated with it being viewed as the visible trappings of a cult whose swift acceptance and adoption explained the rapid transmission of these artefacts across Europe. Perhaps, it was added, the significance of the Beaker lay more in what it had once contained than in those who made it.

Some of the assertions previously made now seem less than compelling. It seems doubtful, for example, whether the existence of new immigrants could ever have been established by physical anthropological means, even if such studies were not firmly out of fashion, for by this date any previously distinct strains which may have existed in the Western European population would have become largely submerged. The introduction of metallurgy to Britain by Beaker immigrants has also yet to be established. While the first metal objects assigned to the grave are associated with Beaker pottery, the adoption of the ubiquitous copper axe is not similarly tied and may or may not be due to Beaker involvement. We have also seen that individual interment with grave-goods beneath round barrows may also antedate the first datable Beaker context in Britain. While these developments limit the number of new features to be anchored firmly to an introduction in the Beaker phase, the ready acceptance of Beaker migrant, pottery, cult or custom may well have owed much to the fact that society was already moving towards a greater recognition of the individual and the living, laying less stress upon the community and the dead. We have seen, too, that many of the major undertakings of the period were associated with the insular pottery styles and not with Beaker. The erection of Stonehenge II stands apart, but there must now be considerable doubt as to whether the bulk of the blue stones, if these indeed do originate in Preseli, were transported from that source at this time, for a block of blue stone was incorporated within Bowls Barrow (Wiltshire), an earthen long barrow likely to have been erected at least half a millennium earlier than the blue stone monument at Stonehenge. Whatever else post-War excavation has demonstrated, it has shown clearly enough that the early farming communities were active, well organised and capable of undertaking massive communal works without direction by newly implanted Beaker 'overlords'.

The very nature of archaeological evidence probably precludes a final judgement as to whether the earliest Beakers and such classic Beaker-related artefacts as tanged copper knives and v-perforated buttons reached Britain through actual settlers or by way of exchange to those eager to demonstrate their position by acquisition of exotic objects of prestige. But hard on the heels of these events came some limited colonisation. The settlement at Ballynagilly (Co. Tyrone), dating to around 2000 bc, was that of a group of immigrant farmers practising a mixed regime of agriculture and stock-raising, and using Beaker pottery in clear distinction to the insular Neolithic population. Sites like those around Hockwold (Norfolk) or Willington (Derbyshire) show similar separate Beaker-using communities of a later date. Such discoveries are entirely in keeping with what is known of the Beaker ceramic tradition itself. New insular Beaker styles were developed, often alongside those introduced from the Continent, as the ditch sequence at Mount Pleasant (Dorchester) has demonstrated. But Beaker pottery remained always distinct. The desire of the native potters to emulate these products can be seen already appearing in the latest bowls of Mildenhall style, in the

24 Pottery Beaker, a perforated stone wrist-guard and part of a bone ring from a grave at Hemp Knoll, Bishops Cannings (Wiltshire). The height of the Beaker is 27.3cm (10.7in.). Both the wrist-guard and ring were already old and broken when placed in the grave.

Ebbsfleet and Mortlake styles of Peterborough Ware and also in Grooved Ware. Such features became still more pronounced in the Food Vessel and Urn pottery of the succeeding phase. But it is noticeable, too, that it was the decorative features, not the technology, which were copied, and there is no difficulty in distinguishing these products apart.

The Wessex Culture and the Earlier Bronze Age

Knowledge of copper-working had been introduced to the British Isles relatively late compared to other parts of Continental Europe, but once established the new industry was able to thrive. The availability of copper deposits, primarily in south-west Ireland but also in western Scotland, North Wales, Devon and Cornwall, provided a ready supply of raw material. Metal analyses have shown that ores possessing arsenical impurities were particularly favoured, no doubt because this natural alloy gave implements a hardness greater than that of pure copper. But the appearance of metal also introduces a basic problem which besets much of British prehistory. While first copper, then bronze were to be used on an ever-increasing scale for a growing list of tools and weapons, relatively few of these survive on settlement sites and those assigned to the grave were chosen for reasons not simply of availability but of appropriateness according to the rites and beliefs then in vogue. Thus, amongst the first products of the metal-smiths, the thick-butted flat axehead and halberd, with but rare exception, never appear in association with traces of the living or the dead, though stray finds and hoards show that these were made in some quantity. What came now to be interred with the dead does record, however, for whatever reason a new emphasis placed on personal possessions, and individual interment was soon to become the norm, though graves might be grouped to form cemeteries or made successively in pit or mound.

The change towards a more overtly ranked society which these outward manifestations seem to imply did not arise everywhere without conflict. Around 1700 bc a massive wooden palisade was thrown up within the circuit of the existing enclosure at Mount Pleasant. Though defensive in intent, this was clearly a failure, for it was destroyed soon after completion. Around the same time a setting of sarsen stones was arranged to mark the place where the former timber structure had once stood. Similar events occurred elsewhere in Wiltshire. A comparable replacement of wood by stone can be seen at the Sanctuary on Overton Hill, while at Stonehenge the creation of a double stone circle made of blue stones was commenced. This monument was never completed, for the scheme was overtaken by a design of still greater magnitude. This was to culminate in the massive sarsen monument whose tumbled remains survive to the present day. The scale of the work involved was immense. Transporting, shaping, jointing and erecting the sarsen blocks, the largest weighing up to 50 tonnes, each hauled a distance of some forty kilometres (twenty-five miles) from the Marlborough Downs, must have absorbed something in the order of 3,000,000 working man-days. Not only was this a feat of engineering, but the whole enterprise would have called for sustained control over a work force of no mean size. Yet amidst these changes can be detected something of a backward glance. In the marking of sites of former timber structures and in the very techniques used in the construction of Stonehenge – the mortice-and-tenon and tongue-and-groove joints more reminiscent of work in wood than in stone – can be seen a positive desire to commemorate and enshrine something of the customs and beliefs which had found ex-pression formerly in wood.

Throughout much of Britain the raising and reuse of monuments to the individual dead became a well-established custom. Round barrows, and ring- and platform-cairns are but some of the variations which were to appear. In southern England many can be seen to congregate around the former ceremonial enclosures, and the area around Stone-henge itself became a focus for such monuments. Cemeteries of round barrows cluster prominently along the slopes of the adjoining downs, and from here and there amongst these came many of the rich grave assemblages on which the pre-War concept of a 'Wessex Culture' had been based. For much of the immediate post-War phase this concept was to dominate discussion of the period, though it was destined to remain a culture of the dead, for attempts to locate the living met with little success. This was, indeed, a concept to catch the imagination. The Wessex grave assemblages, with their occasional flash of gold, of amber, jet, faience and fine bronze, seemed to offer a glimpse of a more heroic class, of rich warrior–chieftains and their womenfolk, the builders of the final monument at Stonehenge. The belief that this élite had direct contact with the Mycenaean world and that the sarsen phases of Stonehenge might owe something to inspiration drawn from that source no longer commands respect, but the contents of the Wessex graves nonetheless reveal that through the exchange networks of the time fashions and occasional exotic items were transmitted from Central Europe and beyond to those who sought and could afford them.

A less romantic view would now see this 'Wessex Culture' as a phase during which the custom of placing an array of personal items with the dead was practised by one segment of society. Since many of the objects, certainly in the earlier graves, include fine and exotic items unlikely to have been in wide circulation, there can be little doubt that the segment came from the higher echelons of society. Of the objects placed in the graves, many are suggestive of wealth and status, rather than an embodiment of wealth itself. The quantity of gold deposited, for example, is quite trivial compared with the amount used in the manufacturing of the lunulae – which reached neither Wessex nor the grave – but the form that it took shows access to craftsmen of the highest order. Nor in terms of conspicuous splendour does anything in Wessex compare with the cape of beaten gold from Mold (Clwyd), North Wales. The martial aspect, too, can be overplayed. Many of the broad triangular 'daggers' of the early phase make unconvincing weapons, and even the more functional later ogival forms would hardly be the first choice of weapon for a warrior in a period which knew the arrow, spear and the stone battle-axe. Such items would, nonetheless, have given status within the community to those who could possess them, especially when enhanced by an organic hilt itself decorated, like the example from Bush Barrow (Wiltshire), with patterns created with minute pins of gold.

The earlier graves possess the greater array of items, and the daggers in these show strong affinity with contemporary Breton forms. Those in the later graves are the product of insular development, and in many of these graves were placed copies in bone, jet and shale of items originally made of bronze, amber and faience. Many of these copies recur sporadically, too, in graves remote from the Wessex area and mark the spread of fashions and a desire to emulate already now more widely based. It would be wrong to assume, however, that such sporadic finds must relate directly to the level of wealth or poverty prevailing in areas outside Wessex. Post-War archaeology in Britain has done much to reveal the great diversity of evidence between the regions and to underline the dangers of using objects placed with the dead as a secure guide to what was available to the community at large.

It remains difficult to relate these Wessex graves to contemporary events elsewhere in southern Britain. Many of the settlements and cemeteries yielding Deverel-Rimbury pottery can now be seen to run contemporary with the later Wessex graves, yet little can be found to link the two. The Deverel-Rimbury communities practised cremation, rarely placing anything other than pottery with the dead. At the extensive cemetery of Kimpton (Hampshire) the burials could be seen to fall into a series of small successive clusters. These revealed an astonishing continuity of burial practice stretching on over at least a thousand years. The composition of each cluster, with its range of adults, juveniles and children of both sexes, must surely represent the remains of single kinship groups, and other cemeteries can be seen to have much the same structure.

25 Reconstruction drawing of one phase of the Bronze Age farmstead at Itford Hill (Sussex). The main enclosure contained four huts: D appears to have been used as a dwelling, E as a place for weaving and preparing food, F as a work hut and C for animals. Hut G was also used for food preparation. A marks the site of farm buildings used at an earlier phase.

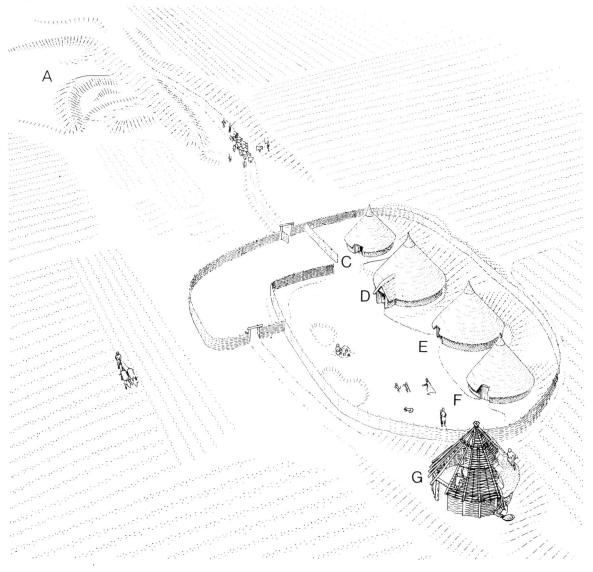

26 A stone 'reave' on Dartmoor fully revealed by excavation. Stones from later land clearance, which have been piled against it, can be seen at the front.

Settlement evidence provides a complementary picture. The chalkland farmstead often comprises a small group of round timber-framed houses, each entered through a short rectangular porch, with ancillary huts built to provide space for a range of household and farming activities including weaving, storage and the preparation of food. The houses themselves usually nestle within a sub-rectangular embanked or bank-and-ditched enclosure and stand amongst groups of small rectangular 'Celtic' fields. Detailed study of the houses at sites like Itford Hill (25) and Blackpatch (Sussex) suggests that such a farm was being worked by a unit the size of an extended family.

But it is the south-west that has produced the most dramatic new evidence for land use and settlement at this period. Intensive survey carried out in recent years on Dartmoor has shown just how extensive the ordering of the landscape had now become. By the middle of the second millennium bc much of Dartmoor was beginning to be farmed, for this was a phase which saw considerable uptake of new land in the upland areas of western and northern Britain, spurred on by increasing pressure on the primary farming lands and a mounting population. Besides land, Dartmoor offered metal ores, for both copper and alluvial tin were to be found in exploitable quantities in the river valleys. Initial settlement may have been a piecemeal affair, but it was not long before the need for a more structured division of the available land was to be felt. Evidence now points to much of the moor being enclosed around 1300 bc as a single planned act. Stone banks or 'reaves' (26) were now used to carve up the land into separate territories. These are particularly obvious along the southern margin of the moor, where each territory had as a core area a steep-sided river valley, separated from the next by a reave following the line of the intervening watershed. Each territory thus defined had access to the high moors, no doubt for common grazing, and this was partitioned off from the lower-lying ground by a reave set to follow a contour of the land. Each territory in turn contained a block of land subdivided by further reaves set parallel to each other. Where this landscape remains well preserved, as in the Dartmeet system, stock enclosures, houses and further pasturage can be seen to form part of the overall pattern. The size of some units was considerable. The Rippon Tor system in east Dartmoor can be traced over at least 3,300 hectares (8,154 acres) and must rank as the largest prehistoric field system so far recovered in Britain, while less well-preserved divisions can be followed around the remaining margins of the moor.

More exploration will be required to establish in detail the true nature of the settlement, for the range of evidence is considerable and few sites have so far seen the spade. In the Plym Valley, where detailed survey has been carried out, settlement can be seen to concentrate in the band between the 224m (800ft) and 336m (1200ft) contours. In the main, traces of habitation are less dense on the higher ground and concentrate more in the valleys. This no doubt reflects a heavy bias in the upland areas towards the management of seasonal pasturage, contrasting with the lower ground, where herds would be tended during the worst of the winter season and where metal extraction would demand a greater resident labour force. In this region cereal cultivation appears to have made only a minor contribution to the total economy. In the initial phase the majority, if not all, of the settlements had been open, but many were later to see enclosure, a move apparently designed to exclude livestock, for where an enclosure has been excavated, as at Shaugh Moor, no evidence has been recovered for the quartering of animals within the walls, a point underlined by the absence of any form of entrance through which the animals could have passed. Throughout the moor the surviving evidence is for round-houses up to nine metres across (thirty feet) whose stone-faced rubble wall-footings are particularly durable, but excavations at Holne Moor have shown that at some sites an earlier phase of timber building can be present, and the Shaugh Moor enclosure, too, showed more than one building phase. Many of the enclosures, then, are likely to have seen long, if intermittent, use. By the beginning of the first millennium, however, the situation was again changing. Over-grazing and a deterioration in the climate were to set in train a process which was to see the gradual encroachment of blanket peat and lead finally to the abandonment of much of the moorland for human habitation.

A similar uptake and later abandonment of land can be seen in other upland areas of Britain – on the North Yorkshire Moors, in the Cheviots and Teesdale, in southern Scotland and parts of Wales – as fieldwork and aerial photography continue to reveal the true extent of this expansion. Nor was an ordering of the landscape confined to these more marginal lands. Similar systems have come to light on the gravels around Fengate on the Fen edge and in Essex. But despite this apparent organisation of the countryside on a grand scale, little survives outside Wessex to suggest major divisions of wealth within the population.

In most areas outside southern Britain we must be content with graves and metal implements to give some impression of this phase, for though evidence for settlement continues to grow, particularly in north-east England and in the Scottish Lowlands, death not life still stalks vast areas of the archaeological scene. It is a period of striking diversity in the pottery selected for funerary use – some, like the Collared Urn, in use over much of the British Isles, others with a more marked regional bias, like the Cordoned Urn, confined to Scotland and Ireland, with only minor penetration of northern England and Wales. The range of burial site and ritual practised is immense and can be seen to vary over quite short distances, though cremation was to emerge as the universal rite. Post-War investigations have made only modest contributions in this field, for after a brief spell of further exploration in the 1950s interest moved firmly away from barrow exploration and the archaeology of death. Nevertheless, information recovered then and more sporadically since provided new and more reliable observation of techniques used in barrow construction and of aspects of ritual and burial practice – an area first pioneered by Fox. In particular, the old 'geological' approach to the interpretation of burial depositions which had rigidly segregated a central (*sic*) 'Primary' burial from 'Secondary' peripheral interments was seen to oversimplify a situation which had more to do with social access than with chronological succession. Excavation of a barrow like West Overton G6b (Wiltshire), with its assortment of near-contemporary burials – Beaker inhumation, urned and unurned cremations – illustrated the complexity likely to be found in many of these funerary monuments. Work ahead of the construction of a new reservoir in the Brenig Valley (Clwyd), North Wales was to underline further problems of interpretation. Here a cemetery spread around the head of a single valley saw almost complete excavation. The time during which the cemetery was in use spans a period when the North Welsh bronze industry was active and flourishing, yet little reflection of this activity or wealth was to be garnered from the graves. If wealth or status was acknowledged, it was expressed in the labour required to erect the mounds, for most had been raised over a single cremation. In this the Brenig cairns contrast with those in the neighbouring counties of Anglesey and Flintshire, where many of the mounds saw use as cemeteries for multiple interments. The Brenig 'cemetery' also contained monuments whose prime function was not burial, offering a rare glimpse at a much broader spectrum of interrelated ritual and belief. Investigations of this type and those currently underway at Radley (Oxfordshire), where areas between and around the main components of a barrow cemetery are being searched, will help to provide a much clearer view of the interlocking of funerary and ritual practices over time which individual barrow exploration cannot hope to recover.

Few settlement sites have emerged to extend our knowledge of how such communities lived. For Collared Vessels, the Fen edge site of West Row, Mildenhall (Suffolk), for Cordoned Vessels. Downpatrick (Co. Down, Ireland), remain the most extensive areas of habitation associated with these types of pottery, but neither site yielded much in the way of structure. Certainly the erection of many barrows and cairns upon ground already abandoned for farming or for habitation reflects the ever-present need to move as land became exhausted. There is no doubt, too, that in the upland areas of Britain the bias lay firmly with stock, not agriculture, and some seasonality in occupation must be assumed. In many areas, as on Dartmoor, what settlement there was of a more permanent nature is more likely to have been concentrated in the valleys, where in most regions later occupation and intensive farming will have combined to conceal and remove much of the evidence.

Later Bronze Age

From a little before the end of the second millennium evidence accumulates for major changes, both social and economic. It is clearly a time of stress. Many of the customs and beliefs which had inspired the building of the characteristic funerary and ritual monuments over the previous millennium were now abandoned or took a form which was to leave no trace. Here and there some minor survival of barrow-building may have occurred, and in the south a few flat cemeteries like Kimpton see some prolongation of their use, but in most areas formal burial as a custom was to disappear over much of the British Isles. It was not just in the upland areas that changes in land use can be seen. In Wessex new land divisions appeared in the form of long linear dykes cutting across the old field systems, suggesting a greater emphasis on stock. Larger settlements are now in evidence, and new forms can be recognised, like Runnymede (Berkshire), set on an island in the River Thames and strategically placed to control a major riverborne trade-route (27). Here and there in the large timber-framed round-houses, twelve or more metres across (40 ft), recovered at sites like Mucking (Essex) and Thwing (Humberside), each set within its own enclosure, may be glimpsed the dwellings of an emer-

27 Reconstruction drawing of one of the Bronze Age stitched plank boats found on the northern bank of the River Humber at North Ferriby (Humberside). The boat was constructed of oak planks set edge to edge and stitched together with yew withies. Greater rigidity was produced by the use of cross braces, which passed through cleats in the keel and bottom planks. Further support was given by transverse formers and one or more lashings which passed transversely round the boat. The overall length was about 15 m (49 ft).

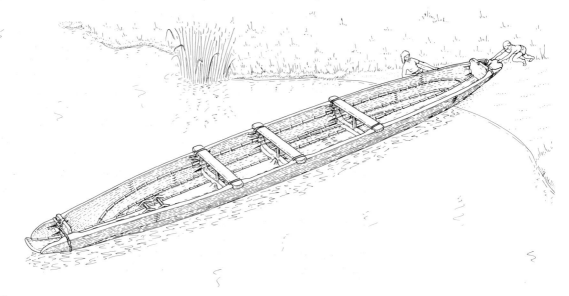

gent ruling class. In Highland Britain the first defensive phase of hilltop settlements dates to this time – a measure perhaps of the unsettled times and the need to safeguard communal food supplies. The bronze-smiths, too, were to respond with an increased range of weaponry. Noticeably many of their finest products come from river beds or once marshy ground, too many to be the product of accidental loss or erosion from riverine or marsh-side settlement. The wetter climate which had forced renewed building of timber trackways in areas like the Somerset Levels and had brought flooding to much of the former farmland around the Fen edge seems now to have led to cults and beliefs centred on river, lake and bog. Some objects, like the curious hollow-bladed barbed spearheads of Broadward type, may even have been made specifically for use in such cult practices, for they are clearly non-functional and occur mostly in watery contexts.

What remains debatable is to what extent external influences had acted as a catalyst to hasten and promote the events now in train. The rise of the great Urnfield tradition had ushered in a near pan-European age of change, and much of this had not been achieved without strife. Some characteristic Urnfield trappings inevitably reached Britain, but Britain, like north-western France, was to remain outside the Urnfield bloc. Unsettled times in Europe had led to some movement of people. Refugees could well have sought sanctuary across the English Channel. If their numbers were sufficient, at a time of high population and growing pressure upon the food supply, their coming could well have had a disproportionate effect.

The first half of the first millennium bc sees a period in which wealth and power become more obviously aligned in the archaeological record with possession of and control over food production and the activities of the metal-smiths. The size of the bronze industry was now considerable, judged even by the biased evidence which has survived. In Lowland Britain, where both copper and tin are lacking, the recycling of metal was of vital importance. Unfortunately for archaeology, the more effective such a system, the less the surviving evidence of earlier phases of metal production. Some drain on this existing metal pool must have been made by ritual deposition of weapons and hoards – for not all hoards can be seen as occasioned by the need to find a temporary home for wealth in times of danger. To make good these losses and to fuel the expansion in markets which was now underway metal was imported, as the recent discovery of a wreck in Langdon Bay (Kent) just outside the modern port of Dover has graphically revealed. Here sank a cargo comprising implements and scrap, which were French in origin and of a type rarely found in Britain. There can be no doubt, therefore, that the shipment was inward bound. The adoption of a new alloy, leaded bronze, on both sides of the English Channel, later to spread to the bronze industries of northern Britain, may not be unconnected with this need to increase the supply of raw material, though this alloy also possessed the valuable technological advantage of a metal which when molten flowed more freely in the mould. The result was that bronze became available in some quantity for tools and implements, but equally significant was the increase in range of weaponry and objects of display. Insufficient evidence exists to be certain that the majority of weapons and objects of parade were the work of specialist smiths working for the warrior and princely classes, but information from two sites lends support to such a view. At Dainton (Devon) and Springfield (Essex) quantities of metalworking debris were recovered. This comprises fragments of clay moulds and crucibles. Certainly at Dainton, and as far as analysis has reached also at Springfield, the products were confined to swords, spearheads, ferrules and baldrick fittings.

The introduction of iron was to bring these bronze industries to an abrupt end. In south-east England in particular scrap metal was dumped in vast quantities never to be retrieved, for the mass market for bronze implements and weapons now quickly collapsed. For a time the bronze-smiths produced a range of basic tools, and added a few 'Hallstatt' features to their swords, but the market was destined never to revive. The very speed of this change did much to mask the basic continuity which can be seen in many other aspects of society at this phase, so that 'Iron Age' studies came to be treated, until recently, as something separate and distinct, a time of conflict and a product of invasion.

The Iron Age: continuity or invasion?

In the period prior to 1945 hillforts had come to dominate Iron Age studies throughout much of Britain. Although not all formed such formidable features of the upland landscape as Maiden Castle (Dorset), the surviving earthworks of ditch and rampart nevertheless made them easily recognised and deceptively simple to classify. Viewed as strong-holds or places of ultimate refuge, it was only natural that what excavation there was should be concentrated upon their defences, which offered not only an insight into defensive strategy and the 'military mind' but also a record of the major events and changes in the hillfort's (military) life. Of all the prehistoric periods the Iron Age came most to be perceived in terms of invasion and response. After all, had not Julius Caesar himself recorded that Belgic invaders had settled in the coastal areas of southern Britain? By extrapolating similar invasions back through time, the appearance of many other features of the later first millennium bc and of obvious Continental derivation could be explained.

In a crucial paper in 1931 Hawkes[9] had offered the first independent formal scheme for the British Iron Age. This, while accepting the major role played by Continental colonisation, was designed to accommodate insular development resulting from the absorption of the new intrusive ideas into the native Bronze Age traditions. The main Continental divisions of Hallstatt and La Tène were abandoned in favour of a tripartite insular scheme using the letters A, B and C, each division reflecting one of the major waves of cultural incursion: A saw a folk migration into the eastern lowlands and beyond in the sixth or fifth centuries bc, introducing hillfort construction, the earliest use of iron and a variation of Hallstatt culture; B marked migrants from Iberia entering the south-west in the fourth century, bringing a variant form of hillfort construction – the cliff castle – and a La Tène culture. Close on their heels came other La Tène migrants, this time a warrior élite from north-eastern France occupying eastern Yorkshire and spreading some way south along the Jurassic scarplands. Finally, in the early first century BC, had come that invasion described by Caesar of Belgic tribes from northern France into south-east Britain, introducing the C phase.

It remained to find sites which could be tied into what limited historical record was perceived to exist. Two seasons of excavation in the region of St Albans (Hertfordshire) and a ten-year programme at Colchester (Essex) recognised two pre-Roman tribal settlements. The extensive dyke system at Wheathampstead (Hertfordshire) was confidently identified by Mortimer Wheeler as the final stronghold of the territorially ambitious Cassivellaunus, Chief of the Catuvellauni. Its capture by Caesar in his campaign of 54 BC marked the acceptance of defeat by the tribes of southern Britain. Prae Wood (Hertfordshire), just outside the Roman town of Verulamium, was designated the tribal centre of Tasciovanus, Cassivellaunus's successor, while the dyke system at Colchester was identified as the tribal capital of the Trinovantes established by Cunobelinus, the son of Tasciovanus, when he achieved supremacy as king or high chief of the southern tribes. In the south-west excavations at Maiden Castle revealed remains of Roman siege-works outside its defences and a 'war cemetery' complete with a skeleton transfixed by a Roman projectile-head. Maiden Castle must then have been one of the forts recorded by Tacitus as having held out against the Roman advance till subdued by Vespasian in his campaign of AD 44. Beyond, in Scotland and the west, an upland landscape dominated by hillforts suggested turbulent times, which accorded well with the fragmentary historical evidence of warring tribes and the recurring threat posed by new immigrants. It was with this accepted chronological and culture–historical framework, with the division between the end of the Bronze Age and beginning of the Iron Age set around 500 BC, that post-War studies were to commence. New discoveries, it was confidently felt, could be dovetailed in to fill out a picture the outline of which was well established.

In practice the period since the Second World War has turned out very differently. By the 1960s attempts to adapt the A B C scheme to fit the new and often conflicting evidence then accumulating had led to disenchantment. Against a growing swell of anti-invasionist thinking a fresh approach was demanded. A reappraisal of artefacts and settlement at the beginning of the period argued, it was claimed, for continuity, not introduction by an invading Hallstatt horde. Equally, a Marnian invasion in the third century was not easy to reconcile with known developments in metalwork. Yet invasions or migrations were still to play an important part in the two new syntheses which appeared in the mid-1970s. D. W. Harding still argued for three invasions with a three-fold cultural division of the period, while Barry Cunliffe accepted

Marnians in Yorkshire and Belgic settlers in the south-east. Not all were to agree, and with a growing belief that the historical record was itself not above refutation, the Belgic invasion of 75 BC began to look more suspect.

Over the past twenty years an alternative approach has taken shape, using archaeological evidence, particularly pottery, to suggest regional groupings. Regional studies aimed at producing a series of relative sequences began to replace the national frameworks. With a growing list of radiocarbon dates, the beginning of the period could be pushed back in time, and continuity with the later Bronze Age clearly documented. Trade was seen as being as much a catalyst for change as migration, while the idea took root that Britain was but one part of a broad North-West European cultural province. If so, many social, economic, political and even religious developments might appear more or less simultaneously within this zone without the need to involve folk movement.

With the expansion of environmental studies a much fuller picture has emerged of changes in climate and environment during the latter half of the millennium. But the picture remains uneven and complex. After 500 BC many areas beyond the settled chalklands were subjected to widespread clearance and much marginal land was brought into cultivation. Yet in other areas a different pattern emerges. Dartmoor stayed abandoned due to increased acidity and the formation of blanket peat, while the North Yorkshire Moors may have remained uncultivated. Much of this changing land use is now seen as due to over-exploitation of land with subsequent erosion of soils rather than simply a response to deteriorating climatic conditions. Whatever the cause, the change may well have taken place gradually over an extended period of time. Evidence from the Cat's Water sub-site of Fengate, for example, suggests a prolonged struggle against rising water-levels (28). Here ground water was sufficiently low for areas below the 3m (10ft) contour to be permanently occupied from the fourth–third centuries BC through to the Roman Invasion and then again for a short period in the second century AD. The thorough and repeated recutting of drainage ditches and an apparent migration of the site to the driest area enabled the settlement to survive until the rising water table eventually forced its total abandonment before modern drainage of the Fens once again made occupation possible in the eighteenth century.

Interest in settlement had been greatly stimulated by the publication of the excavation of the farmstead enclosure at Little Woodbury (Wiltshire) in 1940. This report had unequivocally demonstrated that area excavation was capable of recovering the surviving ground-plans of timber structures far more successfully than the narrow slit trenches hitherto in fashion. The excavation had also provided evidence for different types of timber structure: a palisaded enclosure, post-built round-houses and rectangular four-post structures. From the ground-plans recovered it became possible to attempt reconstructions of those above-ground structures which no longer survived and to begin to assign to them different uses. Aerial photography in turn provided

28 An imaginative reconstruction of life in part of the settlement on the Cat's Water site, Fengate (Cambridgeshire) during the Late Iron Age, viewed from the north-east. After Pryor

Lying at the Fen edge, flooding was a hazard which increased as the water-table rose and finally led to the abandonment of the site. Drainage ditches were repeatedly recut and extended as the need arose. Hedges may also have been established or developed naturally so providing shelter from biting north and east winds.

Not all of the round-houses were inhabited. Some may have been used to shelter animals and others for produce and implements. It has been estimated that a family of four or five persons could have lived in a round-house, so the total number living in this corner of the settlement may have varied from four to thirty, if all of the huts were occupied simultaneously. Because of the high water-table, water was readily available from shallow wells. However, it precluded the use of deep pits for storage.

Stock-rearing was the main agricultural occupation, chiefly cattle, with sheep (or goats) and pigs. Animal products, wood, reeds and clay were available for a variety of processes and crafts. Grain, salt, metals and stone were amongst the most important commodities which had to be obtained from sources outside the settlement.

the mechanism whereby lowland sites could be recognised in both soil and crop marks. The result was a vast increase in the number of sites recorded in these areas, and similar crop mark patterns of ditched enclosures, clusters of more or less superimposed hut circles and pits came to be recognised in many other parts of Britain. Yet aerial photography and fieldwalking have been shown to have their limitations. They favour thin soils, particularly those where chalk and gravel underlie areas under arable cultivation. Excavation of sites on clay like Little Waltham (Essex) and on the alluvium of the Fens have underlined the danger that certain areas may receive too little attention. The degree to which recovery is biased will vary, but the Oxford Unit has calculated, for example, that the photogenic river terraces of the Upper Thames Basin have received twelve times the attention that their actual area warrants to give an even coverage over the whole region.

Whatever the bias, a feature of the evidence now available is the great variety of different settlement types recurring over much of Britain: open, enclosed and defended; dispersed, concentrated and nucleated. Much of this new information remains to be digested and difficulties abound. Attempts to classify according to crop mark shape may aid recording but are unlikely to provide a sound basis for interpretation. Not all features show up either as soil or crop mark, so that basic information is often incomplete. Without excavation, differences due to population size, function or chronology cannot be distinguished. Complexity may stem from a site having served a number of different roles with a high population over a restricted period, or may reflect successive changes over a more extended time-span. The very size of a settlement at any one time may be difficult to deduce. At Mingies Ditch, Hardwick (Oxfordshire) the inhabited structure, represented by a ring-gully and circle of postholes, occupied at least four different positions, migrating over time in an anticlockwise direction within the ditched enclosure area. Without excavation such a settlement could have been interpreted as comprising four contemporary huts. Yet even total excavation may fail to provide definitive answers, for within a settlement it can be difficult to establish an overall sequence to include every feature. Total excavation at Gussage all Saints in Dorset (29) failed in this respect, while extensive excavations currently under way at Danebury (Hampshire) have shown that such sequences survive only in limited areas just within the defensive circuit. Difficulties of definition are also evident. How open was an open settlement? Some degree of protection against wild herds and predators would have been necessary, and it is possible that some areas would have been enclosed by hurdles or hedges hardly traceable in the archaeological record. Enclosure, on the other hand, may mark a change from arable to pastoral farming or the introduction of some form of pastoral activity requiring stock control, thus making enclosures and trackways necessary. But equally, it may indicate an increased population, leading to the need to define holdings more rigidly.

Functional specialisation has often been assumed for different forms of settlement, but this has not always been endorsed by excavation. 'Banjo' enclosures, with a ditch system funnelling towards a single narrow entrance leading to a circular enclosure, had been assumed to be the product of large-scale stock control, used perhaps for seasonal cattle round-ups. Yet the site at Bramdean (Hampshire) on excavation revealed a habitation occupied from the Middle to the Later Iron Age. Other interpretations seem more plausible. The series of scattered huts and sites spread over the lowlying flood plain of the Thames at Farmoor (Oxfordshire) seem very much a lowland version of the upland shielings, for these are set amongst open grassland and were used seasonally for perhaps no more than five consecutive years.

But though recent prospection and excavation have provided a somewhat unbalanced picture, they do suggest a very much more widespread and denser settlement pattern than had hitherto been considered, with a general trend from open and ill-defined settlement in the early first millennium to enclosed settlements defined by ditches,

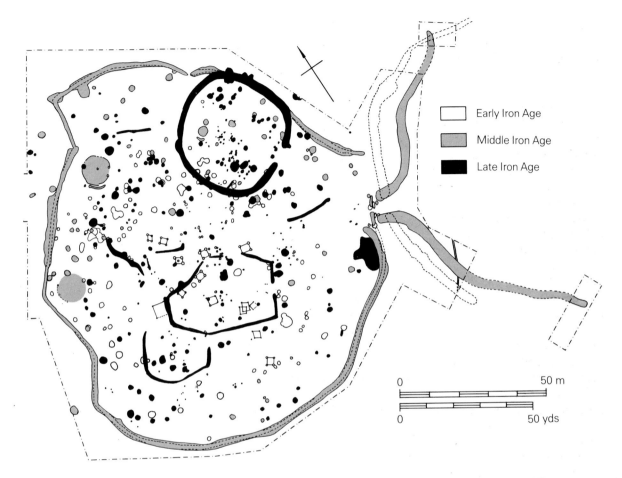

Early Iron Age

Middle Iron Age

Late Iron Age

0   50 m

0   50 yds

29 A plan of the settlement at Gussage All Saints (Dorset) showing the three structural phases. In contrast with Danebury Hillfort (Hampshire) and the Cat's Water settlement (Cambridgeshire), Gussage is a much smaller unit, possibly a farmstead, occupied by a single extended family group. After Wainwright

with or without the addition of a palisade, from the Middle Iron Age onwards. By the later Iron Age concentrated rural settlements with ditched trackways, rectangular enclosures and ring-gullies appear widespread throughout Lowland Britain.

Elsewhere, in the north of England, many small fortified settlements have been recorded and some excavated. Hownam Rings (Borders), for example, started life as a palisaded enclosure, was then walled in stone and developed into a multivallate fort, but ended as an undefended settlement. Pastoralism seems to have predominated, but artefacts are few and chronology relies heavily on radiocarbon. Similarly, in Wales the Iron Age culture seems to be virtually aceramic, and dating is uncertain until the arrival of Roman pottery. In the west and north of Scotland major excavations at Jarlshof and Clickhimin (Shetland) led to new theories about the development of brochs (30) and wheelhouses. Here typologies abound but the rarity of datable artefacts and sparsity of radiocarbon dates combine to inhibit a convincing reconstruction of the period.

Hillfort studies, in contrast, have developed strongly in post-War years. Not only have radiocarbon dates shown that hillfort construction

30　Reconstruction view of the Clickhimin Broch (Shetland) as it may have appeared between the first century BC and the second century AD, with the stone-built broch towering over its encircling wall and the entrance defended by a massive rectangular blockhouse. The islet lies close to the southern shore of the loch from where all of the building-stone had to be ferried. Despite problems of access, flooding and shortage of raw materials, the site had been favoured for occupation since perhaps the eighth century BC as farmstead and fort. After Hamilton

Brochs have been defined as tapering circular towers whose overall height could be in excess of 15 m (50 ft), built of dry-stone walling using an unusual hollow-wall technique. At the base, the main wall is solid, at Clickhimin over 5 m (16 ft) thick, but upwards it tapers and divides, with separate inner and outer walls bonded together at vertical intervals by horizontal stone slabs which form floors running within the walls. The various floor levels are connected by flights of steps, but whether these galleries were specifically constructional features combining the functions of bonding with scaffolding, or had additional uses, remains uncertain. It is unlikely that the method of roofing will be discovered since no wall survives complete. Timber-framed huts around the inner wall provided the living

accommodation.

Brochs had evolved uniquely in Scotland by about 100 BC. They now survive as impressive monuments to the skills and organisational abilities of their builders. Nearly five hundred have been identified around the coastal margins of the north-western mainland and the islands of the Hebrides, Orkneys and Shetlands. Despite this geographical spread these defensive buildings share considerable uniformity in design and construction and this, combined with their coastal distribution, has led to one theory, by no means universally accepted, that they were built by a cohesive maritime power for both defence and prestige.

began at a much earlier phase than hitherto supposed, but open area excavation within the interior of the forts was to reveal in many cases a very different role to that of the temporary refuge once assumed. Prior to the Second World War, excavations at Maiden Castle had produced evidence of extensive occupation. Excavations in the 1960s in the Welsh Marches, at Croft Ambrey, Credenhill and Midsummer Hill were to suggest that intensive ordered occupation over an extended period might for many be the norm. Work at South Cadbury Castle (Somerset) further supported such a view but later came excavations at Balksbury and Winklebury (Hampshire) revealing a different picture – of occupation, but over a more limited span of time.

With well over a thousand hillforts known from Britain, extending in size from as little as four to over a hundred hectares (10–250 acres) and with defences varying from the simple to the highly complex, the likelihood that all could have served the same function throughout their lives was always fairly remote. Exploration was to show that while many possessed storage pits and above-ground four-post 'granaries', suggesting that storage of surplus agricultural produce, principally grain, could have been one of their primary functions, others like Crickley Hill and Danebury had developed into something more, becoming defended permanent settlements occupied over several centuries. The Danebury excavations, in their sixteenth year in 1985, have in particular offered a yardstick against which to test many of the ideas and assumptions deduced from more limited excavation elsewhere.

Danebury (31), which had been built in the middle of the sixth century BC, had remained in occupation until the first century BC (32). While other hillforts along the southern chalklands passed out of use, Danebury, in company with a small number of other forts, gained in importance, passing from an enclosure formed by a simple timber-framed rampart and ditch to one defended by a massive V-cut ditch and dump-constructed banks. The timber gates at the eastern end, re-modelled more than once, must have been imposing. The fort within reveals ordered settlement with signs of incipient urbanisation. A road ran across from the eastern to the western gate, with two subsidiary roads running parallel to the rampart in the southern sector. The circular houses, 6–9m (20–30ft) across with single entries and walls of wattle or split vertical planks, clustered around the inner side of the ramparts. Over 2,000 grain-storage pits have already been excavated and four-post 'granaries' abound, scattered in the early period but concentrated later in the southern sector of the site. At the centre, four rectangular buildings suggest shrines comparable to those found at South Cadbury (Somerset) and Heathrow (Middlesex). Winter-sown spelt and hulled six-row barley were the principal cereals stored; sheep, cattle and pig the main stock animals, but detailed study of the domestic rubbish shows the diet extended by a long list of fruits and berries, fish, birds and venison.

The Danebury project has provided an opportunity to compare the

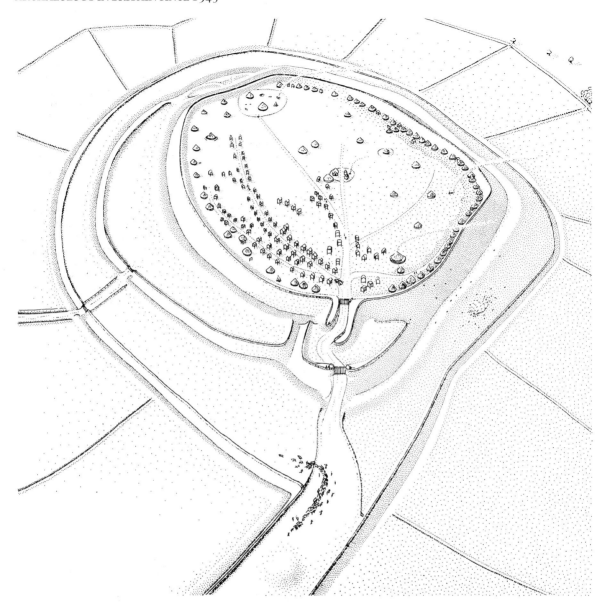

life within the fort with that of the scattered farmsteads of the region. Little so far suggests any marked disparity in quality, either of living-structure or of objects to hand, but quantity is a different matter. Certainly in terms of food, the amount stored is well in excess of that likely to have been produced in the immediate locality, and detailed analysis of the weed seeds surviving amongst the stored grain shows that crops were derived from both the damp river valleys and fields set on the clay-capped hills to the north. As yet the evidence is not sufficiently conclusive to show whether Danebury was the seat of local power to which a client population brought its surplus in the form of tribute, or whether here was the communal food store, guarded and overseen by a resident population. Perhaps both are simply aspects of the same situation. Whatever the final judgement, study of finds recovered has offered

31 A bird's-eye view of the Danebury Hillfort (Hampshire) as it may have appeared in its late phase, 400–100 BC, when it was defended by multiple circuits of ditches and banks (from the east). The round-houses may have been inhabited, and the population has been estimated at between 200 and 350 at any one time. Smaller square structures may have been used for storage, along with large numbers of bell-shaped storage pits. At the centre the larger rectangular structures have been interpreted as religious shrines, while a larger hut complex, isolated from the main settlement areas, may have housed the head man and his entourage.

32   A selection of pottery which illustrates changing and proliferating vessel-shapes and decoration at Danebury Hillfort (Hampshire) from the sixth to the first centuries BC. Since no clay was available within the hillfort, clay and finished vessels had to be brought in. For most of the period of occupation, however, the inhabitants used handmade vessels made from clay available within a day's walk of the site. By the first century BC imports had reached the Wessex region – containers of wine from Italy, wheel-thrown cordoned and graphite-coated fine wares from Brittany and Normandy, while vessels ornamented with curvilinear patterns were brought in from the area of the Glastonbury and Meare Lake villages (Somerset). After Cunliffe

Top row Ceramic Phases 1–3 (Early Occupation, *c.* 500–450 BC). The basic vessel-form was rather shapeless with a tall upright neck or rim and slight, rounded shoulder. On the left, the utilitarian pots, large jars for storage and cooking were poorly finished and plain, ornament being confined to fingernail impressions along the top edge of the rim. In contrast, on the right, the small cordoned and decorated bowl is both shapely and carefully made, with a bright red glossy burnished outer suface.

Middle row Ceramic Phases 6–7 (Late Period, *c.* 400–100 BC). The basic form was widemouthed and bucket-like, shapelessness being taken to an extreme. Rims have been reduced to a narrow bead. Generally, the vessels were more skilfully

formed and better finished than in the earlier periods. Conical saucepan pots and shallow open bowls were particular innovations of the Wessex region and immediately adjoining areas. Similarly, with the increased use of burnished ornament, regional decorative patterns and styles emerged, simple eyebrow and intricate herring-bone motifs being specialities.

Bottom row Ceramic Phase 8 (Late Period). Techniques of wheel-throwing and wheel-finishing were introduced during the first century BC. They facilitated the development of markedly curvaceous vessel-forms and the use of horizontal raised cordons to emphasise and complicate the shape. Decorative patterning was much simpler.

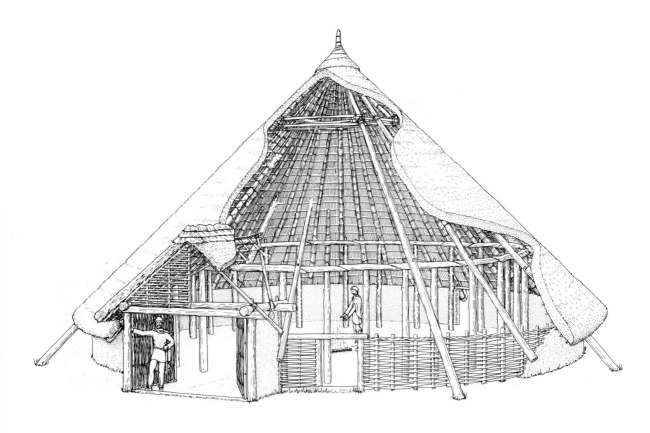

an opportunity to assess the degree of self-sufficiency and need for contact that such an Iron Age community might achieve and require.

Experimental work, too, has added much to our understanding of how an Iron Age community might have functioned. The Butser Ancient Farm Research Project was set up on some fourteen hectares of chalkland near Petersfield (Hampshire) to establish an experimental Iron Age farmstead with reconstructed houses (33) and adjoining grazing and arable land. The project was designed to explore theories and ideas generated by archaeological discovery and useful data has already accrued on a wide range of topics, from house construction to animal husbandry and crop storage. From these and other lines of research it has become clear that, while many of the basic needs – for example, of wood, clay, bone, leather, wool and straw – could have been met by many communities, at least in Lowland Britain, from the resources of the immediate locality, other raw materials would have had to have been brought in from adjoining regions, no doubt through exchange. Of these iron and bronze would, of course, have figured large.

One of the more interesting products of post-War excavation has been the growing number of settlements to yield evidence of ironworking. Slags, crucible and furnace fragments, as well as actual ironwork, appear regularly amongst the finds recovered. Clearly, both smelting and smithing often took place on the same site. Although iron ore was

33 Drawing of the round-house constructed at the Butser experimental Iron Age farm, which was itself based on the ground-plan of a post-built hut excavated at Pimperne (Dorset). After Reynolds

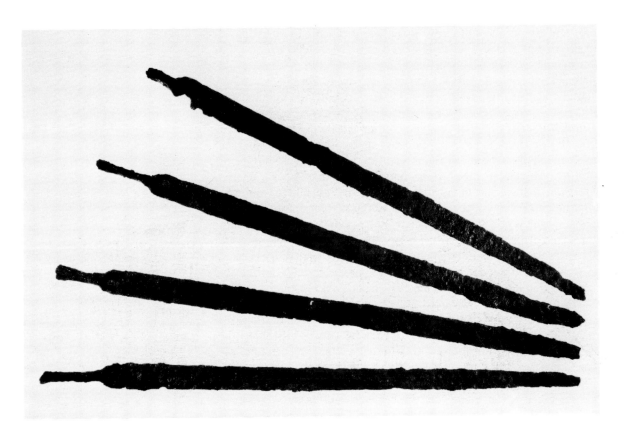

34 Four iron 'currency bars', portable ingots of forged iron, probably dating to the first century BC. 'Currency bars' appear to have been forged to a fairly standard pattern and size, with a 'handle' formed by bending over the edges towards each other. These examples weigh from 490 to 550 grammes, vary in length from 78 cm to 83 cm (30–32 in.), while the width is approximately 4 cm (1.5 in.), large enough for a sword. A smaller size was also produced. Examples found recently at Orton Meadows, Peterborough (Cambridgeshire) still held traces of wood within the 'handle'.

In the *Commentaries*, Julius Caesar notes that the British tribes used bars of iron as coinage or currency, hence the use of the term 'currency bar'. They are now considered to have been ingots prepared from smelted down iron ore ready for smithing into tools and weapons etc. Since sources of good quality iron ore were limited, 'currency bars' may have been distributed widely from their point of origin.

available over much of Britain, early methods of ironmaking required ores of high grade, and these were of much more limited occurrence. The bulk of the metal probably came on site in raw state, but part was traded as smelted iron in the form of 'currency bar' ingots (34), made to specific sizes and weights. Some idea of the scarcity of iron and the value placed upon it is shown by the fact that iron tools and weapons were not carelessly discarded when broken or worn out. Sites like Danebury have shown that repairs were attempted and tools reshaped for other use. A study of these pieces also reveals something of the blacksmith's craft, for not all were skilled or knowledgeable in the selection of blooms suitable for quenching and tempering.

Bronze-working, too, has seen considerable attention. The largest and most varied collection of bronze-working debris has come from the site of the small farmstead at Gussage all Saints. From the fragments of clay moulds recovered we know that sets of horse-harness for chariots or carts were being made, comprising horse-bits, rein rings and linch-pins. No fewer than 3,583 items are represented, yet despite the total examination of the site not a single example of the finished product, or indeed of comparable piece, was discovered: all had been removed from the site. The range of raw materials required for such an output makes interesting reading: beeswax for patterns, clay for crucibles and moulds with sand for tempering, oak for charcoal and other woods for hearths, bone and iron for the smith's own tools, copper and tin or, more likely, bronze as raw material, as well as iron to make iron fittings, for the Gussage smith worked both metals. Much of the required bronze would no doubt have been acquired in the form of recycled scrap, and the fact that all fragments had been removed before abandonment of the farm underlines the scarcity and importance now attached to the metal. Yet if Julius Caesar's claim that Cassivellaunus had a force of four thousand chariots is correct, the sets of rein rings alone would have called for one-and-a-half tonnes of bronze for their production.

Other commodities were no less important. Suitable stone for querns was often not available in the immediate locality and had to be sought from neighbouring regions, as was salt from the coast. Small luxury items – armlets of Kimmeridge shale, glass beads, amber and coral – moved far further from their sources of origin, but how far these and the fine metalwork produced in gold as well as bronze were distributed in society or moved down the social scale is less easy to estimate. Exchange, tribute, gift and plunder would have given such objects some mobility, but in a period largely divorced from formal burial, and with other aspects of wealth and power hardly to be observed, such questions remain difficult to assess. Fortunately, formal burial was to reappear in the latter half of the millennium, and this offers a glimpse, first in Yorkshire, later in south-eastern England, of stratified societies.

Though formal burial also re-emerged in the form of cist graves in the south-west, it is the 'Arras' culture cemeteries of eastern Yorkshire which offer the greatest wealth of information. The rite was inhumation.

35 Two of the chariot-burials discovered in 1984 in an extensive Iron Age inhumation cemetery at Wetwang Slack (North Humberside).

The iron tyres and knave hoops from the wheels and the five graduated bronze and iron terrets from the yoke pole survive *in situ*, showing that the chariot was dismantled before being placed in the grave. Linch-pins and horse bits were added later.

Left The grave of a woman accompanied by her iron mirror, iron and gold dress-pin and decorated bronze canister (see 36).

Right The grave of a warrior accompanied by his iron sword in its decorated bronze and iron scabbard and seven iron spearheads.

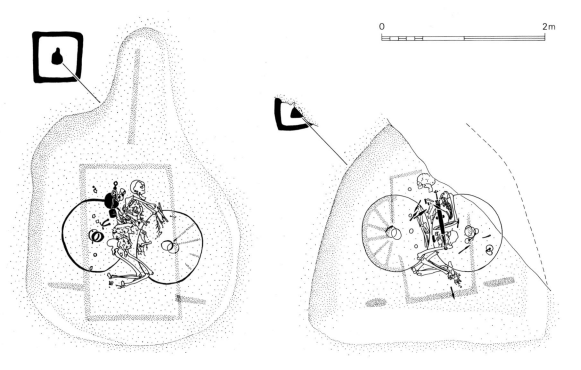

36 Decorated bronze canister sealed at both ends, with a suspension chain, found in a chariot burial at Wetwang Slack (North Humberside) (see 35).

The cylinder was made from one piece of sheet bronze secured with dome-headed rivets. Three similar rivets secured the top in place, while the bottom was sealed by a rolled seam. 'Top' and 'bottom' are indicated by domed studs of red glass or 'enamel' of different size, each held in place with a circular repoussé setting and a central rivet. A loop on the 'top' holds 14.6cm (5.75in.) of suspension chain while there is a second loop on the side. The ornament comprises a scroll of interlocked s-shaped motifs, simply executed in incised lines infilled with cross-hatching, parallel lines and stipple. The design was amended to fit the circular field of the top and bottom surfaces. It is a fine example of early Celtic art.

Its function remains unknown. Since it is a hollow canister it could be a container, but as it is sealed, it cannot have been for everyday use. Investigation with x-ray has revealed no solid content, but it may still contain decayed organic material. Whatever its function, whether ritual or merely decorative, it was sufficiently prized or significant to be included amongst the personal belongings of a woman whose status warranted a chariot-burial.

Distinctive cemeteries of square ditched barrows are now known through aerial photography in almost every dry valley in the Wolds, and cemeteries at Burton Fleming, Garton and Wetwang Slack (Humberside) have seen extensive excavation. By Continental standards the burials revealed are poor. Half have yielded no evidence for objects placed with the dead, unless these were made of organic substances that have left no trace. Most of the remainder held only a simple pot, a joint of meat and sometimes the brooch which had secured at the shoulder the clothing of the dead. Changes both in the organisation of the cemeteries and in the burial rite have been noted. At Wetwang and Garton the earlier burials were set into larger and more widely spaced barrow areas, with the burials themselves placed at no great depth. As the cemetery developed and space became more limited, the barrows were reduced in size and jostled more closely together, while the graves became deeper. Whether such a sequence reflects a growing poverty, pressure on available land or some change in religious attitude is difficult to say. But amongst the burials in Yorkshire are a small number which have always stood out as of a different and higher status, with the body placed upon a dismantled cart accompanied by harness fittings. Until recently no

37 (*below*) Upper part of an iron sword in its bronze scabbard found in a pond at Little Wittenham (Oxfordshire). The waterlogged conditions in which it was discovered had helped to preserve the bronze in excellent condition.

The top panel of the scabbard is decorated with a typical curvilinear repoussé design, while the remaining length has chased laddering on either side of a central rib.

38 Bronze mirror with decorated back and cast bronze handle, dating to the late first century BC or early first century AD, found at Aston (Hertfordshire).

The design on the back was executed with scriber and graver using a similar technique to that shown in detail in 39. The handle was cast separately with prepared slots at the top into which the mirror plate was fitted.

It was found in two pieces in 1979; the mirror plate by chance after ploughing and the handle during the subsequent archaeological excavation. The mirror may have originally been placed with a cremation burial.

Decorated bronze mirrors are amongst the finest achievements of Celtic craftsmen in Britain and they are unmatched on the Continent. Fourteen provenanced examples have been found; each is unique with a different design on the back and, where they survive, a different shape of handle. At least eight examples have been found in graves, four each in cremation and inhumation burials dating to the late first century BC or the first century AD. They are considered to be prestige items belonging to women of high status and wealth.

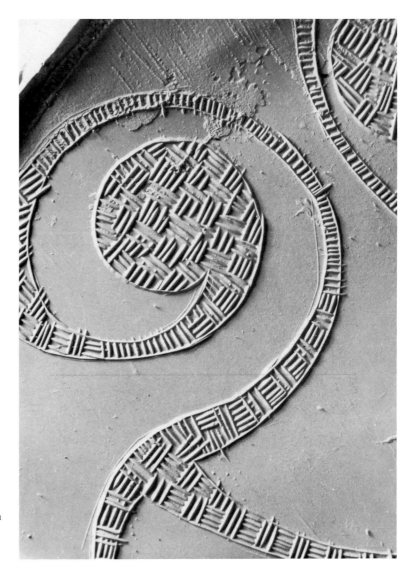

39   Detail of a silicone rubber mould of
the decoration on the back of the mirror
found at Great Chesterford (Essex).
   The fine 'guide-lines' of the design were
lightly incised with a fine-pointed scriber
and then infilled with an intricate basket-
weave effect of broader strokes made with
a graver which had a chamfered cutting
edge. Such techniques were widely used
by bronze- and goldsmiths in the Late Iron
Age to produce decorative items like the
Aston mirror (38) and the Snettisham torc
terminals (42).

weapons had been found with such a burial, but in 1984 at Wetwang
Slack (35) a group of three came to light and these included two iron
swords in decorated bronze and iron scabbards and seven iron spearheads. In this society both men and women qualified for such burial,
and it was the woman's grave at Wetwang which yielded the richest
items – rein rings decorated with coral, a dress pin enhanced with gold
and a canister magnificently decorated with Celtic art motifs (36).
   It had been the similarity between these burials of the 'Arras' culture
and those of the Champagne region of France that had led many to
argue for the arrival of an invading warrior élite who, having settled,
had imposed their burial rites upon the native populace. Yet many
differences exist between the rites of the two regions, and others have
preferred to argue that the Yorkshire burials represent just a local version

of what had come to be the practice elsewhere in North-Western Europe. Whatever the origin, the Yorkshire cemeteries give clear evidence of a hierarchical society in which objects of value were, at least in death, only for the few.

Elsewhere the number of items of fine metalwork discovered since the Second World War has grown steadily, and both new and old finds have been subjected to more critical study to discover methods of manufacture and techniques of decoration. Notable discoveries have been the bronze scabbards from Little Wittenham in Oxfordshire (37) and Isleham (Cambridgeshire), and decorated mirrors, such as those from Holcombe (Devon) and Aston (Hertfordshire) (38). The mirrors in particular have seen much detailed examination, and the distinctive marks left by many of the craftsmen's tools can now be recognised with some confidence (39). Occasionally in southern Britain such choice items reached the grave, for over much of south-eastern England during the first century BC the rite of cremating the dead was now adopted. The majority were buried in a pottery urn without other grave-goods in groups ranging in size from a few graves to extensive cemeteries of nearly five hundred burials. Less is known about the settlements which they served, but at Baldock (Hertfordshire) and at the smaller settlement of Owslebury (Hampshire) ditched cemeteries adjoin the inhabited enclosures. As in Yorkshire, within this general tradition stand a small number of graves set apart by the richness of the objects placed within them. Three in particular at Hertford Heath, Welwyn Garden City and Baldock, all in Hertfordshire, have added to our knowledge of this phase, offering a fair impression of the range of imported goods and fashions now reaching south-eastern Britain through contact with the Roman world. Many of the items relate to drink – Italian wine amphorae, bronze jugs and strainers and fine silver drinking-cups – but other high-quality items are also present, like the pillar-moulded glass bowl from the Hertford Heath grave. Particularly rich was the Welwyn Garden City grave. Into this went five amphorae, thirty-six pottery vessels, a silver cup, a strainer and dish of bronze, wooden vessels with bronze and iron fittings, as well as a remarkable set of twenty-four decorated glass gaming pieces – items which would not have disgraced the household of a provincial Roman citizen. But other items from these graves, like the fire-dogs (40) and wooden bucket with decorated bronze binding strips from the Baldock grave (41), offer an insight into a different world, into that of the native smiths and how they responded to the needs and demands of this insular aristocratic market, which marked the passing of the dead with such conspicuous display.

In other regions the display of wealth was to take other forms. Perhaps the most dramatic increase in fine metalwork seen since the War has been in the number of gold-alloy torcs which have come to light, all as chance discoveries. In the autumn of 1948 and 1950 a series of hoards was discovered in Norfolk, comprising an array of complete and fragmentary torcs, bangles and coins. One of the hoards yielded the finest example of the Iron Age goldsmith's craft so far recovered from Britain –

40   Oxhead terminal of an iron fire-dog, one of a pair in a cremation burial dating to the mid-first century BC found at Baldock, Hertfordshire (see 41).

The head has been modelled in the round with nostrils, jaw and eyes skilfully shaped and emphasised to produce a particularly impressive example of the blacksmith's craft. It surmounts one upright of a freestanding H-shaped frame, about 70cm (27.5in.) high and 69cm (27in.) wide, and is matched by another head on the second upright. The frame was forged from three iron bars, using tools like those found at Waltham Abbey (43). Each upright has a square mortice into which tenons on either end of the crossbar were fitted.

Other pairs of iron fire-dogs have been found in cremation burials in East Anglia. Their precise function is unknown but they may have been used in pairs with fuel heaped over the crossbar and the horns helping to support spits for roasting meat or hooks for suspending a cauldron. Of the examples discovered to date, only that from Baldock has been accompanied by a suitable metal cooking vessel, a bronze cauldron.

41 Reconstruction of a late Iron Age cremation burial discovered at Baldock (Hertfordshire). The burial was found during building operations. The objects were smashed and most fragments removed and dumped on a traffic island undergoing construction at the time. During the subsequent archaeological excavation the grave was located and the original arrangement of the grave-goods worked out by combining information given by the discoverers with the position of *in situ* fragments and iron and bronze stains surviving on the floor of the grave.

The bronze cauldron containing the cremated remains of an adult male had been placed in the centre of the grave with the other grave goods encircling it – a ceramic wine container, a pair of shallow bronze bowls, a pair of wooden buckets sheathed in bronze bands, a pair of iron fire-dogs (40) and the carcase or part of the carcase of a small pig.

The buckets were the most unusual finds since they appear to have stood on three rectangular wooden feet. Made of wood, the outer surface was entirely sheathed in sheet bronze bands, three broad and two narrow, while the feet were covered with rectangular bronze plaques decorated with a simple geometric repoussé design. Each bucket had two very similar but not identical handle mounts fixed over the rim. The mounts are in the form of a helmeted human head with prominent, lentoid eyes, triangular nose and narrow slit mouth. Each head has a mortice hole at the back in which the semi-circular cast bronze handle pivoted.

The wine amphora or container had originally been used to transport wine from Italy to southern Britain. It may have been full when placed in the grave, a status symbol ready for use in the afterlife; alternatively, the wine may have been used during the ritual accompanying the interment. Wine was clearly important in burial rites in the first century BC and early first century AD, for two cremation burials found about 20km south of Baldock, near Welwyn, each contained five amphorae and all the paraphernalia associated with decanting, straining, mixing and drinking wine, much of which had to be imported from Italy or Gaul since there were no alternative sources closer to hand.

42 A multi-strand ring-terminal torc made in gold alloyed with silver, from Hoard E, found on Ken Hill, Snettisham (Norfolk).

It weighs 1083.3g. and has a maximum diameter of 19.5 cm (7.8 in.). The hoop comprises sixty-four lengths of gold wire twisted together in groups of eight, with the ends then soldered onto the terminals, which were made using the lost-wax process. A pattern or model of each, complete with its intricate ornament of motifs in relief and basket-weave infilling, was made in wax and then covered in clay to form a mould. The molten gold melted and replaced the wax when it was poured into the mould.

Five hoards, Snettisham Hoards A–E, were found in the same area between 1948 and 1950 during deep-ploughing. This multi-strand torc was found in Hoard E with a decorated bracelet and about half of a second plain torc threaded through the ring terminals. In all there are the remains of at least sixty-three torcs and bracelets and 158 coins, many made of gold or a gold and silver alloy, as well as miscellaneous fragments and lumps of molten gold and tin. The whole group may have been buried at the same time in the second half of the first century BC and may have been the stock of a smith. However, torcs were apparently more than prestige ornaments since they have been portrayed around the necks of Celtic deities. There may, therefore, be a ritual aspect to the Snettisham Hoards.

the Snettisham torc (42). The hoop of this torc was made of eight ropes of wire twisted together, each rope comprising eight wires similarly twisted. At each end a massive cast hollow terminal had been attached. Since 1950 a further twelve torcs have been discovered, six, probably from a single hoard, at Ipswich (Suffolk). All appear to date to the first century BC and leave no doubt as to the wealth they represent – the six Ipswich torcs alone weigh almost 5.5 kg (12 lb). But less easily explained is the concentration of these finds in East Anglia. Nothing else in the archaeology of the region would point to the presence of a wealthy aristocracy or suggest why this region in particular should have attracted a greater wealth than elsewhere. Whatever the reason, the torcs, along with the coins which now appear, demonstrate that in the first century BC gold and silver were available in greater quantities for items of prestige than at any time since the Later Bronze Age. Perhaps it is significant that the torcs so far discovered fall outside the areas where burials of Aylesford type occur.

Little mention has been made so far of religion or of formal shrines, but these have received attention, too, in the post-War period. The ritual deposition of weapons and shields in rivers and marshes already established in the Later Bronze Age clearly persisted. Many of the more spectacular examples of Iron Age weaponry have come from rivers, particularly the Thames and Witham. In recent years new deposits have been found near Peterborough at Orton Meadows during gravel extraction in an old stream bed of the River Nene. Swords and scabbards predominate, but domestic items are also represented, including an iron sickle and large iron ladle. Blacksmiths' tools comprised a further deposit (43) found in the River Lea at Waltham Abbey (Essex). Such discoveries confirm an impression gained from the hoard found during the

Second World War on the margin of a lake at Llyn Cerrig Bach on Anglesey (North Wales) that offerings were by no means confined to the spoils of battle or prime objects of military display. But ritual and religion are an area where later written record and recent archaeological discovery mesh badly. While the classical writers speak much of groves, archaeology has produced increasing evidence for shrines and temples. Pre-Roman use has been established beneath the Roman temples at Harlow (Essex), Uley (Gloucestershire), Frilford (Oxfordshire) and Brigstock (Northamptonshire). Even the typical square 'Romano–Celtic' temple with portico may have been in use before the Roman Conquest, for similar structures have been excavated at Heathrow, within the fort at South Cadbury and are also perhaps represented within the fort of Danebury.

In southern Britain the abandonment of hillforts like Danebury, the flourishing of trade with the Roman world, the appearance of rich graves of Welwyn type and the emergence of recognisable tribal centres (*oppida*) at sites like Braughing and St Albans (Hertfordshire), Colchester, and Silchester (Hampshire) mark the culmination of a period of reorientation in which settlement became more concentrated and tribal power more

43 A selection of tools for forging iron from a hoard of tools, implements and weapons found during gravel extraction along an old course of the River Lea at Waltham Abbey (Essex).

From left to right 1) pair of iron tongs, the handles of which may have been deliberately bent before deposition, total length 56cm (22in.); 2) sledge hammer-head, length 12cm (4.7in.). Grooves on two faces could have been used for rounding metal wire; 3) iron file, length 23cm (9in.); 4) iron anvil with a dual function: rods and bars could be bent over it, while two grooves on one face could be used for rounding wire.

The hoard also included spatulae, chisels, a bill-hook and poker, along with a whetstone for keeping edges sharp. It may have been the tool-kit of an itinerant blacksmith, for the number of heavy tools is limited and some are multi-purpose. The watery context and the deliberate spoiling of some items suggests that it may have been a ritual deposit made some time in the first century AD.

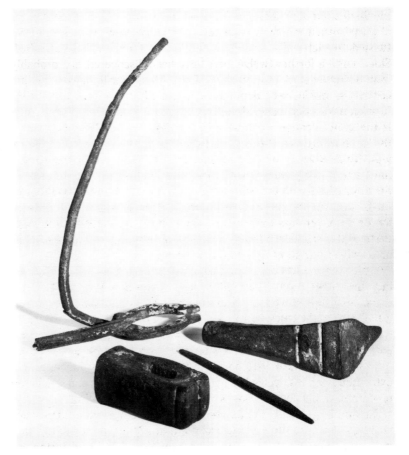

overt. Though still dependent upon a wide range of client farms and settlements, the *oppida* were to bring within their boundaries many of the activities associated with regional administration. The tribal system chronicled by Julius Caesar may not have been of long standing, but that it existed finds corroboration in the coinage now minted in the *oppida* and elsewhere.

The discovery of stone weights at Winklebury and Danebury, together with the better-known 'currency bar' ingots, which appear to have been made to definite standards, implies that some Iron Age communities were already familiar with the concept of weights and measures as an aid to exchange and payment. Some coins, too, may have reached southern Britain in the wake of trade, as objects of rarity and curiosity rather than as a form of agreed value. But the main impetus for the acceptance of coinage appears to have been payment for mercenaries serving in the Gallic Wars. Dating of the Gallo–Belgic and native series has remained fluid and, as a source of historical reconstruction, debatable, but the coins do record for the first time the actual names of the kings and tribes which were the reality of the century before Christ. Regrettably, what light they shed falls only on southern Britain, and such detail serves more as a reminder of the profound gaps which elsewhere are all too evident.

Despite an immense increase in new data and concentrated effort by prehistorians over the post-War period, a new and integrated picture of the British Iron Age remains something for the future. In terms of regional sequence, most progress has been achieved in Wessex, and search has been made of the southern coast as a natural 'contact zone' for sites which might yield positive evidence for trade with lands beyond the English Channel. One such site, now under excavation at Hengistbury Head (Dorset), is proving particularly fruitful. But many problems stubbornly persist. The isolation of Iron Age metalwork from the new pottery sequences is one, perpetuating problems already met in the previous period. But of greater concern are the vagaries of chronology and the realisation that at present no agreed criteria exist for assessing the archaeological record as to whether an invasion or migration has taken place. In these areas, at least, not all our innocence has been lost.

NOTES
1 D.L. Clarke, *Analytical Archaeology* (1968), p. 3
2 *Ibid.*, p. 22
3 *Ibid.*, p. 663
4 *Antiquity* XLVII (1973), p. 18
5 *Antiquity* XLIX (1975), p. 44
6 D. Clarke, 'Archaeology: the loss of Innocence', *Antiquity* XLVII (1973), pp. 6–18
7 S. Piggott, *The Neolithic Cultures of the British Isles* (1954)
8 D.L. Clarke, *Beaker pottery of Great Britain and Ireland* (1970)
9 C.F.C. Hawkes, 'Hillforts', *Antiquity* V (1931), pp. 60–97

*Radiocarbon dates expressed as bc are uncalibrated.

2 A Roman Province: Britain AD 43–410

Discoveries and ideas

Britain, brought under direct Roman control from AD 43, was never an illustrious province, nor have we inherited a rich legacy of standing monuments. Much of Hadrian's Wall is still incomparably majestic, but visitors to one of northern Britain's tallest standing Roman buildings, the Ravenglass baths (Cumbria), may well be disappointed by this modest little structure, especially if they have seen the vast and magnificent Caracallan baths in Rome or the huge Antonine baths in Carthage. Similarly, those who have sat in the elegant theatres of, say, Orange or Sabratha will find Verulamium's little theatre, charming though it is, rather trifling by comparison. Impressive monuments there are in Britain, not least the well-preserved and massive defences of some of the Saxon Shore forts that dot the coast of south-east England, but most of our Roman remains lie long buried beneath town, city or countryside and were, for the most part, a very pale reflection of the architectural glories of richer provinces.

This has had an important effect on the way that archaeological studies of this period have developed in Britain. In the Mediterranean the excavators of Pompeii, Ostia, Timgad and elsewhere saw their main priority in clear and unmistakable terms: to lay bare these spectacular remains. One can only admire their achievement as one wanders through the streets, squares and houses of a remote North African frontier town like Timgad, one of the most complete town-plans known to us from the Roman Empire. What this work did not do, however, was take into consideration the niceties of layer-by-layer investigation. More often than not late buildings were disregarded, dating relied upon the chance discovery of an inscription rather than upon the recovery of coins and pottery from floors and foundations, and no account was taken of buildings that may have been constructed in more ephemeral materials, such as wood. Structures made of timber *do* exist in regions like North Africa, but only very recently has this been demonstrated.

In Britain, on the other hand, excavators always had much less to work with and soon found themselves grappling with complex problems of interpretation: buildings where the stone had been removed completely, others made wholly of now perished wood, and, everywhere, structures that had been replaced time after time. Making sense of all

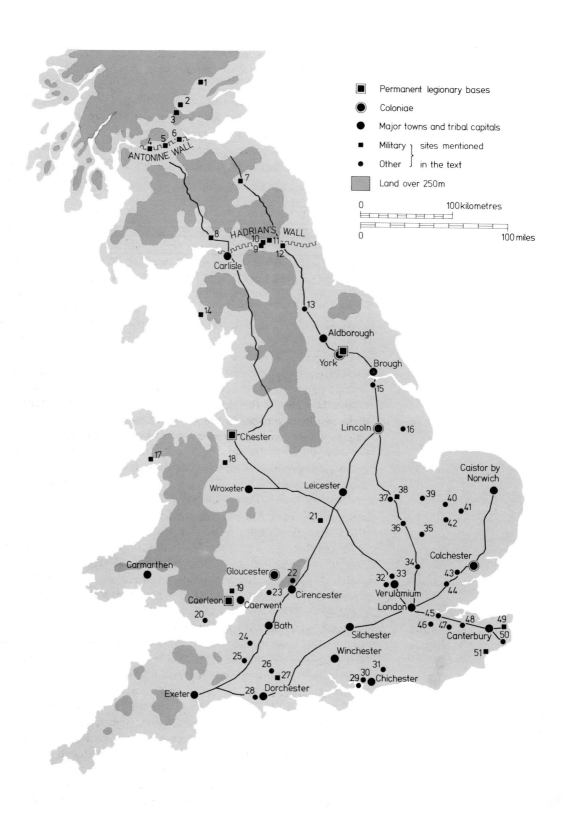

ANTONINE WALL

HADRIAN'S WALL

Carlisle

Aldborough

York

Brough

Lincoln

Chester

Wroxeter

Leicester

Caistor by Norwich

Carmarthen

Gloucester

Cirencester

Caerleon

Caerwent

Bath

Colchester

Verulamium

London

Silchester

Winchester

Canterbury

Chichester

Exeter

Dorchester

■	Permanent legionary bases
◉	Coloniae
●	Major towns and tribal capitals
■	Military ⎫ sites mentioned
●	Other ⎭ in the text
▨	Land over 250m

0 ————— 100 kilometres

0 ————— 100 miles

this meant developing refined techniques of excavation. Prominence is
always given, rightly, to the contribution of A.H.L.-F. Pitt-Rivers and
his work at Cranborne Chase (Wiltshire). This began in 1880, and the
publications had an immense influence upon Mortimer Wheeler and
others who followed.[1] But, for Romano–British archaeology, equally
significant things were soon happening elsewhere. In 1890, at Silchester
(Hampshire), the Society of Antiquaries of London initiated an imaginative project to strip the entire Roman town (still the most extensively
excavated urban site in Britain), while in 1896 the Society of Antiquaries
of Scotland began digging at the Roman fort of Ardoch (Tayside). Ardoch
is a site that is even now conspicuous for its magnificent ditches and
ramparts, fossilised in pasture, but one that is completely devoid of
standing remains. The report, promptly published in 1898, describes
how the 'Clerk of the Works' began to notice lines of circular pits and
was soon to work out that these had held timber uprights for wooden
buildings.[2] The published plan, with its barracks and headquarters
complex, was an unheralded triumph. Meanwhile, other excavators
were also identifying postholes at the Scottish forts of Bar Hill, Camelon,
Newstead and elsewhere, although none was as successful in restoring
complete plans. Nevertheless, the prevalence of timber buildings in these
northern forts was well recognised, as was the presence of several
periods of occupation, dated mainly by imported pottery. In 1919
George Macdonald, the pioneer of Antonine Wall studies, summed up
these results in a paper in the *Journal of Roman Studies*.[3] Here he was
able to isolate two main periods of fort-building, the earlier of which
could be related to the campaigns of Agricola (governor between AD 78
and 84) as described for us by his son-in-law, the historian Tacitus, and
the second to the frontier of Antoninus Pius. It was an important step,
not least because conclusions derived from detailed excavations were
being firmly set within a known historical framework.

Another giant of the time was Francis Haverfield, whose *Romanisation
of Roman Britain* (1912, originally a lecture given in 1905) developed
another important theme in Romano–British studies. Ideology and
archaeology have always been deeply interwoven, as the 'Marxist',
'social' and 'economic' schools of today clearly show; it may be no
accident that so many contemporary archaeologists in Britain are pre-
occupied with the reconstruction of ancient economies in these days
when talk is dominated by words like 'inflation', 'balance-of-payments'
and 'monetarism'. Indeed, it is revealing to go back to the end of the last
century and read the words of J. Toutain, writing about the classical
remains of Algeria: 'The better we understand what the Romans accom-
plished in their African provinces, then the better we shall be able to
direct our efforts and more speedily ensure their success.'[4] In other
words, the French saw their colonial role as identical to that of the
Romans, whose remains lay everywhere, and consequently ignored the
native tradition. Haverfield, by contrast, was fascinated by the mix of
Roman and native in Britain. Whereas it was only as recently as 1976
that a serious study (by a Tunisian, M. Benabou) was published on the

indigenous African contribution to Roman North Africa,[5] Haverfield ensured that, in Britain, this was a pivotal theme of Romano–British studies, whether in art, architecture, religion or in social matters. It was to prove a vital intellectual contribution.

It is an absorbing exercise to take the pages of the books and learned journals of the period between the two World Wars, and to see how Romano–British archaeology grew into the status of a serious academic discipline. In 1921 the Roman Society started to publish annual accounts of work-in-progress, and there began the slow process of what today we would call model-building: the integration of all this new data into historical schemes and explanations. Excavations burgeoned, prompted mainly by chance interest. For example, at the town of Venta Icenorum, Caistor-by-Norwich (Norfolk) parching of the grass in 1929 'revealed the complete lay-out of the town, the barley being devoid of colouring matter wherever walls and streets lay beneath the surface'.[6] An excavation committee was set up, funds were raised, and between 1929 and 1935 extensive digging took place. This was just one of a number of large-scale projects up and down the country, and in 1932 two assistant keepers at the British Museum saw fit to draw together the results of contemporary research. 'Prehistoric studies require an interim report', they wrote, but 'our knowledge of Roman Britain has advanced some way beyond this and . . . it is actually the stage of historical revision that is setting in'.[7] Similarly, a review published in the *Journal of Roman Studies* for 1933 on a general study of Roman Britain considered that the section on Hadrian's Wall was 'a clear and spirited statement of difficult problems that are nearing solution'.[8]

The work in question was by R.G. Collingwood, one of the brilliant thinkers of his age. A philosopher both by training and profession, Collingwood will always be Roman Britain's most distinguished 'amateur' scholar. It would be facile to sum up his contribution in a few lines, for it was enormous. What matters for our purposes is that Collingwood published several syntheses which were to hold the field until quite recent times. One dealt with the archaeological evidence – classifications of pots, brooches and the like, and of the sites that yielded them[9] – while others neatly integrated the evidence of archaeology and history into a narrative of Roman Britain.[10] This was 'model-building' on a grand scale, which, if criticised for 'driving the evidence hard' and 'building upon it a series of conclusions whose very artistry disguised the inherent weakness of foundation', nevertheless provided the main textbooks down to the 1950s and early 1960s.

Those words,[11] written in 1943, are of Ian Richmond who, with Wheeler, Simpson, Bushe-Fox and many more, were bringing excavation techniques towards the standards of the modern day. Their styles differed vastly. Bushe-Fox dug sites like the great fort at Richborough with huge squads of workmen and few supervisors and published prodigiously and well, with meticulous attention to his finds; Wheeler brought order and method (still coined in many countries as a catch-phrase) into the subject, and with a series of highly publicised campaigns, promptly and elegantly written up, injected new, influential and easily digested information into the arena; while Richmond and Simpson – also methodically – posed problems in their patient way and went forth to solve them. It is astounding to see how many sites that Richmond in particular tackled, normally with a few workmen, a carefully defined quest in mind – and almost always with brilliant results.

If aspects of these projects may not always please the excavation specialists of today, it is nevertheless the case that many vital sites were carefully examined. Sequences for Hadrian's Wall were worked out, sanctuaries received serious attention and villa-studies were placed on a firm footing. Moreover, new and important sites were being discovered or elucidated by the then infant craft of aerial photography. In the Lincolnshire and Cambridgeshire Fens, for example, duty flights by the Royal Air Force had registered an extraordinary wealth of detail concerning a plethora of native-style settlements, together with field divisions, ancient water-courses and much more. 'The only obstacle to clearing up the whole question of the Roman occupation of the Fens was the sheer magnitude of the task', one scholar was later to write,[12] and it is indeed sad that so little excavation of consequence was undertaken on the Roman sites of that now highly damaged landscape. Nevertheless, a start was made, and it is significant that the Fenland Research Committee, founded in 1932, included not just prehistorians and Roman archaeologists, but scientists – especially botanists – as well. It was the first major step in the widening of the discipline so that it incorporated environmental evidence into a wide and multi-period study of a specific landscape. Haverfield and Macdonald had earlier castigated those Roman archaeologists whose command of Latin was insufficient and who thereby misrepresented the written sources;[13] now, in the Fens of the 1930s, the non-classical scholar was beginning to impinge on spheres of interest that had always been traditionally those of the classicist and ancient historian.

The Second World War interrupted most things, but it also brought opportunities. In London some 20 hectares (50 acres) of the area enclosed by the Roman walls (which totals about 133 hectares, or 330 acres) had been devastated by bombing, and the Society of Antiquaries and the Ministry of Public Buildings and Works were quick to realise the possibilities: 'It was seen that there must be some interval before new buildings could be erected in these areas; for the first time therefore opportunity was provided for archaeological excavation in controlled conditions, free from the cramping limitations of time and builders' needs which had prevailed formerly'.[14] An excavation committee was set up, and despite acute shortages of time and money, work continued ceaselessly from 1947 until 1962. During this period truly spectacular finds were made, particularly the Cripplegate Fort and, above all, the Mithraeum – visited, it was estimated, by 35,000 people on one day alone in 1954. These brilliant excavations truly brought home the meaning of the term 'rescue archaeology' and, at the same time, led the way in the study of Britain's historic town centres. In the post-War period systematic investigation was put in hand on many towns with Roman origins, bringing forth a deluge of new information. Approaches to urban archaeology also changed, so that at Verulamium, St Albans (Hertfordshire) in 1957–60 'at first the method of excavation was to dig comparatively small trenches . . . but great difficulty was experienced in correlating the timber buildings . . . from trench to trench. In subsequent seasons, therefore, efforts were made to open up much wider areas'.[15] Henceforth many excavations were to become ever bigger, and the neat array of baulks that had so characterised work before the War were increasingly abandoned.

Tragically, however, the generally augmented scale of investment in excavation in no way matched the scale of destruction. In London during the 1960s heroic efforts, often by weekend volunteer teams, could not really stem the onslaught of the developers. There was no time and little money: the Guildhall Museum estimates for excavation in 1970 were just £500! 'The years up to 1972 now seem like a bad dream', recently wrote one of the leading figures in the salvage of London's past, 'to see an elaborately decorated Roman mosaic destroyed without being able to uncover and record it, is a tragic experience'.[16] Happily, things were to change, and by the mid 1970s some sixty professional archaeologists employed by the new Museum of London were at work. Elsewhere in Britain were many other professional teams, variously charged with the investigation of sites both urban and rural; it was an astonishing transformation.

It would be easy to dwell on these recent changes, and their implications, at some length. But our task is different, for we must now stand back a little, and attempt to gauge the wider significance of this explosion in data and these developments in technique. Is the way that we see and understand Roman Britain really so different from the picture that Collingwood painted some fifty years ago? How have our approaches to the past changed, and are they right? And what sort of future do we envisage for the Romano–British archaeologist of the century to come? Not easy questions, and as the vast number of recent books on Romano–British archaeology quite clearly show, they are not ones that always elicit consensus. But, nevertheless, they are questions which, in these interrogative days, should and must be posed.

Today's approaches

It takes only a visit to virtually any museum in Britain to appreciate the quantity of new information that is now available to us. Were, for instance, Haverfield, who died in 1919, or Collingwood, who died tragically young in 1943, to pass through the British Museum's Roman Britain display of today, they would recognise few of the major exhibits. The great late Roman treasures of Mildenhall (Suffolk), Water Newton (Cambridgeshire) and Thetford (Norfolk) are all post-War acquisitions, as are the Christian wall-paintings from Lullingstone (Kent) and the Hinton St Mary (Dorset) pavement with its head – almost certainly a bust of Christ – and chi-rho monogram. New, too, would be the temple

45 Decorated silver jug from the hoard of Christian silver found at Water Newton (Durobrivae) in 1975. Altogether there were twenty-eight objects, all but one of silver, dating mainly to the fourth century. Height 20.3 cm (8 in.).

finds from Uley (Gloucestershire), with the spectacular limestone head of Mercury; a wide range of finds from Hockwold (Norfolk), including a hoard of superb early Roman silver cups; and the Vindolanda writing tablets, the oldest group of documents known from Britain, from a fort near Hadrian's Wall. Nor should we forget hoards of coins, like that from Bredgar (Kent), where a soldier in the invasion army of AD 43 buried no less than thirty-seven gold aurei, perhaps as a precaution before going into battle.

Many local and regional museums also have their 'new' star pieces, like the sculpture and metalwork from the Walbrook Mithraeum, now in the Museum of London; the chest of armour in the site museum at Corbridge (Northumberland); Newcastle's splendid display of the finds from the mithraeum at the fort of Carrawburgh on Hadrian's Wall; or Dover's 'painted house' and Fishbourne's mosaics. All these are major post-War discoveries and it is a list that could easily be extended. Encouragingly, a good many of these discoveries are not chance finds but were made in the course of systematic programmes of excavation. Highly important objects have, of course, come to light through building, ploughing and, increasingly, through treasure-hunters using metal detectors, but the enormous number of sites that have been properly investigated since the Second World War have provided most museums with large collections of material recovered under controlled conditions. This in itself is also a reflection of the fact that there are now many more archaeologists around, most of them admirably skilled in excavation techniques, as well as a great deal more money to fund their work – nothing like enough, particularly in the difficult days of the 1980s, but much more than in, say, the 1930s or 1940s.

The vastly increased tempo of fieldwork is also matched by the rate at which new sites are being discovered. Here aerial photography has been the main factor. For example, in the course of the last fifty years or so the number of forts and camps in Wales has been trebled, as has the number of forts in northern Britain. Similarly, whereas only 26 marching camps were known in northern Britain in 1931, by 1978 this figure had risen to no fewer than 127.[17] Our map of Roman Britain, while no doubt still very incomplete, has nevertheless been transformed – due largely, let it be said, to Cambridge University's quite outstanding programme of aerial reconnaissance, backed up now by what seems like a legion of other fliers (46).

Along with this explosion in the quantity of data, there have also been significant changes in the way that we approach this information. The seeds for many of these ideas were undoubtedly sown by pre-War scholars, some of them working in fields other than Roman Britain. But, from the 1960s especially, in tandem with a general boom in the amount of work being done, came new directions – and doubts. The way was paved by various works of synthesis upon both general aspects and more specific topics, such as villas, other forms of rural settlement, temples and towns. Much of this was seen as an updating of Collingwood's *Roman Britain*, the definitive version of which had been published in 1937. But the vast mass of new data meant, in the words of one reviewer published in 1968, 'that Collingwood's wider conclusions need to be re-tested against the whole body of the evidence as it stands today'.[18] Whether there really was an economic decline in the towns in the third century, what archaeology now tells us about the interaction between Roman and native, how far physical geography can explain real or apparent regional differences in settlement and cultural patterns – these are but some of the issues.

Equally, long-held concepts began to come under close scrutiny: the troubled years of the later 1960s also had their counterpart in the more rarefied world of academic debate. While prehistorians were busy rejecting the well-established idea that it was successive invasions from the

46 The Saxon Shore fort of *Branodunum* (Brancaster, Norfolk), taken in June 1978. To the right, part of the civilian village, with its streets, shows clearly.

Continent that accounted for cultural changes in Britain, Romanists were starting to question the very historical framework that had for so long governed our accounts of the province. One has the impression that, in the past, a good many archaeologists set out to prove what the documentary sources said: thus a Cambridge undergraduate writing at the time of the Melchett Expedition of 1929:[19]

> Oh! Garstang, take your spade and go:
> Prove every scripture true!
> Find me the walls of Jericho
> That fell before the Jew!

By the early 1970s, however, a certain reluctance to relate archaeological episodes to historical events as stated in, or implied by, the written sources was becoming apparent. The main impetus came from those working on the northern frontiers, particularly Hadrian's Wall. In 1972 pottery studies demonstrated that Hadrian's Wall and the Antonine Wall could not have been held simultaneously, as had long been believed, while other reappraisals of the evidence came up with interpretations which often differed strikingly from the 'traditional'

81

view. Equally fundamental was the attack on the standard chronology, which envisaged two great destructions of Hadrian's Wall, in AD 197 and 296, at the hands of the northern tribes – 'two of the essential, established pegs on which Wall chronology hangs'.[20] Both were hypothetical historical 'events', the idea being that troops were taken away from the frontier to fight in (known) battles elsewhere, giving the northern tribes the chance to overrun the Wall. Signs of destruction were identified 'everywhere', including an attempt to lever out a gate-post of Milecastle 37, and were used to back up these supposed historical events.

As doubts grew, both the dates and the notion of destruction-levels came under attack. Reappraisal of the finds did not really support the dates, and the harder one looked, the less universal became the evidence for destruction. Ashes *could* derive from hearths, buildings *might* have been fired accidentally, new structures *could* be explained in lots of other ways; and, as far as the gate of Milecastle 37 was concerned, 'the Caledonians were hot-blooded tribal warriors, not trained demolition-squads . . . far from seeking the arduous tasks of heavy demolition, the highlanders streamed south for plunder, pillage and rape'.[21]

In the course of the 1970s this scepticism about the value of historical sources achieved a firm footing amongst many archaeologists. 'Text-hindered archaeology' became something of a catch-phrase, while an attempt to relate building sequences at the fort of Dover (Kent) to actual or inferred events on Hadrian's Wall provoked comments like the following: 'This is a spirited attempt to relate the archaeology of the site to known, or assumed, historical events . . . But should the attempt have taken place? . . . To try to relate any archaeological 'happening' to any historical event is, to say the least, hazardous'.[22] Or, more extremely: 'If the *Notitia Dignitatum* says the [the Saxon Shore fort at] Lympne was garrisoned at the end of the fourth century and, on excavation, as is the case, the coins and the pottery clearly state that there seems to be no occupation at the end of the fourth century, [then] the *Notitia Dignitatum* is wrong'. These historical sources, the writer points out, suffer from 'scribal errors, military incompetence, imperial bias, sycophancy and all. Fascinating: but to the student of a particular villa, or a pottery industry, or a cemetery, or a town, just about irrelevant'.[23]

Echoing these doubts about the value of some of our sparse historical data came questions about the validity of the archaeological evidence. The use of statistics, now a feature of everyday life, began to make an impact on archaeological studies, particularly in prehistory, in the mid-1960s. By the 1970s everyone was aware of concepts like 'sample size' and their implications, and it took not too much thought to realise just how little had been properly excavated (and published): virtually no villa had been related to its outbuildings and fields (although Richmond had stressed the need for this long before); our large trenches in towns were in reality only small parts of the total occupied area – at Verulamium, for example, one of the most extensively explored sites of modern times, just 8 hectares (20 acres) out of 80 have been investigated – while, of the fort sites, at very few has a complete plan and sequence been recovered. Even where the sample is larger, the results may not always give rise to consensus: 'In spite of extensive excavation and considerable evidence for the plan of the fort [it is not possible] to match up the garrison and the fort-buildings with complete satisfaction. The total excavation of forts provides the only hope of advancement . . . but even where this has been achieved . . . the evidence is not always unambiguous'.[24]

Some will find these rather pessimistic overtones in accord with the spirit of our age; others will see them as healthy and challenging: 'Textbooks on Roman Britain to date make the subject appear like a nice sand-pit in which toddlers can safely be left to play. I am thankful that it is instead a wild overgrown garden in which anything may happen', as one scholar recently put it.[25] Certainly there are some new trends and directions which are of particular interest and potential, and it is worth commenting briefly upon them.

One is the study of the environment, as reflected by seeds, pollen, snails, diatoms, bones and much more. This is a very young subject as far as Roman Britain is concerned, but the results are already fascinating. The long-held notion that Roman soldiers did not eat meat has been firmly scotched, and important distinctions can now be drawn between the meat diet of the indigenous population and that of the 'Romans'– although the distinction becomes more blurred as time went on. In addition, we now know that Roman York was a considerably cleaner place than its Viking successor; that some parts of Hadrian's Wall were buit over cultivated land or pasture with, at Wall Knowe, near Carlisle (Cumbria), 'a patchwork of open fields bordered by hedges and ditches', and nearby, 'poorly drained ground . . . covered by alder and fringed with hazel/alder scrub';[26] and that vines were grown in some parts of the south. Moreover, experimental work suggests that late Iron Age farms were probably producing a very large surplus of grain – perhaps an additional reason for the Conquest – and that the so-called corn-drying ovens were more likely to have been used for a process such as malting.

The manner in which these disparate data will eventually be stitched together is not easy to predict at this stage of research, but the results could well be spectacular. For example, hints are beginning to emerge that, while the Conquest itself changed little in the day-to-day running of the farms, there may well have been major innovations in crops and their cultivation around the end of the third century AD. If so, this might begin to explain why the fourth century saw the heyday of the Romano–British villa, a feature in stark contrast with the picture from most other provinces. Similarly, methodical but exciting research is now going on that is attempting to measure the impact of man upon the environment and landscape, a matter of no little concern to all of us today.

Indeed, it is issues such as these that take us into another important area of current enquiry: namely, the reconstruction of ancient landscapes. There is a natural temptation to think of Roman Britain as a series of towns, villages, villas or farms and, of course, forts, linked by road and tracks. In reality, as today, these were just places within a medley of fields and forests, rivers and marshes, all of them controlled by a particular authority, public or private. Without written testimony we can only guess at who these owners might have been – whether a town council, the emperor or, perhaps, the family that farmed a particular villa estate – but at least we can try to see how a landscape was divided up and what man tried to do with it. It is here that a combination of aerial photography and fieldwalking has begun to make an immense contribution. Given the right soils, the right crops and the right weather conditions, an astonishing amount of detail can show up from the air, much of it quite unsuspected. Temple complexes like Gosbecks Farm, near Colchester (Essex), can be seen to be the centre of a formally laid-out complex, beyond which were small ditched fields; towns like Silchester can be shown to have had earlier and quite different defensive circuits; and forts like Old Carlisle turn out to possess not only an extensive civilian settlement around it but also trackways leading to substantial 'native' farmsteads and their field systems. This work, from which 183 native sites have recently been identified in an area of some 690 square kilometres (260 square miles), with the forts being 'limited islands within a rural sea',[27] is of particular importance. Here a carefully designed programme of research involving flying, field survey and limited excavation has produced not only spectacular maps of the Roman-period landscape, but has also provoked a series of intensely interesting questions about the effect of Roman upon native.

This work is matched by a project in another area dominated by 'native-style' settlement, the Cambridgeshire and Lincolnshire Fens. As we mentioned earlier, aerial photography in the 1930s, combined with botanical and geological studies, had demonstrated how this vast alluvial basin had dried out in the early Roman period and was colonised on an enormous scale. Visible from the air were canals, roads, fields and settlements consisting of ditched enclosures and containing wooden buildings, while on the ground were prodigious quantities of pottery, bones and other finds. Mapping all this was a slow process – much of it done by amateurs, working independently – but in 1960 the Royal Geographical Society sponsored a fellowship, so as to draw the results together. A volume appeared in 1970[28] and was a major step forward in landscape studies, documenting just over 2,000 square kilometres (800 square miles) of Fenland. Currently this is being followed up by a field survey that takes account of all periods – prehistoric, Roman and medieval – and much more detailed mapping of the soils, extinct rivers and archaeological features. Sadly, however, it is only now that systematic excavation on any scale has begun to take place – sadly, because most of the grassland sites have now been broken up, and the late and mid-Roman structures must in many cases have gone for ever. Indeed, there is a crying need for still more digging, not least to investigate the network of Roman canals and roads that are still so conspicuous from the air.

The Fens are of special importance because they form a geologically discrete landscape and, in addition, there is reason to believe that in Roman times they also comprised a single administrative unit of public land. They also yield well-preserved finds of wood and other organic material conserved by waterlogging, underlining the point that, at long last, archaeologists have realised that they must give priority to such sites. To have visited the remains of the magnificently preserved wooden quays beside the River Thames in London, or the amazing early Roman wooden buildings preserved beneath modern Carlisle, is to appreciate how much an ordinary dry-land site has lost. At long last, too, we are beginning to possess the facilities and knowledge to conserve and store all this organic material – no mean task, when one object can take five months to treat.

Other examples of landscape maps could be quoted – for example, that being built up for the gravels that fringe the River Thames – and it is hugely encouraging that this is so. These maps incorporate traces of

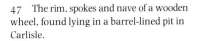

47   The rim, spokes and nave of a wooden wheel, found lying in a barrel-lined pit in Carlisle.

human activity over many centuries, and thus provide a unique glimpse into the past. But what of the finds that these sites yield? Although the value of finds for dating has long been recognised, one can sometimes detect a certain cavalier attitude towards the objects. In part it is sheer bulk that is the deterrent. 'It is one of the characteristics of the organisation of British archaeology that . . . at the end [of an excavation] the Director is left with fifty or a hundred chests of material and no resources for their disposal', wrote one author in his preface to a volume with a model account of the finds.[29] Happily, this situation is changing and the 'post-excavation' component is now an essential feature of most budgets. As a result, ever-more detailed accounts are being prepared of every class of find, from lorry-loads of brick and tile to tons of coarse pottery, to the animal bones (no less than 250,000 from an area of just 70×30 m (230×100 ft) of the temple site at Uley, for example). Quantification, analysis and scrupulous illustration is now the name of the game, generating vast reports and, with them, one of the present crises of British archaeology – how to publish these mounds of information?

Future generations will no doubt pass verdict on current attitudes towards all this detritus from the past. But have things got out of perspective? Certainly it is now a daunting prospect to mount an excavation in the knowledge that it may generate material for perhaps forty or fifty different specialists. Nevertheless, most archaeologists would agree that much of this work is yielding highly significant information. Obviously, objects can be crucial when it comes to assessing the social standing of the inhabitants of a site, just as they are often the principal key to judgements about cultural matters. But it is the implication for economic studies that is perhaps the major breakthrough of recent years. Here it is important that students of Roman Britain have to a large extent liberated themselves from a certainly insularity of approach, particularly at grass-roots level. Markets in antiquity could be local, medium or long-range, so that a province such as Britain could and did import from far afield – including North Africa and the eastern Mediterranean. Even our poor Fenland villagers drank the occasional glass of Spanish wine.

Studies of the different sort of amphorae that carried commodities such as olive-oil, wine, fish sauce (garum) and dried fruit are now much in vogue. Many of the amphorae can be assigned to production areas, approximately dated and their contents can be deduced. As a result, we can begin to see how one province fared *vis-à-vis* another and draw conclusions about broad economic implications. Even many ancient historians, so often sceptical of the value of archaeological evidence, have awakened to the worth of such studies.

Pottery generally, once its origin (if possible the kiln site) and its distribution have been worked out, can therefore be a highly valuable tool in the reconstruction of Roman marketing patterns. This necessarily involves much laborious counting, weighing and measuring, and probably scientific analysis as well, but the results can give an impressive insight into the organisation of ancient industry. Similarly, numerical work on the distribution of coins is beginning to provide crucial infor-

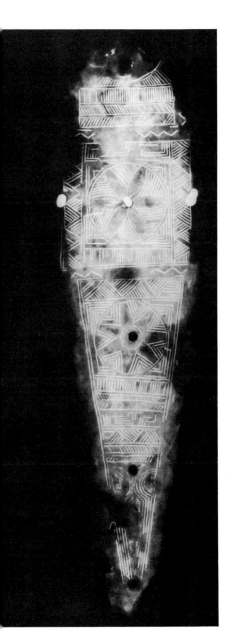

48 X-ray of a dagger from the fort at Hod Hill (Dorset). The technique clearly brings out the intricate silver inlay.

mation about questions of supply and circulation, not least the impact of a monetary economy upon peoples who did not use coinage.

These advances, which extend right across the board of artefact studies, are at the least dramatic, and they open up whole new fields of study and understanding. They are just part of a gigantic reappraisal of Romano–British archaeology, which has revealed a hitherto unsuspected complexity – and potential. If we are now less certain how to integrate all this new information, then it is only because we are much more aware of the difficulties of our task. Some do try to write 'textbooks' and syntheses; some believe that we should be trying to write history from the archaeological evidence: but the job becomes ever more daunting – and more stimulating – each year.

Roman Britain today

Over recent decades there have been thousands of excavations and an enormous amount of publication. Particularly notable have been the first volume of *Roman Inscriptions of Britain* (1965, a project originally initiated by Haverfield) and *The Placenames of Roman Britain* (1979) – both corpuses of lasting importance – and, from 1970, the annual appearance of a journal specifically devoted to Roman Britain, *Britannia*. Whilst publication has lagged well behind the fieldwork, nevertheless a prodigious amount of new information has been made available. Here certain categories of site will be considered which highlight some of the principal achievements and advances – invidiously, since no brief survey can possibly do justice to so large a body of fresh data.

The military aspect

It is appropriate to begin with military matters, since it was the Roman army that shaped so many aspects of Roman Britain. Although soldiers comprised only a small proportion of the total population (perhaps just a few per cent), their stamp is found in all parts of the province. Most striking, perhaps, is the revelation that a high proportion of the towns of Roman Britain, both large and small, had military antecedents. The identification of early Roman forts beneath the civilian buildings at Verulamium, Cirencester, Winchester and a good many other urban sites in the south of England, is one unmistakable pointer towards this. Not that all of these forts became successful towns, while many military sites were abandoned in the years following the Conquest and never reoccupied. Precisely what factors favoured the development of one site rather than another is a matter that has seen much debate: market forces or governmental manipulation? No doubt both played a part.

To the north and west the pattern changes. Urban centres and affluent country estates became much rarer, and the military presence increasingly overt. Nevertheless, there can be no simple distinction between the 'developed' lowlands of the south and east and the army-controlled uplands of the north and west; the pattern is much more complex than that. Wales is an important area in which to study these processes. At first sight it is tempting to regard Wales, with its rugged topography and skein of military posts, as a self-contained and heavily garrisoned frontier region, where Romanisation had little effect. But this would be wholly to misrepresent a very involved situation. Neither can Wales be considered in isolation from the rest of the province – events in the north, in particular, had major repercussions upon the garrisons of the Welsh forts – nor was it under tight military control for the whole of the Roman period. That said, it is becoming ever more difficult to fit the available evidence into any very convincing overall picture, since the known sites yield what has been well described as a 'bewildering kaleidoscope of changing patterns'.[30]

We must first bear in mind that a good many military sites no doubt remain to be discovered, a point that is underlined by the comparatively recent identifications of major legionary bases at Usk (Gwent) and Rhyn Park (Salop). Nevertheless, we can now begin to relate the main phases of the Conquest to the sites on the ground and see how a network of forts and roads was evolved to control the region. Some see this as a process of experimentation in the prelude to the Conquest of the north: certainly it is the 70s, the period when the main northern thrust began, that sees the consolidation of the military organisation of Wales. Most notable was the building of two legionary fortresses, at Chester and at Caerleon (Gwent); these were the heirs to a series of short-lived legionary stations and were to stay as bases for a large part of the remaining centuries of Roman rule in Britain.

During the second century there were, however, considerable changes in the military dispositions in Wales. We no longer believe that the region was completely drained of troops when southern Scotland was reannexed and the Antonine Wall was built in the 140s, nor that there was a massive redeployment of troops in Wales when the frontier-line returned to Hadrian's Wall later in the second century AD. But we can infer a substantial reduction in the size of the resident garrison in Wales during the second century, particularly in the south. This can now be very satisfactorily correlated with archaeological evidence for a gradual spread of Romanisation. Thus, the fort and its civilian settlement at Carmarthen (Dyfed), in south-west Wales, was converted into a town at some point during the second century, and some of the native farms came increasingly to take on characteristics of very simple villas. Rectangular buildings, for instance – normally regarded as a 'Roman' trait – first appear in these farms in the second century and become more widespread. Many would regard this as a telling comment on the way that some of the native population began to integrate with these intrusive elements and share more in the changing social and economic climate. Whilst there was always an army presence in some parts of Wales, increasingly the danger came not from within but from overseas.

A thumbnail sketch of this sort can hardly do justice to what is an extraordinarily complex picture of changes and developments. Much of the evidence comes from small excavations, but at some sites the work has been more extensive, and it is worth now looking at some of these, both in Wales and elsewhere. One major area of advance has been in our knowledge of legionary fortresses. A type that was completely unknown until twenty years ago or so is the so-called vexillation fortress, namely, ones garrisoned by various troops on detachment. Fourteen examples are now known from Britain, and more undoubtedly await discovery. All except for one date to the first century AD, and that at Longthorpe, near Peterborough (Cambridgeshire), has been partially excavated. This proved to consist of a turf rampart within double ditches, enclosing an area of 10.9 hectares (27 acres). This size is about average for the vexillation fortresses but is roughly half that of the normal legionary base. Within the ramparts were a series of wooden buildings, including the headquarters complex, granaries, a house for the commandant, storage areas and barracks – one of them very eccentrically laid out. Analysis of this plan, and of the finds, suggests that the fortress was probably designed to accommodate about 1,800 legionaries (that is, one third of a legion, almost certainly the IXth Hispana), and perhaps 1,000 auxiliaries (the non-citizen supplementary troops of the Roman army, usually recruited from the provinces). These were brought together as a battle unit, with the vexillation fortresses providing both a base for stores and winter quarters when the campaigning season was over.

The fortress at Longthorpe was founded between about AD 44 and 48 and was held until about AD 61. About that time its size was drastically reduced, probably because of troop losses in the Iceni revolt led by Queen Boudica, and shortly afterwards it was put out of commission. Similarly short-lived was the fortress at Red House near Corbridge (Northumberland). This site, which may have covered about 8–9 hectares (25 acres; the full limits are not known) has yielded storage buildings, workshops and barrack accommodation, constructed in the late 70s. Nearby was a stone bath-house. Given its position on the main eastern route to the north, there is no difficulty in identifying the fortress as a supply base for the army of Agricola, as it set about the conquest of the north in the period AD 79 to 84.

The special interest of these fortresses lies in the fact that they can often be linked to particular campaigns known from literary sources. In addition there were the main legionary bases, one for each of the four legions (later reduced to three) that came to Britain in the original invasion force in AD 43. Over the last few decades a good deal has been learnt about the complex mosaic of successive fortresses. The early fortress beneath the later colony at Colchester has now been securely identified; a base of 15 hectares (38 acres), built for the IInd Augusta legion, has been found at Exeter, with magnificent baths of about AD 60–80; while at Usk, in South Wales, a carefully planned fortress, probably for the XXth legion, has been partially excavated.

Pride of place, however, must go to the results of the work at Inchtuthil (Tayside) in Scotland between 1951 and 1965. Here stood a 21.5-hectare (53-acre) fortress (49), constructed by Agricola's army from about AD 83 and still not quite completed when it was totally demolished around AD 86–87. Its importance lies partly in the completeness of the plan, as reconstructed from systematic trenching, and

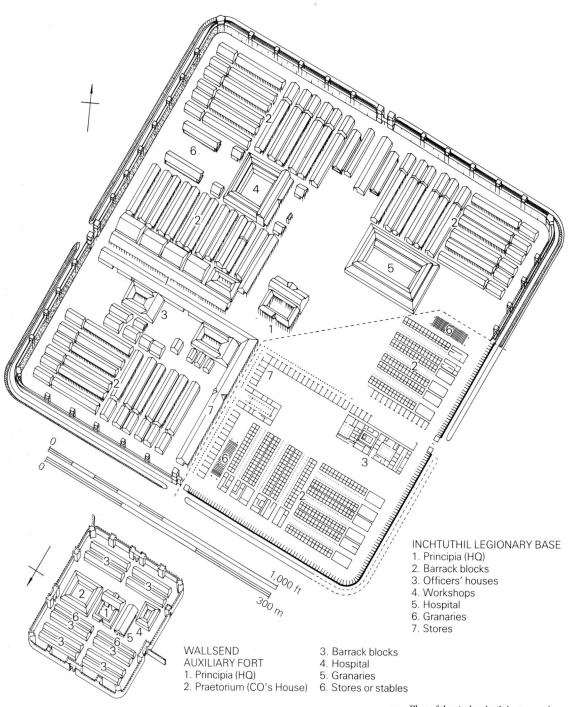

INCHTUTHIL LEGIONARY BASE
1. Principia (HQ)
2. Barrack blocks
3. Officers' houses
4. Workshops
5. Hospital
6. Granaries
7. Stores

WALLSEND
AUXILIARY FORT
1. Principia (HQ)
2. Praetorium (CO's House)
3. Barrack blocks
4. Hospital
5. Granaries
6. Stores or stables

1,000 ft
300 m

49 Plan of the timber-built legionary base at Inchtuthil in Scotland (late first century AD) and the stone-built fort of an auxiliary regiment at Wallsend on Hadrian's Wall (second century AD), drawn to the same scale.

also in the fact that it was a one-period site, unencumbered by later features, whether Roman or medieval. As such, it is unique not just in Britain but in the whole empire.

All of the fortress was built in timber, except for the extra-mural baths and the defensive wall. Accommodation was provided for a full legion, around 5,000 men, with neatly arranged groups of barracks and quarters for the centurion of each 'century' of 80 legionaries. There were also four houses for the tribunes (the senior officers), as well as a small and probably temporary headquarters building, a hospital, work-shops and storerooms, a *schola* or 'club-house' and six granaries. Two more granaries, the commander's residence, two houses for tribunes, a training hall and permanent baths remained to be built, however, when the orders came to withdraw. There followed an astonishingly system-atic programme of demolition, epitomised by the burial of the famous hoard of some one million nails, so that nothing would be available to enemy scavengers.

Also of importance were features outside the fortress, including a labour camp, where the men were housed in tents, and other compounds, one with buildings for the senior staff: these can all be convincingly regarded as the temporary accommodation while the fortress was under construction. Overall, therefore, Inchtuthil provides a remarkable in-sight into the army at work, and it is satisfying that so close a correlation can be made with campaigns that are attested in the historical sources.

Of the other full legionary fortresses in Britain, ten of which are now known, only those at Caerleon and Chester have been sufficiently exca-vated to provide a reasonably coherent plan. Both sites have a heavy overlay of later buildings, but sustained programmes of excavation have identified the position of a good many of the main buildings. Even so, basic questions remain, not least the later histories of the sites. Legionary occupation for a large part of the second century seems not in doubt, but the size of the garrison in the third century is problematic and the fourth-century history of both fortress sites is extremely difficult to interpret. Indeed, current excavators are at pains to emphasise our *lack* of understanding rather than our advances in knowledge.

Turning to the forts of the auxiliary units, the rarity of very extensively excavated sites still hampers our knowledge. The well-entrenched view that the layout of military bases followed precise textbook patterns has been conclusively destroyed – the variety of fort plans is remarkable – but detailed analysis is only possible at a very small number of sites. For the period of the Conquest we are still heavily reliant upon the exca-vations during the 1950s at Hod Hill, a fort planted in one corner of the great Dorset Iron Age hillfort. Occupied from about AD 44 for less than a decade, the fort covered an area of 4 hectares (10 acres). All the buildings were of timber and were laid out around a T-shaped arrangement of streets. There were barracks, a granary, and a headquarters building, as well as three courtyard houses in the central area. One may have been a hospital and it has been suggested that the other two were for the commanders of, respectively, detachments of legionary soldiers and of auxiliary troops – appropriate types of equipment and fittings for both have been recovered – but there is no certainty about this, something that underlines the difficulties in interpreting such remains.

Equally problematic to explain are some of the structures at the rather later fort at The Lunt, near Coventry. Built in the early 60s but soon modified, the fort contains a good many standard buildings, such as the headquarters building, barracks and granaries; but it also includes a curious wooden structure, 32.7 m (107.5 ft) in diameter, with a funnel entrance at one side. This has been interpreted as a *gyrus* or training arena for horses, and it may be that the whole fort was designed as an army training school. This in itself is of great interest, but the importance of the site is further enhanced by some fascinating experiments in the reconstruction of part of the turf rampart and of the east gate, as well as of a granary and the *gyrus*. Although many of the details are necessarily speculative, these attempts to simulate the Roman buildings are highly valuable for what they tell us about the logistics of construction and about the wear-and-tear of the structures.

The irregular features of these early auxiliary forts are in strong contrast with those of the Flavian period (AD 69–96), particularly the forts built in the governorship of Gnaeus Julius Agricola (AD 78–84). The network of military stations laid down in this period, when Wales was finally pacified and most of Lowland Scotland was brought under Roman control, is astonishing, both for the number of forts and for the meticulous planning behind their disposition. At Pen Llystyn (Gwynedd), in north-west Wales, the complete plan of a 1.8-hectare (4.5-acre) fort was re-covered while the site was being quarried for gravel in the late 1950s and early 1960s. Probably founded in AD 78, its arrangement of build-ings – for example, a central range of commandant's house, head-quarters building and a pair of granaries – and their design are for the most part typical of military planning in this period. Similarly, in Scotland excavation has considerably advanced our knowledge, building on the classic pre-War work at the fort of Fendoch. At Strageath, for example, a significant proportion of the fort's interior has been systematically investigated in recent years, disclosing that it was first laid out in about AD 80 under Agricola and that it saw two subsequent periods of occu-pation, around the middle part of the second century.

These considerable advances in our understanding of the Agricolan military dispositions are matched by work on the frontiers that were to succeed them. Early experimentation is attested by a series of watch-towers along the Gask Ridge in Scotland, again constructed under Agricola. With the withdrawal to the Tyne–Forth line soon after Agricola's departure in AD 84, a not dissimilar arrangement of towers, backed up by forts, was laid out along the Stanegate road. Vindolanda, with its rich harvest of early second-century documents, mostly written in ink on thin sheets of wood (50), was amongst these forts. The successor to the so-called 'Stanegate frontier' was, of course, Hadrian's Wall, a massive work of engineering, the study of which has almost become a discipline in its own right.

50 One of some two hundred writing tablets dating to the early second century AD, from the fort at Vindolanda, near Hadrian's Wall. They are mostly official military documents written in ink upon wood, and comprise the oldest group of written documents from Britain. Length 18cm (7in.).

Certainly, 'Wall studies' have moved forward immensely over the last few decades, both through excavation and through thinking and re-thinking the highly complex problems. As we noted earlier, scholars these days tend to be suspicious about applying a 'standard' division into periods to all sites on the frontier; although some decisions (for example, the move north about AD 140, which led to the building of the Antonine Wall) undoubtedly did affect all garrisons, notions such as the overwhelming of every fort by northern tribesmen at the same time are plainly ridiculous. Each site needs to be evaluated on its merits, not fitted into some largely hypothetical framework. This means very large-scale excavation, of the sort that has been carried out with conspicuous success at forts such as Housesteads and Wallsend (49), as well as at some milecastles and turrets and on the Wall itself. If the great achievement of a previous generation of scholars was to define the broad anatomy of the frontier, then the current task is to build upon, expand and question this framework.

Indeed, discoveries of fundamental importance are still being made. One of the most interesting concerns the coast of north-west Cumbria. While the Wall itself stops at the fort of Bowness-on-Solway, it has now been established that a system of fortlets, spaced at intervals of one Roman mile with two towers between each, carried on down the low-lying Cumbrian coast. In places it has been shown that these were linked by a wooden palisade and a military road. Just how far these frontier works continued is still a matter of debate, but they have been proved to extend for at least twenty-five miles beyond the end of Hadrian's Wall and may well carry on much further. But, whatever the truth of that, they underline the grandiose nature of the design of the whole frontier – and the massive task that the unravelling of it poses.

Just why Hadrian's Wall should then have been replaced by a new frontier, some hundred miles to the north, is a matter that continues to perplex, but the much shorter and less elaborate Antonine Wall is no less interesting. Particular attention has been paid in recent decades to defining and deciphering successive phases in the frontier's 'blue-print'. In 1949 the first fortlet (resembling those on Hadrian's Wall) was identified, and since then they have multiplied. Now there is good reason to think that they may have been placed at intervals of one Roman mile, imitating the measured layout of Hadrian's frontier. Turrets have yet to be found, despite specific searches, but many of the forts have been subject either to reinterpretation or to new investigation. At Bearsden

51 Stone slab, measuring 97 cm by 76 cm (38 × 30 in.), found in 1969 at Hutcheson Hill, on the Antonine Wall. It records building work carried out by the Twentieth Legion. A female figure places a wreath of victory in the beak of a legionary eagle, while to left and right are barbarian captives with bound hands.

(Strathclyde) for example, as near total an excavation as was possible of this small 1.1-hectare (2.8-acre) fort has disclosed barracks, stables, store buildings, a workshop and two granaries – but no headquarters or commandant's residence. There was a bath-house in a separate compound and much of the fort was laid out in multiples of Roman feet, but it is the non-standard arrangement that is so thought-provoking, emphasising, as it does, the dangers of the generalised conclusion from an inadequate sample. Fascinatingly, too, methodical botanical and biochemical research on sewage deposits suggests that the soldiers' diet at this fort was largely vegetarian, and included wild strawberries, raspberries and figs, as well as opium poppy and coriander seeds as flavouring.

A major area of controversy, fuelled by the result of extensive excavations on other Antonine forts elsewhere in Scotland, such as Birrens (Dumfries and Galloway) and Strageath (Central) concerns the phases of occupation of the Antonine frontier. Were there two periods or three, and what dates should be assigned to them? When was Hadrian's Wall finally reinstated as Roman Britain's northern perimeter? Many currently believe in only two periods, the latter terminating in the early 160s, but the matter is hardly decided.

Much more could be said about the military occupation of the north, not least about the archaeological evidence for the campaigns of the emperor Septimius Severus and his sons in north-east Scotland in the early third century, and about the later Roman buildings at sites like Housesteads. But it is the south-east of Britain that is archaeologically more significant in the later third and fourth centuries. With the exception of highly interesting second-century forts in London and Dover (where a squadron of the British fleet was based), there is no evidence in this region for army activity after the 60s. From the 270s or so, however, a series of massively defended forts were constructed around the south-east coast. Known as the forts of the *Litus Saxonicum*, the Saxon Shore, they were clearly designed to repel sea-borne attack from these Germanic pirates. Much work has gone into assessing these sites and, following on from the pre-War investigations at Richborough (Kent), there has been a good deal of excavation, of which the most extensive has been that at Portchester (Hampshire), where one eighth of the interior has been examined. Probably constructed about AD 285–90, the fort was occupied, perhaps intermittently, for much of the fourth century. However, although large quantities of refuse were found, as well as ovens, pits and hearths, there were disappointingly few traces of buildings, something that cannot easily be explained unless they were of very flimsy construction. Indeed, taken as a whole, we know all too little about the internal arrangement of these 'Saxon Shore' forts, although headquarters complexes at some imply a more recognisable pattern of military organisation. Nevertheless, it is not impossible, to judge from present evidence, that some of the forts were occupied by mercenary troops, perhaps even with their families, suggesting an altogether more relaxed system.

Seen overall, however, our understanding of the distribution and history of the military sites of Britain has advanced considerably since the days of Collingwood – even if one net effect has been to make us increasingly cautious about the conclusions that are drawn. Moreover, this must be set alongside other highly valuable work upon the epigraphic evidence for garrisons and their movements, upon individual soldiers' careers and also upon military equipment. Our knowledge about armour and the ways in which it changed has, in particular, been transformed, as the many reconstructions now in our museums remind us.

Town and country

We remarked earlier upon the pervasive influence of the army on many aspects of life in Roman Britain, and it is now time to examine this and the civilian development of the province. There were some twenty-five 'planned' towns in Britain – a figure to be contrasted with Italy's total of more than four hundred – as well as a great many low-status, smaller settlements. One of the largest and most important was Verulamium, a site which has also played a critical role in the evolution of our views about the towns and their history. The first Romano–British town to receive proper layer-by-layer investigation, by the Wheelers between 1930 and 1934, Verulamium furnished much of the data for Collingwood's view about the urban history of the province. Particularly influential was the Wheelers' picture of Verulamium in the second part of the third century, when, it was claimed, economic crisis had struck, the city walls were in ruins and the place 'must at this time have borne some resemblance to a bombarded city'.[31]

In the event many of the Wheelers' inferences, including their dating both of successive defensive circuits and of the forum, as well as their views about third-century Verulamium, have either been challenged or proved wrong. But the project did create a semi-historical framework (particularly as synthesised by Collingwood) and also stressed the need for large-scale stratigraphical study of urban sites. Moreover, since so many of the Roman towns lie beneath rapidly developing modern centres, this provided – and still does – an additional incentive for excavation. The post-War work at Verulamium has here been of particular importance, both as a corrective to many of Wheeler's conclusions and as a model for presenting and interpreting the investigation of an urban site. Briefly stated, we can now see how this substantial Roman city originated as a major late Iron Age centre. Soon after the Conquest a fort was planted there (and was to influence the subsequent development of the street-grid), but by about AD 50 the decision had been taken to create a town. Before long this had attained the size of nearly 50 hectares (125 acres) and possessed its own defences. Indeed, it has been inferred from the plan and constructional techniques of the early multiple blocks of shops that a good deal of official aid was available to the first settlers. Verulamium entered recorded history when it was sacked by Boudica's warriors in the uprising of AD 60 – the burnt-down buildings are encountered wherever one excavates in the central part of the city – and it took a long time to recover. But in AD 79 the forum was dedicated (perhaps replacing an older, temporary structure), and before the end of the first century AD there were temples and a market, all in masonry, and most probably other public buildings as well. Verulamium, with a population of perhaps 15,000, many (to judge from a small sample of graffiti) with Latinate names, was well on the way to becoming a Mediterranean-type classical city.

The theatre, one of the very few known from Britain, was built in about AD 140 on what seems to have been a reserved space from the earliest days of the town. Its proximity to a temple underlines the religious role that such buildings often played. Around the middle of the second century new earthwork defences, enclosing 93.6 hectares (231 acres), were constructed, but soon afterwards, in about AD 155, some 20 hectares (50 acres) of the central part of the city was engulfed in a great fire. The calamity left its mark for many decades, but eventually new houses began to appear, so that third-century Verulamium, rather than being a 'bombarded city', was in fact a rather prosperous place. Many of the new houses were large and elegantly appointed (and built of fire-proof materials), and the construction of three monumental arches and stone town walls (probably datable to about AD 265–70) is a further sign of affluence.

In Collingwood's day fourth-century Verulamium (52) had been seen as initially wealthy and successful, but by the mid-fourth century 'the greater part of Verulam was uninhabited, a waste of empty land and ruined houses. Here and there squatters lived among the ruins. The

52   The Roman city of Verulamium, near St Albans, showing all buildings known to have been standing in the fourth century AD.

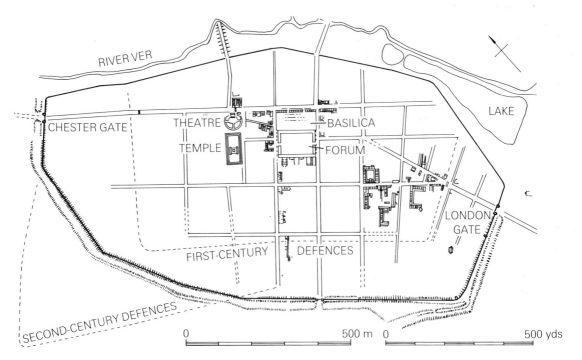

theatre had become a rubbish tip . . . close around it a shrunken and impoverished population lived in slum conditions'.[32] Not surprisingly, this evocative picture soon achieved the status of orthodoxy, and it was not until the excavations of 1955–61 and their assessment that another perspective was achieved: that the theatre was not abandoned until about AD 380–90 (and then probably because of its pagan associations in a now Christian world), and that fourth-century Verulamium saw a good deal of building in the private sector. Indeed, it was one of the triumphs of this work to demonstrate that city life (including the maintenance of the water supply) continued well after the formal end of Roman Britain in AD 410 and probably into the later fifth century.

It has seemed appropriate to dwell on Verulamium at some length, since we can compare pre-War and post-War conclusions and offer some sort of narrative account of its history. Its plan may be much less well known than, say, Silchester or many famous Roman cities of the Mediterranean, but the archaeological evidence is such that we can trace the fortunes of the town in some detail.

Increasingly, this is also becoming possible at other Romano–British urban sites. Just four of these were *coloniae* – settlements set up for retired legionary veterans and the highest in rank of the various classes of Roman town – namely, Colchester, Gloucester, Lincoln and, the latest foundation, York. All have seen major programmes of excavations, illuminating both their origins as legionary bases and the transition to civilian status. Much of the advance in our knowledge is due, as at Verulamium, to the meticulous and skilful quality of the excavation and to the much more refined possibilities of dating that an infinitely greater knowledge of the objects – particularly coarse pottery – has brought. But, if many of the excavations have taken place through chance factors of redevelopment, there has also been a healthy tendency to frame and then test hypotheses.

Both in the *coloniae* and in lesser-ranking towns one particular preoccupation has been with their defences. Many were very obviously the product of more than one period of building and, since town walls could not be constructed without Imperial permission, it was of importance to see whether towns were provided with defences at the same time – perhaps in response to a particular threat. As it turns out, very few circuits can be dated to the first century, but there does seem to have been a concerted thrust to encircle towns with earthen ramparts in the late second century, quite possibly as a result of the unsettled conditions that prevailed at that time. Subsequently at most towns the ramparts were cut back and a stone wall inserted. This was a slow and expensive job which took decades, but where close dating is possible it seems that the bulk of the work took place in the later third century, partly preceding and partly coinciding with the construction of the Saxon Shore forts, the defences of which they often resemble. Again, the political crises of the period may have been the catalyst, although the presence of earlier stone walls at sites like Cirencester warns against complacent and wholehearted acceptance of the idea.

Another area of investigation and debate concerns the way in which the main towns of Roman Britain came into being. This is a matter of particular interest, since Rome's 'urbanising policy', whether in Italy or in its provinces, was a crucial element in shaping the development of the empire. Indeed, one has only to reflect on the fact that so many cities and towns of today, both in Britain and elsewhere, can claim their structured origin to Roman engineers, to appreciate the significance of these early decisions in urban planning.

At some sites with military origins it can be shown how the defences, streets and sometimes even the buildings were retained in use when civilian status was granted. At both Lincoln and Gloucester, for example, the army headquarters was replaced, appropriately enough, by the main administrative buildings of a Roman town, the forum and basilica. This was not always the case, but it must often have seemed the sensible and logical choice, as long as no very radical replanning, as at Colchester, was required.

These new perspectives on the origins of towns (which have also attracted some interesting, if speculative, attempts to recognise measured layouts of blocks of land, in Roman feet), must be set alongside another area of current interest, namely the later history of these urban centres. There was a time, particularly in the 1950s and 1960s, when it was fashionable to look for evidence which prolonged the life of Romano–British towns well into the post-Roman period. The work after the Second World War at Verulamium, discussed above supported this, as, apparently, did the results from sites like Cirencester and Catterick (N. Yorkshire). Some, on the other hand, received Saxon settlers, as at Canterbury, a conclusion that began to dispel the notion that the Germanic invaders totally shunned all Romano–British towns. All this, let it be said, was totally in contrast with Collingwood's picture of complete urban decay by the middle of the fourth century.

More recently, however, the pendulum has started to swing again, back towards Collingwood's position. As more and more data are made available, it is becoming clearer that many towns yield rich evidence for buildings of the early Roman period but comparatively little for the later third or fourth centuries. London, for example, has seen great advances in our knowledge of its layout and main buildings; however, while a late Roman riverside wall is known, there are very few signs of contemporary buildings, public or private, either in the City or in the suburb now covered by Southwark. Instead, many of the second-century buildings are buried by a layer of dark soil, of the sort that forms in gardens. This 'black earth', as it has come to be known, is not only found in large parts of London, however, but has also been recognised at many other towns, such as Winchester, Cirencester and Canterbury, to name but a few.

The apparent overall sparsity of fourth-century buildings in the towns, together with these hints of substantial areas within the walls being given over to agriculture, has led some to a provocative thesis: put simply, it suggests that the economic and political crises characteristic of a large part of the third century, particularly on the Continent of Europe, resulted in the flow of money away from the towns and into country estates. As we shall see, the fourth century was indeed the heyday of the villa. As a consequence, many towns entered a period of shrinking population and wealth, echoing what seems to be an equally well-defined drop in the fortunes of many towns in France, Italy and elsewhere. The pattern was by no means even – at Wroxeter (Salop), for instance, a remarkable sequence of wooden buildings, some of them rather grand in scale, were being built from the later fourth century onwards; but, it is argued, the general trend was for a steady decline in the role of the major towns, beginning in some from early in the third century.

Views such as this have, as can be imagined, provoked sharp controversy, running counter, as they do, to the predominant lines of thought of the 1960s and early 1970s. They introduce parodoxes, not least the idea of a falling urban population at a time when many towns were being fortified in stone, and it could well be thought that we have investigated far too little to permit much in the way of generalisation. But the merit of setting the evidence from Britain within the broader context of the Western Empire is obvious, particularly because there is now becoming available an increasing body of well-excavated information from, for example, Rome, Ostia, Lyon and Carthage.

Until now the towns that we have been considering have been primarily those of high rank – the colonies, those with municipal status and the centres of tribal administration (the 'civitas capitals'). In addition to these there were a considerable number of small towns and villages. As with the major urban centres, the army seems to have had a considerable hand in their foundation. Forts, planted very often in or near to major native centres, provided a stimulus to the local economy and a focus for settlement. As aerial photography vividly demonstrates, these were not planned communities. Very few have any hints of regularity in their street pattern, and most seem to have grown up in a haphazard and uncontrolled way. At Durobrivae (Water Newton, near Peterborough), for example, a variety of buildings line the Ermine Street, the Great North Road of Roman Britain. Many were no doubt shops and taverns, catering for the through-flow of travellers, and one larger structure may have been a mansio, or wayside inn and posting station. Leading away from the main road were various side-streets, most of which probably grew up piecemeal as the settlement expanded towards the 18 hectares (44 acres) that it eventually covered. This sort of pattern is typical of many of these sites, and what have been identified as mansiones have been excavated at Chelmsford in Essex (53) and Godmanchester (Cambridgeshire).

Water Newton is unusual in that it was to develop into the largest pottery-manufacturing centre in Britain, with a separate industrial complex and a great many rich suburban houses. It also became an important centre for Christianity, if the discovery in 1975 of a hoard of silver church plate is any guide. But at most small towns and villages

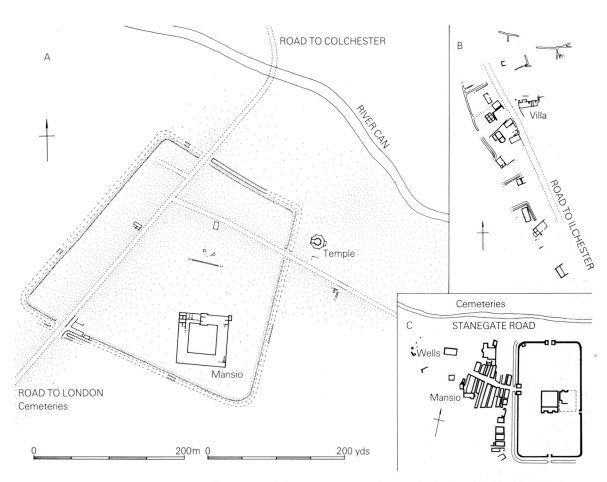

ROAD TO COLCHESTER

A

B

RIVER CAN

Villa

ROAD TO ILCHESTER

Temple

Mansio

ROAD TO LONDON
Cemeteries

Cemeteries

C   STANEGATE ROAD

Wells

Mansio

0   200m 0   200 yds

53 Plans of smaller settlements, drawn to a common scale. A is the small town of Caesaromagus (Chelmsford), on the road from London to Colchester. Few individual buildings have been excavated, but the stipple reflects their whereabouts. B is Catsgore (Somerset), a hamlet where there were a number of individual farmsteads. C is the civil settlement (*vicus*) outside the gates of the fort at Vindolanda, just south of Hadrian's Wall.

the economic base was more or less exclusively agricultural. At Catsgore (Somerset), to take one recently studied village site, thirty-seven buildings were identified, belonging to perhaps as many as twelve adjacent farms (53). Grouped around the road leading to the nearby town of Ilchester, with corn-drying ovens, barns and yards, they represent a class of site that seems to have been fairly common in some parts of the province. Others were larger, like Cambridge or Braughing (Hertfordshire), and contained more elaborate buildings, but despite the demonstrable presence at some of suites of baths or temples, none has yielded the trappings of a proper town, such as a forum and basilica. Whilst they may well have had a role as a local market centre (and could in some cases have served as a base for low-level administrative work), they were in the Roman hierarchy places of no real consequence. Only in the later centuries of Roman Britain may this have changed. As with the larger towns, a considerable number of the small settlements – even diminutive Horncastle in Lincolnshire (2.8 hectares, or 7 acres) – were provided with defences. At a few, earthen banks were thrown up towards the end of the second century, but the majority have masonry walls only. These seem to have been constructed over a long period during the third and early fourth centuries, and at half-a-dozen or so external towers were subsequently added. Some of these fortified sites, Horncastle amongst them, may have been connected with the Saxon Shore defences discussed earlier, since they lie close to the east coast, but the overall significance of the small walled towns is not easy to assess. Quite possibly they imply the evolution of a more localised system of administration, and it may be that larger towns like Durobrivae were promoted to the status of a tribal or *civitas* capital; but these are questions that we cannot as yet resolve.

So far we have been mainly considering the settlement of the more southerly part of Britain. In the north towns become much rarer. The military bases at Carlisle and Corbridge were eventually to be converted into places with civilian status, and Carlisle may well have become the *civitas* centre of the tribe of the Carvetii; this is a matter that current excavations in Carlisle on sites with long sequences of buildings and, towards the bottom, magnificently preserved organic remains, will surely illuminate. Otherwise, the main agglomerations of the civilian population lay in the vicinity of the forts. We have already commented upon the settlement (*vicus*) around Old Carlisle, near Wigton (Cumbria), a site that so far has been mapped only from aerial photographs. At Vindolanda, on the other hand, extensive excavations have thrown much light on the layout and history of one of these *vici* (53). Initially it consisted of a cluster of buildings, one of them probably a *mansio*, lining the street that leads out of the fort's west gate. There was a bath-house and the whole complex was enclosed within a clay rampart.

Whether this was properly a *vicus* of civilians or a military annexe is a matter that is open to question. What is clear is that it was eventually demolished and subsequently replaced by a much larger settlement. Here were long residential 'strip houses', evidence for industrial activity and, no doubt, shops, taverns and temples. The *mansio* and bath-building were maintained in use, and the overall impression is of a thriving community, presumably consisting mainly of soldiers' dependants (since regulations by then permitted marriage).

The chronology of the *vicus* at Vindolanda has still to be decisively demonstrated, but the excavations have provided an important insight into a common class of frontier settlement. Moreover, as aerial survey and fieldwork continues, the relationship between these military communities and the native sites is coming increasingly into focus. The pioneering work of systematically mapping and investigating the native farmsteads began in the north-east part of the province and is now being extended elsewhere. There seems to be quite pronounced regional variation. In the Cheviot Hills, for example, oval or circular stone-walled enclosures predominate and usually contain several round buildings and yards. Initially timber was used for the construction, but at most sites stone was subsequently preferred. South of Hadrian's Wall, on the other hand, a rectilinear plan was more usual, with perhaps four or five stone-built structures within an enclosure of 0.1–0.2 hectares (0.3–0.5 acres). The finds from these farms underline the poverty of the inhabitants, for 'Roman' objects are almost always rare, but it is interesting that there is growing evidence to suggest that the population of the region south of the Wall, whilst maintaining a life-style and economic system that did not differ significantly from pre-Roman days, nevertheless increased sharply in size during the Roman occupation. If this is a correct interpretation, then it may be a clear pointer towards the benefits that could accrue from a controlled frontier and a series of permanent garrison posts.

The way in which these native farmers exploited the land is just one of many current lines of research, aided by mapping of field and enclosure boundaries and by analysis of environmental evidence. There has also been much similar enquiry upon the rural landscape of many other areas of the province. The country villas, with their mosaics, elegant courts and bath-suites, have long been one of the best-known features of Romano–British archaeology, but it was only in the 1930s that the first systematic attempts to study their evolution were put in hand. Since then there have been major discoveries of individual sites, most spectacularly the later first-century 'palace' at Fishbourne, near Chichester (Hampshire), and a huge amount of excavation both of villas and of contemporary 'native' settlements. At the same time there have been important studies of the mosaics, enabling the identification of various 'schools' of craftsmen, and some absorbing essays which seek to analyse the social structure that villa buildings represent and the nature of the relationship between town and country. If the net result has been somewhat to blur our once neat definitions of what a villa is, then it is perhaps no more than a comment upon the vast array of data now available in interim or more digested form.

Close on a thousand probable villa sites are known. The majority lie in the south, although clusters in regions like southern Wales and northeast England demonstrate the falsity of an over-sharp distinction between the so-called 'military' and 'civilian' sectors of the province. A very high proportion of these villas has seen some form of investigation – probably more than in any other country – but at very few has even the central residential and farming complex been adequately explored. One important exception is Winterton (Humberside). Here an initial programme between 1958 and 1967 exposed much of the main buildings and determined the main phases of the villa's history. It was shown how the first buildings consisted of three circular houses in native tradition, one with a rectangular structure attached to it. Constructed early in the second century AD, they lasted without significant modification until late in the century, when there was a radical rebuild. This included the laying out of a residential wing with mosaics (a great rarity in British villas of this period) and a bath-house, as well as farm buildings. Winterton had, in effect, been 'Romanised' and, despite various alterations and additions, retained its basic plan down to its abandonment in the later fourth century.

Outline histories of this sort have been or are being established for a considerable number of villa sites. However, at Winterton a second phase

of large-scale investigation is attempting to set the central complex within a much wider context. Aerial photographs suggest that around the villa were enclosures, fields and trackways extending over some 25 hectares (62 acres). Excavation of this landscape is a massive task, but a good deal has already been achieved. Circular houses pre-dating the first known period of occupation have been identified, as have a series of additional buildings, some set well away from the main complex. Much has been learnt about the system of enclosures that surround the villa, and an industrial area and a number of burials have been found. Work is still in progress, but there is real hope that, for the first time, a study that integrates the villa with its estate can be made.

Equally significant has been a long programme of work upon villas in the vicinity of Verulamium, offering the fascinating chance to examine the relationship between town and country. Two excavations stand out both for their large scale and their archaeological importance, those of Gadebridge (55) and Gorhambury (Hertfordshire). Gadebridge lies only 8 kilometres (5 miles) to the west of Verulamium and was founded

54 Aerial photograph, taken in July 1976, of the courtyard villa at Chignall St James, Essex.

about AD 75, a little later than the city. Between this time and the mid-fourth century the villa went through six main episodes of building or reconstruction, gradually becoming increasingly elaborate. Naturally, there is no way of knowing who its owners may have been, but, if from a single family, it was one whose fortunes rose steadily. Special interest attaches to the construction of a large bathing-pool (about AD 325), the dimensions of which approach those of the Great Bath at Bath. Was this vulgar ostentation of the sort much favoured in the Roman world, or was its significance more arcane and perhaps religious? We do not know, but it is interesting that within three decades or so the baths and the villa were systematically pulled down and the area given over to cattle pens and stockades.

Gorhambury lies even closer to Verulamium, under a mile from the walls. The 2 hectares (5 acres) that have been excavated have shown how the villa originated as two conjoined enclosures, constructed in late Iron Age times. This basic layout was retained for much of the site's history and served to divide the main residential area from the farm-workers' quarters. Whether this can be taken to imply a native family gradually adopting Roman ways is a matter for conjecture, but the first masonry villa can be dated to about AD 100 and there were major rebuilds in the late second and fourth centuries. Like Gadebridge, they suggest a slow accumulation of wealth. Meanwhile, in the outer compound, amongst other buildings, a pre-Roman aisled hall has been identified – a very rare discovery, since the 'native' architectural tradition strongly favoured a circular plan. In the mid-second century AD this was replaced by another aisled building, which may have housed the estate workers, and around AD 300 a simple bath-suite was added nearby. This was the prelude to what seems to have been a prosperous fourth century, and it is thought that the villa may well have been functioning as such into the fifth century, matching the history of Verulamium itself.

Gadebridge and Gorhambury are two of six villas to have been well excavated in the vicinity of Verulamium, lending a pleasing sense of design to the research. Many other recent villa investigations stand more in isolation but are of no less interest. Whether the site of Whitton (55) in Glamorgan, South Wales, may properly be referred to as a villa is open to debate – the excavator prefers the term 'Romanised farmstead' – but it is of importance since the whole area within a rectangular bank and ditch was examined. The report (which, interestingly, stresses the negative side of the results as much as the positive) traces the evolution of the site from its foundation in about AD 30 to its abandonment around AD 340. Round-houses in timber were preferred until the early to mid-second century, when the first rectilinear building with masonry foundations was constructed. This architectural style remained the norm from then on; however, their design was distinctly rustic, the two hypocausts that were built seem never to have been fired, and although some painted wall-plaster was found, it was conspicuously rare. We seem, therefore, to be dealing with people who

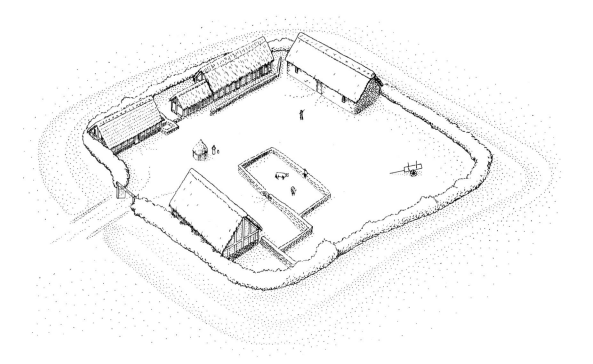

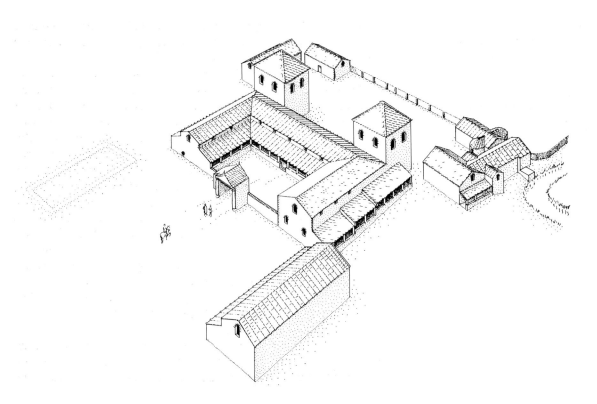

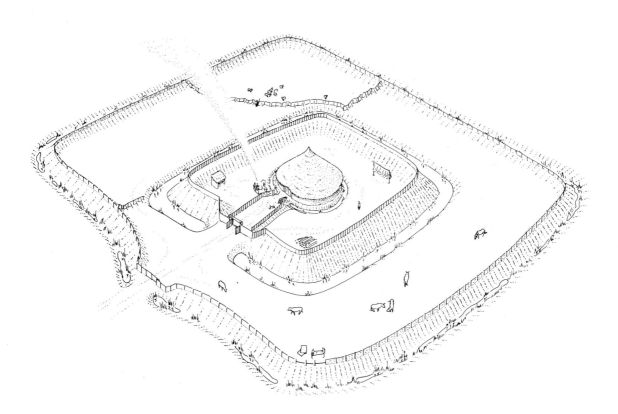

55 Late third-century Roman villas and farms, drawn to the same scale. They reflect a wide range of social rank.

Top left the moderately Romanised farmstead at Whitton (South Glamorgan).

Bottom left the elegant mansion of Gadebridge Park (Hertfordshire).

Above the native farmstead at Burradon (Northumberland).

aspired to some of the trappings of 'Romanisation' but who were unable to go the whole way – a telling comment, perhaps, on the ambitions and failings of these Romano–Britons.

At Fishbourne, on the other hand, the design of the complex was grand almost from the first. Originally a Conquest-period supply base, this was soon replaced by two spacious wooden houses. Early in the 60s these were in turn pulled down and an elaborate masonry courtyard building, with a suite of baths, was constructed. Then, about AD 75, this was incorporated into an enormous palace resembling a very rich Mediterranean villa, with fine mosaics and formal gardens, and an architectural layout best paralleled in Rome itself (56). Covering more than 4 hectares (10 acres), of which some 2.5 hectares have now been excavated, the palace was clearly the residence of a very eminent man, although who he may have been is a hotly debated matter. Fishbourne, if outstanding for its magnificence, is, however, one of a number of recently studied first-century villas which appear to be considerably richer than the norm. Rivenhall (Essex) and Eccles (Kent) are two of a lengthening list. The type of owner is again the main matter in question: native aristocrat, rich trader or Roman official? Without a suitable inscription, no one can be sure.

Turning away from individual sites (and it would be easy to consider many more of very great interest), it is important to stress more general trends in villa studies in Britain. The application of more refined dating

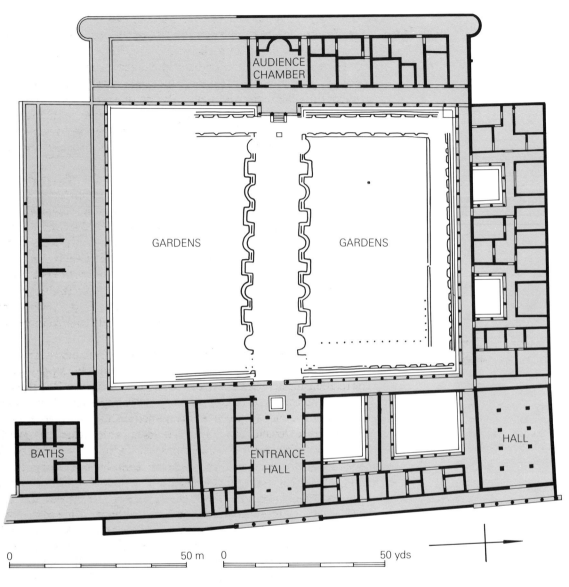

AUDIENCE
CHAMBER

GARDENS

GARDENS

BATHS

ENTRANCE
HALL

HALL

0   50 m   0   50 yds

techniques, particularly the use of pottery, has sharpened our under-standing of the histories of the sites, and serves to support the long-held notion of a fourth-century heyday for the villa in Britain. There is less certainty about the processes of their eventual abandonment, although some stimulating attempts to trace Saxon estate boundaries back to Roman times open up new lines of enquiry and deserve more investi-gation. Equally, there have been some important essays on the recon-struction of villa economies. Approaches have varied. Many are based on the evidence of animal bones and plant remains, while for Bignor (W. Sussex) Carolingian registers, the Roman agronomists, practical experiment and study of the sizes of the farm buildings have all been pressed into service in a necessarily speculative but fascinating analysis.

56   Plan of the palace at Fishbourne, as it was in the last quarter of the first century AD.

Similarly speculative but of no less significance have been a number of recent attempts to examine the social implications of the villas. Villa owners might be drawn from the native aristocracy, from peasant free-holders who prospered, from others who made money from crafts and industry, or from retired soldiers – the likeliest explanation, in some eyes, for the villas of the north-east. The way in which many sites show a gradual increase in architectural elegance certainly would seem to support the idea of families making good and perhaps buying up the property of their neighbours to create a larger farm – a phenomenon as well attested in antiquity as it is today.

Other 'social' studies have concentrated more on the villa plans themselves. These, it has been suggested, indicate at least two forms of land-ownership. One, common both in Britain and in Gaul, involved joint proprietorship, represented architecturally by two villa residences on the same site, sometimes with shared major buildings: the well-known villa at Chedworth (Gloucestershire) is considered an example. The other, characterised mainly by a large central hall, is taken to imply a rather different social unit, possibly an extended family. Interestingly, by the fourth century the distinction becomes blurred and the dual house unit largely disappears, perhaps because one family had acquired the entire estate.

The merits of these ideas have yet to see full debate but, at the very least, they inspire questions which future excavation may help to resolve. The relationship between the villas – the houses and farms of the success-ful – and the poorer rural sites is clearly of key importance here. Much attention has gone into discovering, mapping and investigating these low-ranking settlements of southern England in recent years, particularly in the Cambridgeshire and Lincolnshire Fens. This was a region made habitable by the receding of the coastline towards its present position during the earlier part of the first century AD. It was slowly colonised, mainly it would seem by salters. Later, probably under Hadrian, the scale of settlement increased dramatically, although the sites, where investigated, suggest a low level of material culture. A number of canals (but so far only one dated by excavation to about the time of Hadrian) and roadways were constructed, lending support to the attractive if unproven idea that these were state-owned lands – Hadrian was well known for his interest in developing regions of marginal potential.

Once thought of as a corn-growing area, the Fens can now be shown to be an area where peasant farmers were engaged mainly in animal husbandry, particularly the raising of sheep. Moreover, it is not imposs-ible that a curious site at Stonea (Cambridgeshire), which had some buildings constructed of stone and tile, the materials being brought from the Peterborough region, was intended as an administrative and market centre – a *forum* (57). Laid out in Hadrianic times, it has been extensively excavated in recent years and invites comparison with the contemporary town of Forum Hadriani, Arentsburg, in the Dutch low-lands.

The Fens make an important area in which to work in that they form

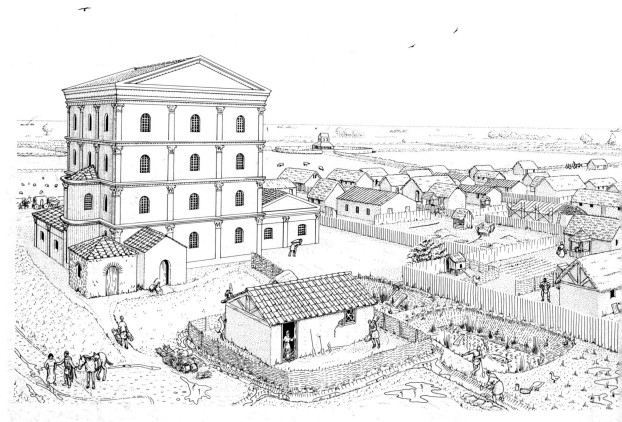

57 The settlement at Stonea, in the Cambridgeshire Fens, as it may have been in the late-second century AD.

a discrete landscape (and were possibly so regarded in Roman times) which, through aerial and ground survey, as well as excavation, offer the chance of reconstructing a complete landscape. Good organic survival at some sites enhances the value of the research, which is already providing other intriguing hypotheses. For example, it would appear that the complex at Stonea was demolished in about AD 200, and it is conceivable that the stone cottages that appear in later Roman levels at a few of the larger villages mark the adoption of a new system of management, namely through *conductores* or local 'middle-men'. But there is still much to do, and it is a race against time as the plough bites ever deeper and the organic deposits continue to dry out.

Hand-in-hand with this work on rural settlement has gone much investigation into industry: the mining of metals, the production of salt and the manufacture of pottery, tiles and other goods. Increasingly, the role and scale of these different industries are coming into perspective. Systematic recording of the makers' stamps of *mortaria*, large mixing bowls, is for example helping to establish the range and extent of their markets, some of which were surprisingly long-distance. Similarly, we are now beginning to have a much better idea of the manner in which salt was produced and distributed in different parts of the province.

Much of this work may seem laborious and mundane, but this is to belie its immense significance in grappling with the difficult subject of ancient industry. Much more obviously spectacular have been the advances in our knowledge of religious cults and their sanctuaries. Major excavations have been numerous. Investigations have taken place at temples like Uley, with its fine cult statue of Mercury; at cult-centres such as Springhead (Kent) and Gosbecks (Colchester), the latter possessing its own theatre; at villas such as Lullingstone (Kent), with its pagan temples and Christian house-chapel; at temples of Mithras like that at the Walbrook (London) and at Carrawburgh on Hadrian's Wall; at the

58   The marble busts from the villa at Lullingstone (Kent). They date to the second century AD, and were probably made in a Mediterranean workshop. They are likely to represent members of the family that owned the villa. Heights 41 cm (16 in.) and 75 cm (29.5 in.).

spa complex at Bath, the urban temples of Colchester, and on a Christian *martyrium* at Canterbury. To these should be added a rich array of portable finds, not least the Water Newton church plate (probably the oldest yet known from the Roman world), and the Thetford late Roman treasure, with its abundance of references to the central Italian deity, Faunus, best known from the works of much older Republican writers such as Virgil and Ovid.

The range of new information is enormous and has provoked a number of recent attempts at synthesis. These have been accompanied by significant advances in technique, such as the meticulous plotting of the position of every find, as at Uley and Hayling Island. As a result, new data can be set alongside new perspectives. One pleasing tendency has been to ignore formal chronological frameworks, and thus to search for both the pre-Roman ancestry of religious sites and their post-Roman history. Uley, for instance, a remote hilltop in Gloucestershire, proved to have been a ritual centre from the first century bc until well into post-Roman times. Whilst a strong element of continuity is implied by much of the evidence, such as building alignments, the site is also remarkable

59 Over-life-size limestone head of the god Mercury, from the temple at Uley (Gloucestershire). It is a fine example of good-quality provincial work, based on Hellenistic prototypes and dates to the second century AD. Height: 29 cm (11.5 in.).

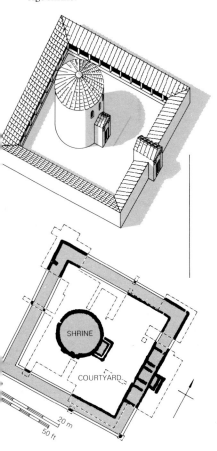

60 The Romano-British sanctuary on Hayling Island, which overlies an Iron Age shrine.

for its successive manifestations of religious beliefs. Late prehistoric sanctification, represented archaeologically by an enclosure containing wooden structures, was eventually followed towards AD 200 by the construction of two ranges of stone buildings. These were later demolished and, by the mid-fourth century, a structure recognisably of temple plan, together with other stone-built complexes, had been put up. A wealth of votive material, including lead curses, bronze figurines and some magnificent items of sculpture, leave no doubt that from the second to the later fourth century the principal deity was the classical god Mercury (59). Then all this was swept away, to be replaced by further structures, including what may be a wooden church. If so – and the identification is an attractive one – then religious activity certainly persisted well into the fifth century and probably later.

At Hayling Island, too, where a circular wooden shrine of late Iron Age date was followed soon after the Conquest by the construction of a stone Gallic-style temple (60), it is the sanctity of the site – not the physical manifestations, whether architectural or votive – that is the striking feature. In combination, both sanctuaries demonstrate how elastic were the boundaries between one religion and another, and that sacred foci, once established, tended to outlast any political upheavals.

Work at Colchester has been of particular interest in this and in many other respects. Before the Conquest the pre-eminent late Iron Age centre of Britain (Camulodunum) and then the first colony (Colonia Victricensis), Colchester has now yielded evidence for a grand temple to Claudius, seven Romano–Celtic temples, one or two small rectangular temples and a possible shrine to a martyr. In addition, there were two suburban sanctuaries. At Gosbecks an important Iron Age complex gave way to a large Celtic-style temple set within a sacred precinct (61). Nearby was a theatre, and there may have been ornamental gardens; this then must have been a religious focus with space for fairs and other entertainment, of a sort familiar from Gaul. Similarly, at Sheepen the Iron Age centre was replaced by a scattered series of temples, some within enclosed precincts. We may reasonably suppose that these Roman-period sanctuaries (where the worship of both Jupiter and Mercury can be demonstrated) were the heirs to earlier cult-centres. In the *colonia* itself there was a mingling of classical- and Celtic-style temples, as though to symbolise the eclecticism of the Roman approach to religion. Although all too little is known about the deities that were worshipped here, they were no doubt numerous and may well have involved the familiar twinning of classical and Celtic gods and goddesses. This theme is best illustrated at Bath (Aquae Sulis), where a magnificent sanctuary built in the classical style was dedicated to the local deity of the spring, Sul, and to the goddess Minerva. Patient and difficult excavation, hampered not least by a lethal virus present in the waters, has refined our knowledge of the layout of the sanctuary in a remarkable way, and recovered thousands of votive objects.

Bath was a spa town, and its *raison d'être* was essentially religious. Some other settlements, too, seem to have developed primarily for non-

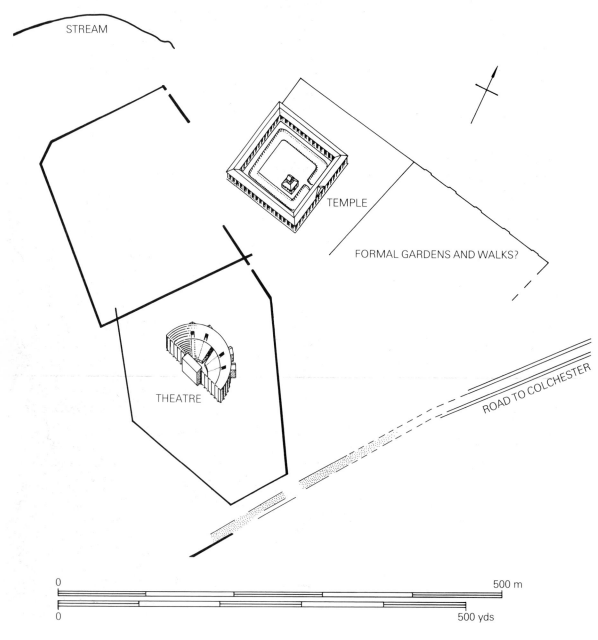

STREAM

TEMPLE

FORMAL GARDENS AND WALKS?

THEATRE

ROAD TO COLCHESTER

0   500 m

0   500 yds

secular reasons. At Springhead, for example, the inspiration behind this extensive roadside complex is surely to be found in its centrally placed group of temples and shrines. Although a pre-Roman origin for the sanctuary is suspected, it seems likely that the settlement flourished mainly from the visits of through-travellers along Watling Street, for whom there seems to have been both accommodation and other facilities.

The work at Springhead epitomises the prevailing view of today that it is crucial to set the temple within the context of both its precinct and the ancillary buildings. Often other considerations rule this out, as with

61   The Romano-British religious complex at Gosbecks, near Colchester, which included a theatre.

62 General view of the excavation of the west baths in Bath.

the Walbrook Mithraeum in London (one of several sites which expand our knowledge of this widespread and intriguing Oriental cult); but, where attempted, the results have always been of interest, not least the recovery at some sites of nearby cemeteries.

There is in fact still an enormous amount to be learnt about the burial grounds of Roman Britain. Cemeteries like Poundbury, near Dorchester, where over 1,000 burials have been excavated, and Lankhills (Winchester), with 451 graves, stand out for the large size of the sample – and for the interest of the discoveries. Poundbury's mausolea, one with wall-

63 The great gold belt-buckle from the Thetford Treasure. It shows a satyr holding a bunch of grapes. It dates to about AD 390. Height of plate 5.2 cm (2 in).

paintings, probably mark the tombs of Roman Dorchester's richer burghers, while at Lankhills some graves may be those of foreign elements in the population, perhaps Saxons and Sarmatians from south-eastern Europe. The future will surely see more attempts at total excavation of cemeteries, and an increasingly refined analysis of the wide variety of burial rites to be found in the province.

It is perhaps appropriate to conclude this section, however, with a comment, not on death, but upon the spread of Christianity within Roman Britain. No one can fail to be struck by the enormous quantity of new information that has come to light in recent years. Spectacular individual finds like the Water Newton treasure, the Hinton St Mary mosaic and the Lullingstone villa chapel, together with many more portable objects, are to be set alongside the excavation of churches and cemeteries, as at Icklingham (Suffolk). Despite unequivocal evidence, such as the Thetford treasure, for the strength of pagan beliefs in late Roman Britain, there is no doubt that the Church was well established.

Britain may appear to lack the great cathedrals of, say, Trier, and ecclesiastical buildings are hard to identify with certainty, but the sheer bulk of Christian finds is witness to its importance. Moreover, the view that the Romano–British church was totally extinguished with the arrival of the Anglo-Saxons is coming under increasing scrutiny. It is particularly striking, as recent studies have emphasised, to see just how many later churches overlie Roman sites, not least in the centres of some major towns of the province. Some continuity from sites already venerated by pagan worship is not implausible. Indeed, at the cathedrals of Wells (Somerset) and St Albans, and at the church of St Martin's at Canterbury, there is a real possibility that they originated as Roman *martyria*, while some villas, like Rivenhall and Lullingstone, were to develop as post-Roman foci of Christian worship. Just as the early fifth-century see at Whithorn (Dumfries and Galloway) must surely have been a Romano–British foundation, so much of the shape of the Christian England which was eventually to follow may well have had its roots in the ecclesiastical organisation of the fourth century and earlier. It is an intriguing hypothesis for archaeology to test.

Roman Britain: the future

The diversity of recent discoveries, and the varied way in which they can be woven into a broader canvas, is both stimulating and daunting to summarise. Romano–British studies have now been firmly elevated into the status of a proper academic discipline, taught up and down the country. But no seminar group, whether in school, university, extramural class, or anywhere else, could or should be stilled into consensus. The possibilities are much too numerous for that. Here we have touched upon just a few of the sites and interpretative ideas that come up time and time again in current debate. Other writers may well have chosen differently, reflecting their experiences, interests and specialisms. But no choice could be properly representative and, in any case, it seems in some ways unimportant. What Haverfield, Collingwood, Richmond and so many other great scholars of the past would probably have found rewarding today is the high level of expertise, both in excavation and in the study of the material remains; the great degree of interest and commitment in the subject; and, no doubt, the shape of current perspectives. That there is so lively a state of affairs is very much due to the sure base that they, and many contemporary scholars, have laid.

Indeed, the Roman period in Britain continues to exercise a peculiar and perhaps disproportionate fascination for layman and professional alike that is not easy to explain. The Romans are, of course, both famous and notorious, but, whether one is a volunteer on an excavation, a visitor to a museum, a treasure hunter, a teacher or a student, or a full-time field archaeologist it is an area that always seems to hold the prospect of a major new discovery or a novel perspective. All these groups have their role to play, and it is a responsible one. None should forget the destructive forces of modern development and agriculture; the depredations of that small, avaricious body that plunders sites, not for knowledge, but for financial gain; nor the awesome costs of a properly conducted and fully published research project. Most people must wonder, at some time or another, whether it is all worth it; if Romano–British archaeology – or any archaeology – is not just an increasingly expensive recreational activity of our time. If so, it takes a not very extended glance at the literature, or perhaps one lecture, to realise that this is a wholly absorbing area of study which, if we are ever to understand even the basics, will keep us busy for a very long time yet.

NOTES

1 A.H.L.-F. Pitt-Rivers, *Excavations in Cranborne Chase, near Rushmore*, 4 vols (1887–1898)

2 D. Christison, J.H. Cunningham, J. Anderson and T. Ross, *Proceedings of the Society of Antiquaries of Scotland* 32 (1898), pp. 399–476

3 *Journal of Roman Studies* 9 (1919), pp. 111–38

4 Cf. M. Bouchenaki, *Cités antiques d'Algérie* (1978), p. 9

5 M. Benabou, *La résistance africaine à la romanisation* (1976)

6 *Journal of Roman Studies* 18 (1928), p. 201

7 T.D. Kendrick and C.F.C. Hawkes, *Archaeology in England and Wales 1914–1931* (1930), p. 209

8 *Journal of Roman Studies* 23 (1933), p. 101

9 R.G. Collingwood, *The Archaeology of Roman Britain* (1936)

10 R.G. Collingwood, *Roman Britain* (1932); R.G. Collingwood and J.N.L. Myres, *Roman Britain and the English Settlements* (1936; 2nd edn, 1937)

11 I.A. Richmond, *Proceedings of the British Academy* (1943), p. 476

12 C.W. Phillips, 'The Fenland Research Committee, its past achievements and future prospects', in W.F. Grimes (ed.), *Aspects of Archaeology* (1951), p. 261

13 F. Haverfield and G. Macdonald, *The Roman occupation of Britain* (1924)

14 W.F. Grimes, *The excavation of Roman and medieval London* (1968), p. 1

15 S.S. Frere, *Verulamium Excavations I*, Society of Antiquaries of London (1972), p. 5

16 P. Marsden, *Roman London* (1980), p. 205

17 Cf. *Britannia* 11 (1980), pp. 442–3

18 A.L.F. Rivet, *Journal of Roman Studies* 58 (1968), p. 247

19 Harold Cooper, privately published (1929)

20 C.M. Daniels, *Britannia* 10 (1979), p. 362

21 *Ibid.*, p. 363

22 D.J. Breeze, *Britannia* 14 (1983), p. 373

23 R. Reece, *Archaeological Journal* 139 (1982), p. 455

24 D.J. Breeze, *Britannia* 8 (1977), p. 460

25 R. Reece, *art. cit.*, p. 456

26 N. Balaam, *Britannia* 9 (1978), p. 56

27 G.D.B. Jones and J. Walker, 'Either side of Solway', in J.C. Chapman and H.C. Mytum (eds), *Settlement in north Britain 1000 BC – AD 1000*, British Archaeological Reports 118 (1983)

28 C.W. Phillips (ed.), *The Fenland in Roman Times* (1970)

29 S.S. Frere, *Verulamium Excavations I*, Society of Antiquaries of London (1972), p. 2

30 V.E. Nash-Williams (revised M.G. Jarrett), *The Roman Frontier in Wales* (1969), p. 21

31 R.E.M. Wheeler and T.V. Wheeler, *Verulamium: a Belgic and two Roman cities*, Society of Antiquaries of London (1936), p. 28

32 R.G. Collingwood and J.N.L. Myres, *Roman Britain and the English Settlements* (1937), p. 206

3 Anglo-Saxon England
AD 400–1100

Unlike those of the Roman or medieval periods, the visible remains of the Anglo-Saxons do not present a high profile.[1] Compared with the Roman Wall's ruthless march across the Northumbrian landscape, or the looming bulk of Durham cathedral, even such substantial standing Anglo-Saxon monuments as Offa's Dyke, on the borders of England and

64   Map of principal sites mentioned in the text.

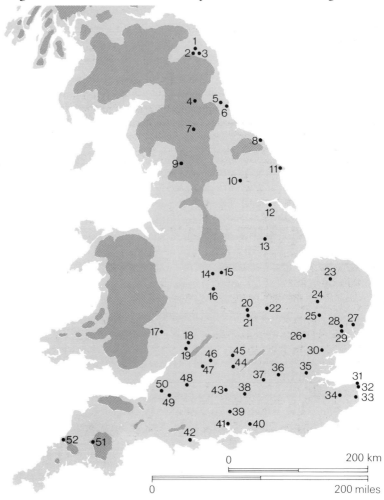

Wales, or Brixworth parish church (Northamptonshire) seem at first glance modest exercises, unable either to achieve the scale and organisation of Rome or to anticipate the architectural feats of the Middle Ages. The impression of decent obscurity is heightened by the quantity of Anglo-Saxon surviving structures, which, apart from the stone sculpture and such original fabric as remains in churches, are relatively few in comparison with their Roman and medieval counterparts. The majority of Anglo-Saxon monuments must be sought out patiently; they do not in general impose themselves dramatically upon the traveller's eye.

This seeming reticence is further compounded in the popular historical imagination by such factors as the use of the term 'Dark Ages', and the success of J.R.R. Tolkien's *Lord of the Rings* trilogy and its many sword-and-sorcery imitations. Thus is nourished the romantic notion of a murky void between the civilised grandeur of Rome and the complex fabric of the Middle Ages – a Germanic twilight of heroic exploits, chiefly memorable for battles and characters with comically obscure names, straight out of *1066 and All That*. At worst, indeed, Anglo-Saxons seem to feature in popular tradition as a kind of decent suburban Viking; King Alfred is doomed forever to be remembered as an incompetent cook, not for his outstanding administrative and military achievements or his intellectual reforms.

Even in those areas where it is relatively abundant, for instance the jewellery of the pagan period, the archaeological spoor of the Anglo-Saxons has tended to reinforce the widespread but misleading picture of a simple society whose dreary rounds are occasionally relieved by events of barbaric splendour, such as the Sutton Hoo ship-burial. It was, as we shall see, the very abundance of grave-goods surviving from the period AD 400–700 which dominated Anglo-Saxon archaeological studies until the 1950s and 1960s, when a new generation of excavators and researchers began to examine the subject in a quite different way, extending its boundaries into virtually unexplored areas. The prolific and sometimes spectacular results have brought about fundamental changes in our understanding of the nature and development of a complex and fascinating society in a period of rapid and profound changes. It is the aim of this chapter to outline the development of Anglo-Saxon archaeology as a discrete discipline and to highlight some of the recent work and approaches which have radically transformed the subject.

Early approaches

As early as the sixteenth century antiquarians had begun to take a serious interest in Anglo-Saxon history. Anxious to stress England's new-found independence of the Catholic church, and papal authority in particular, a number of Protestant apologists, such as Archbishop Matthew Parker began to explore the origins, thoughts and customs of the Reformed church in England. With this began the systematic study of the language of the Anglo-Saxons, Old English, and their history and institutions. But although early antiquaries such as Richard Verstegan and William Camden, writing in the sixteenth and early seventeenth centuries, displayed an interest in the history and standing monuments of the post-Roman period, the first account of an Anglo-Saxon archaeological investigation did not appear until the seventeenth century when Sir Thomas Browne published his essay *Hydriotaphia, Urne-Buriall* (1658).[2] The urns in question came from an Anglo-Saxon cremation cemetery at Walsingham (Norfolk); though Browne believed them to be Roman, they are the first excavated Anglo-Saxon antiquities to have been described and illustrated. In the manner of his day, Browne saw in these 'sad and sepulchral pitchers' an opportunity for reflection on human mortality and transience, but his magnificently sonorous observations are as pertinent to today's researchers as they were to his contemporary audience; 'much more', he wrote, 'is buried in silence than is recorded, and the largest volumes are butt epitomes of what hath been'. In a period as meagrely documented as this, the evidence of archaeology assumes a particular importance; despite the limitations of this evidence, researchers are now discovering how to probe it with increasingly sophisticated methods.

It was to be almost a hundred years before any more excavation of Anglo-Saxon sites was recorded. Towards the end of the eighteenth century two remarkable men undertook separate and systematic excavation of a number of Anglo-Saxon cemeteries in Kent. The first of these was the Reverend Bryan Faussett, who between the years 1757 and 1773 excavated substantial portions of the Anglo-Saxon cemeteries at Gilton, Kingston, Sibertswold, Barfriston, Bekesbourne and Chartham. His excavation notebooks, which survive to this day with much of his excavated material in the Liverpool Museum, meticulously record the contents of each grave and are accompanied by numerous sketches and plans of the sites. Faussett's researches, though known to a few antiquarians, were to remain essentially unpublished for eighty years,[3] so that it falls to his near contemporary, Captain (later Reverend) James Douglas, to claim the distinction of publishing the first scientific account of the excavation of an Anglo-Saxon site, in his work *Nenia Britannica* (1793).[4] Douglas, originally a military man like a notable number of his more recent successors, began to explore Anglo-Saxon cemeteries following chance discoveries of graves while he was engaged in the fortification of Chatham Lines in Kent. His subsequent researches there and at Greenwich, Ash and St Margarets-at-Cliff led him to be the first to identify the artefacts he and Faussett had found as Anglo-Saxon rather than Roman in origin. Both his text and the exquisite illustrations which accompany it are remarkable by the standards of their day and certainly superior to many of the published investigations of the succeeding century. In their careful and scientific recording of data, both Faussett and Douglas – who enjoyed a cordial friendship – were well in advance of German or French researchers in the equivalent field of Frankish archaeology and set standards in England which were not to be matched for almost a hundred years.

The middle years of the nineteenth century, however, brought a great acceleration in the study of Anglo-Saxon archaeology. In part this reflected advances made in the study of the written sources and a growing interest in the material culture of the society which produced them: the great textual scholar J.M. Kemble, for instance, was the first to recognise the affinities between Anglo-Saxon cremation urns and those from the Saxon homelands of North Germany.[5] The growth of interest was perhaps also partly fuelled by Victorian romantic interest in national identity, as some of the more imaginative contributions to contemporary excavation reports make clear: Wylie's *Fairford Graves* (1852),[6] for example, concludes with a stirring piece of verse invoking the Anglo-Saxons as 'kindred men' whose spirit lives on to inspire the Victorian empire:

> Still sounds the Saxon tongue as erst of old,
>> In Saxon breasts still beats the Saxon heart.
> God bless'd the empire-tree which thou didst plant,
>> And still will bless, and mighty increase grant.

But beyond all this there also lay a simple practical reason for the increased activity: the rapid expansion of urban development and of the railway system led to many more sites being discovered, in a manner very similar to that whereby modern motorway building, housing programmes and inner city redevelopment have led to expansion of archaeological opportunities (and anxieties) in recent years. Unlike modern archaeologists, however, nineteenth-century investigators lacked the advance warnings provided by aerial survey or fieldwalking. Sites came up completely unexpectedly and were all too often disastrously looted by labourers, landowners, locals, and not least the archaeologists themselves. (The first General Meeting of the British Archaeological Association, held at Canterbury in 1844, thought it entirely appropriate to celebrate such a momentous gathering by opening a few Anglo-Saxon barrows on Breach Down for the delight of the assembled ladies – despite a torrential downpour. And as late as 1883 the rich barrow at Taplow (Buckinghamshire) was excavated by local antiquaries with such ineptitude that irreparable damage was done both to the contents of the burial and, perhaps deservedly, to one of the excavators.)

The huge Anglo-Saxon and Roman cemeteries at Kings Field, Faversham (Kent) furnish a melancholy case in point: discovered in the process of laying the Chatham–Dover railway line, the cemetery was completely ransacked with no record whatsoever of the outstandingly rich grave groups; it is largely thanks to the tenacity of a local man, William Gibbs, who bought as much as he could from the navvies and others who had made the finds, that any record at all survives of this major site. It was not all such a dismal story, of course: many sites were competently excavated by the standards of their day, and properly published. Major cemeteries such as those of Bifrons and Sarre (Kent), Long Wittenham (Oxfordshire) and Sleaford (Lincolnshire) were excavated during this period, and a few scholars, such as J.Y. Akerman, the Baron de Baye and the indefatigable and quarrelsome Charles Roach Smith, began to synthesise the results in their works.[7]

Systematic analysis, however, had to wait until the early years of this century, with the emergence of scholars such as E.T. Leeds, Nils Åberg and G. Baldwin Brown. Very different from each other, they exemplify three quite distinct approaches to the material which continued to dominate Anglo-Saxon archaeology until after 1945. Leeds's analyses were primarily historical in direction: he sought to understand the chronology and ethnic divisions of Anglo-Saxon settlement in England through analysis of grave-goods.[8] Åberg's approach was more narrowly typological, concerned with constructing a chronological framework for the development of art-styles, and of schemes of artefact classification.[9] Baldwin Brown, whose monumental work, unlike that of any of his contemporaries, covered the entire Anglo-Saxon period, surveyed the social aspects of the material over a wide range, attempting to define social custom and usage.[10] Other notable scholars of the period dealt with particular classes of material or with its art-historical aspects: among them, J.N.L. Myres's work on Anglo-Saxon funerary pottery and Sir Thomas Kendrick's two volumes on Anglo-Saxon art are outstanding examples.[11]

It will, however, have become apparent from this extremely abbreviated account that up to the 1930s the thrust of Anglo-Saxon archaeology was directed almost exclusively onto one aspect alone: the grave-goods discovered in the cemeteries of the so-called 'pagan' period, that is roughly from the early fifth to the end of the seventh century AD. Contemporary settlement sites were simply unknown until Leeds's investigations at Sutton Courtenay (Oxfordshire) in the 1920s and 1930s (see below, chapter 5). By the late 1940s around 1,130 cemeteries were known, compared with about half a dozen settlement sites. And while architectural historians and art-historians had produced valuable surveys and even corpora of Anglo-Saxon churches and sculpture, metalwork and manuscripts, very little work indeed had been devoted to any other aspect of the archaeology of the later Saxon period. The metalwork, pottery and glass of the early period had been extensively discussed and more classifications were on the way; the archaeological evidence for the date and nature of invasion and settlement of England had been animatedly debated, and there had been some scrutiny of the effects of the Augustinian Christian mission to England. But virtually nothing was known from archaeological sources about how the Anglo-Saxons lived: their houses, their diet, their life-expectancy, their illnesses, their social composition; how they used the land, what crops they grew, what animals they reared; how crafts were organised, how goods were distributed, how and when towns came about; what their monasteries looked like, how their churches were used; what had happened to the Romano–British population – the list could go on almost indefinitely. Of course, the answers to some of these questions remain almost as obscure today; it would be over-bold to claim that archaeology is going to solve every query, but it is encouraging to look back on the work of the last forty years and see how radically our understanding of Anglo-Saxon England has been altered by the new directions archaeology has taken in this period.

One of the undoubted catalysts in the process of change was the foundation in 1956 of the Society for Medieval Archaeology by a small and lively group of scattered enthusiasts. Its creation was both a sign of the ripening of the subject and an enormous stimulus to further growth. Through its conferences and its journal, *Medieval Archaeology*, it has provided an essential forum for debate and for the transmission of discoveries and new ideas in the early medieval period; it has helped to bring current Continental work to an English audience, and has exported our researches abroad; it has in general focused interest and stimulated research. That this chapter can be written at all must owe much to the work the Society has achieved in creating, out of the original scattered efforts of relatively few individuals, a sense of the subject as a whole and its potential. It is now time to turn to the work of these recent years and to examine the new discoveries and directions which Anglo-Saxon archaeology has been pursuing since 1945.

Cemeteries

It may perhaps seem ironic to begin with a discussion of the type of site which has for so long dominated Anglo-Saxon archaeology to the detriment of other sources of evidence, but there are two good reasons for this. The first is the inescapable fact that Anglo-Saxon cemeteries are numerous, rich in artefacts and easier to find than, for example, settlement sites. They are thus more likely to be discovered and to be excavated than other sorts of Anglo-Saxon sites, at least in Lowland Britain. Their very nature makes them vulnerable to grave-robbers ancient and modern, so that once found and publicised it is often necessary for professionals to dig them to prevent unscientific and unrecorded destruction. Certain forms of burial – cremations in particular – are especially vulnerable to modern agricultural practices such as deep-ploughing, and this has also resulted in more such sites being excavated in advance of serious damage. For pragmatic reasons, therefore, cemeteries continue to be an inevitable component of Anglo-Saxon archaeology in the field; but the second reason for their continuing importance is the development of new ways of interrogating the evidence which yield fresh insights into the buried communities which they represent.

As we have seen, it was until recently traditional to quarry cemeteries both literally and metaphorically for grave contents, which were classified and studied primarily to enhance understanding of the documentary evidence for early Anglo-Saxon history. But they have now increasingly become subjects for study in their own right, as an important recent paper by Tania Dickinson[12] has very clearly summarised. She has identified three levels of cemetery data: the graves, their contents and any other archaeological features; the cemetery as a whole, viewed in terms of the spatial and quantitative relations of the constituent parts; and the cemetery as a unit to be related to other data, archaeological or historical. It is particularly at the second level that much recent work has been concentrated.

Sonia Hawkes's spatial and chronological analysis of the Finglesham cemetery (Kent), for example, has produced a picture of the development of a small but prosperous community.[13] It was originally founded by a group of aristocratic people in the early sixth century; the leading family and its adherents continued to dominate the community for about a generation, but seem to have left the area in the later sixth century. Their successors seem to have been less wealthy, though the overall size of the community had grown in the seventh century. These conclusions are based on the identification of related grave clusters, and particularly on the observation of the two distinctive phases of barrow-building on the site.

As this implies, the analysis of the structures which accompany graves in certain parts of the country can be very revealing. The large inhumation cemetery of St Peter's, Broadstairs (Kent), provides a striking instance of the range of mortuary structures which have been recognised as current in north-east Kent during the sixth and seventh centuries.[14] First of all, the various forms of structure – lined graves, graves with corner-posts, graves with ledges or cross-beams, graves surrounded by palisades or ring ditches – have chronological significance, as the horizontal stratigraphy of the cemetery, coupled with analysis of the grave-goods, shows (65). Secondly, this phenomenon also reveals something about forms of status in the community. Clearly, a fence around the grave, a barrow over it or a mortuary chamber within it all express the standing of the dead person, in ways more permanent and more prominent than the objects buried with the dead person, which may in conventional terms seem quite modest. Some glimpse is also afforded, by means such as these, of the fugitive rituals and beliefs which accompanied the burial. The hefty cross-beams which occur in some of these graves were obviously designed to support more than the weight of a wooden lid over the body; they may perhaps have formed some kind of bier on which the body and its accompaniments were exposed before final interment. Many of the ring ditches have entrances, some with a central post, suggesting ceremonial functions.

The clusterings may also suggest family groupings, as at Finglesham. Both the Finglesham and St Peter's cemeteries with respectively 246 and 388 excavated graves are large for inhumation ceremonies. Yet the time-span involved shows clearly that the communities they served were comparatively small. Sonia Hawkes has estimated, on the basis of an average life-expectancy of around thirty years for the buried population, that the sixth-century community at Finglesham at any one time was equivalent to a 'smallish household', while the numbers of seventh-century burials suggest an expansion of population roughly equal to that of a large working farm. Analysis of the skeletal material from the St Peter's cemetery is still in progress, but the chronological

50m

50yds

pattern of graves also suggests an increase in population in the seventh century, with numbers apparently more nearly approximate to a small village.

Other factors may condition the layout and development of a cemetery, however. The large, recently excavated, cemetery at Lechlade (Gloucestershire) in the Upper Thames Valley, with some 230 graves

65 (*left*) Plan of the Anglo-Saxon cemetery at St Peter's, Broadstairs (Kent). It can easily be seen from the plan how there are certain clusters of graves within the cemetery, representing family plots as well as chronological phases. For instance, graves with cross-beams are particularly concentrated in the centre of the cemetery, and graves with ring-ditches are sited on the periphery. The latter group belongs to the latest phase of the cemetery's use. After A.C. Hogarth

66 (*below*) The Anglo-Saxon cemetery at Spong Hill (Norfolk): a family group of cremation urns buried in one pit. The darker fill of the hole can quite clearly be seen. Each urn contained the cremated remains of at least one individual, together with personal jewellery and other tokens, sometimes including food-offerings.

known at present, contains at least one large cluster of sixth-century female graves, though these groups may also of course be linked by family connexions. The massive cremation and inhumation cemetery at Spong Hill, North Elmham (Norfolk), provides a different set of data.[15] Some 2,000 cremations and 57 inhumations were buried on the top of the hill with a commanding view of the valley below. The time-span of the burials covers the fifth and sixth centuries. This in itself suggests that it must have served an extensive local population, but preliminary work on the cremated bone has shown that some of the urns contain the remains of two or three individuals, indicating a total population significantly larger than that suggested by the urns alone.[16] The implications of this, reinforced by data from some of the other large cremation cemeteries, are that such massive cemeteries served the scattered population of a fairly wide area, and that this is a feature found in the earlier phases of the period before larger nucleated settlements had developed[17] and established their own burial grounds.

Spong Hill's size, and the decorative variation of its funerary pottery have also made it an ideal subject for detailed statistical analysis. Study of the various groups of pottery linked by shared stamps has sharpened

the picture of the development of the cemetery suggested by analysis of the grave-goods; this has in its turn implications for the production and distribution of such pottery both within the immediate communities and further afield. Here, too, apparent family groups have been discerned, some evidently interred at one and the same time, and there are abundant, if ambiguous, indications of the ritual and beliefs which accompanied the burials (66).

Another area of cemetery study to which much attention has recently been given is the complex issue of status. We have already seen how in some parts of England barrows and other varieties of mortuary structure apparently indicated the social standing of the dead person, and so give insight into the stratification of a community. There have been various attempts, none of them wholly successful, to construct objective ways of evaluating categories of grave-goods and so refine our understanding of degrees of status.[18] It is increasingly clear that Anglo-Saxons, like the rest of us, had infinitely flexible and various ways of indicating a person's status, which their buried possessions or memorials can only represent in a very limited way, and not necessarily the obvious one. For one thing, status in a community is not simply a matter of wealth, as any priest or pools-winner knows. While it is obvious enough both from the exotic and prestigious grave-goods, and the prominent and unusual manner of burial, that the Sutton Hoo ship-burial commemorates a person of outstanding importance, it is less immediately apparent that the young female buried with nothing but an iron knife in grave 25, Bradstow School, Broadstairs, was also a person of standing in the community, as the substantial enclosure round her grave makes plain. We now know, for example, that women's role in Anglo-Saxon society is expressed in terms of burial by more than just their jewellery; accumulated observations in recent years have identified various items and groups of equipment which define status more precisely. Among these are textile equipment – shears, spindles, weaving battens, wool-combs – and collections of medicinal or magical value, such as the bags of amulets and lucky charms, and capsules containing herbs and fibres, which perhaps signified that their owner was a wise-woman.[19] Many sparsely furnished women's graves are characterised by elaborate chatelaines and bunches of keys, which Hawkes and Fell have argued symbolise the woman's role as keeper of the household stores.[20]

Age, too, as well as sex, has its own particular symbolic accompaniments. Recent examination of existing skeletal data has suggested the age at which a boy could take up arms – spear, shield and sword – was at puberty. A good example of this occurs in the Bradstow School cemetery at Broadstairs, where a part of the cemetery was reserved for well-equipped warriors, a few of them with swords as well as the more normal spears and shields. The owner of the finest sword, an inlaid Frankish import, was a boy aged about fifteen, the youngest sword-bearer yet identified (67).

As we have also seen at Spong Hill, the analysis of the skeletal material is now an extremely important aspect of the study of Anglo-Saxon

67   Reconstruction of the burial of an adolescent boy from an Anglo-Saxon cemetery at Bradstow School, Broadstairs (Kent). His array of fighting gear shows he was of high rank and adult status; a Frankish gold coin found in his mouth was payment for passage to the other world, and a bowl of nuts at his feet symbolised the idea of rebirth.

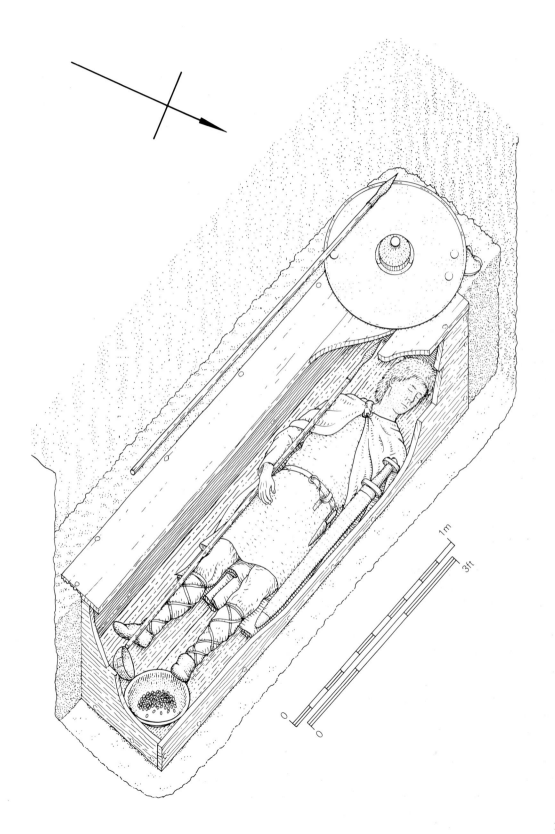

68 A live burial from Sewerby (East Yorkshire). The woman was thrown in on top of the corpse of a younger woman (still unexcavated in this photograph) and weighted down with stones. It seems likely that this was a form of punishment rather than a voluntary act of sacrifice.

cemeteries, though it is regrettable that the necessary palaeopathologists are so thin on the ground that there is an inevitable pile-up of bones waiting to be examined. Vital information about diet (low in sugar until urbanisation starts: Viking town-dwellers have particularly rotten teeth) and mortality can be extracted from the most unpromisingly fragile bone; we are beginning to see, for instance, that the average life-expectancy up to the seventh century is only about thirty years, even in the relatively prosperous south-east of England. A high degree of osteoarthritis of the spine suggests back-breaking field work in a damp climate; and the large number of women dying by their early twenties confirms the grave risks of childbirth. It has also been possible to identify related individuals on the basis of genetically transmitted skeletal anomalies – in teeth, for example – while of course the interpretation of injuries can illuminate the daily hazards of life – broken legs, sword cuts, tooth abscesses, bone infections. Occasionally an extraordinary assemblage demands special interpretation. At Sewerby (E. Yorkshire), a woman aged between thirty-five and forty-five, buried face down on top of the conventional coffined burial of a younger woman seems to have been buried alive: her legs are kicked back, her elbows raised and her fists clenched in an apparent attempt to scrabble free. A chunk of stone quern in the small of her back weighted her down (68). The whole manner of burial suggests punishment for some crime, possibly the death of the woman buried beneath her. She is not the only example of such practices[21]. Decapitations – both before and after death – may suggest at best ghost-laying, but the corpses with their hands tied behind their backs which were recently excavated at Sutton Hoo (Suffolk) look very much like summary executions. Even more extraordinary, a great pile of disarticulated bodies, representing some 250 individuals, was recently excavated at Repton (Derbyshire) under a mound of Scandinavian Viking character. The mound overlay an eighth-century Anglo-Saxon high-status chapel known from this monastic site. The chapel had been reused to contain a high-status Viking burial, round which the disarticulated bones were stacked. Predominantly male, and with some evidence of healed as well as unhealed sword cuts, it was at first thought that these might be the battle-fallen from recorded local Viking engagements in the winter of AD 873–4, a date supported by coins found with charnel. It now seems that if these are mostly soldiery, they more probably died from a winter epidemic. Final interpretation must await full analysis and further excavation, but the investigations at Repton have already indicated that burial practices and circumstances continue to be of the greatest interest and importance to Anglo-Saxon studies long after the conventional end of pagan modes of burial.

This is reinforced by recent work on the later period at Winchester, at Raunds (Northamptonshire) and at Barton-on-Humber, where environmental and palaeopathological evidence has confirmed the value of excavating the unfurnished graves of large middle and later Saxon cemeteries. At Raunds, for example, the evidence of over three hundred late Saxon burials confirms the dismal picture of high infant mortality – one third of all children dead by the age of six – low life-expectancy and physically damaging work that we have come to expect in the earlier period. In terms of mortality at least, the population of Anglo-Saxon England was strikingly similar to much of the Third World today.

The specialised techniques of grave-excavation should not be overlooked here either. Archaeologists in recent years have become more and more adept at sieving the last shreds of information from their deposits; organic samples for radiocarbon dating and for analysis of leather, antler, bone and woods: seeds and pollen to suggest the time of year that burial took place and the nature of the local landscape. Minute scrutiny of grave-goods can be surprisingly revealing, too. At Sewerby the mineralised remains of fly *puparia* on the back of a brooch show that the corpse in question must have lain exposed and unburied for several days. Elsewhere traces of mineralised grasses, moss and bracken found on metal grave-goods indicate that the grave was lined or strewn with plants.

In highly acidic conditions, as at Sutton Hoo, organic remains, especially bone, survive barely at all, bodies being visible simply as stains or 'shadows' in the soil; here the excavator has boldly rejected the traditional approach of scraping these away layer by layer, and has adopted instead a more arduous but much more informative technique which he terms 'sand sculpture'. In this, the body's contours are scrupulously followed, consolidated as necessary with chemicals to hold the friable sand together. The result reveals not only the bone structure but sometimes the more fleshy attributes of the dead person, and, most spectacularly in one burial, a corpse with legs outstretched in the attitude of a plough-man, apparently accompanied by the fugitive traces of a primitive plough or ard (69).[22]

It is perhaps fitting to invoke Sutton Hoo at this point in the discussion, because in many ways it stands at the centre of new directions in Anglo-Saxon archaeology, while at the same time representing the traditional preoccupations presented by a well-furnished cemetery of burials in the pagan manner. The excavations of 1938 and 1939, and

69 Anglo-Saxon burial from the flat-grave cemetery, Sutton Hoo (Suffolk). Bone and other organic material survived here only as stains in the acid soil, which the excavators carefully dug around to reveal the corpses' outlines. The dead person in this grave is accompanied by elaborate wooden equipment, perhaps a primitive plough or ard.

those conducted in the 1960s, concentrated on the elucidation of a number of the barrow burials on the site, two of which contained ship-burials, and on the underlying prehistoric site. An ambitious programme now under way under the direction of Martin Carver aims to set the burials in their physical and historical context – immediate, local, regional and, ultimately, European. Already the excavations have revealed that the sixth- and seventh-century barrow burials stand in a sea of Anglo-Saxon flat graves which may have continued as late as the ninth century; and that these early medieval burials consciously made use of a site which had been used for ceremonial purposes from the Neolithic and Bronze Ages. But the barrow cemetery – and now its accompanying flat graves – are not being investigated in isolation. The significance of the Sutton Hoo research project is that it places the cemetery firmly in its local physical context. In other words, the cemetery is treated as part – an important, probably focal part – of the Anglo-Saxon settlement in the area. The aim both of current work on the site and of the survey and fieldwork in the locality carried out by the Suffolk Archaeological Unit is to understand the nature of Anglo-Saxon occupation in the region, from its royal apex to its peasant base, cemeteries, settlements, palaces, religious centres, trade and communications. The cemetery is of outstanding interest and importance, and because it evidently contains royal burials, there is every likelihood that a settlement of equivalent status lies nearby. How this and other adjacent sites fitted into the landscape, and its riverine and maritime networks, what its relationship was to other royal centres in East Anglia, England and the North Sea at large, we expect to find out. It is arguably this kind of integration of cemetery analysis into the wider study of settlement patterns and land use in a defined area that is the single most important advance that Anglo-Saxon archaeology has made in recent years. How this relates to settlement studies as such we must now examine.

Settlements

Nowhere in the field of Anglo-Saxon archaeology is the post-War shift in emphasis from interpreting archaeological evidence in the context of political history to economic and social history more striking than in the field of settlement studies. The very nature of the evidence that settlements provide is much more grist to the economic historian's mill than to the student of political history: evidence for building techniques, crafts, trade, diet, husbandry, land use, is more abundant, while the fine metalwork finds which provide a basis for the construction of chronologies and for ethnic- and status-related deductions about the cemeteries, are much less common. Indeed, it was to a considerable extent the shift in these underlying concerns which prompted the dramatic increase in activity on settlement sites of all kinds. The history and development of these investigations are discussed in detail in the following chapter, where the development of rural settlement throughout the medieval period is surveyed as a continuity. The development of the medieval town and medieval churches in this period is also discussed in chapter 5. Although Anglo-Saxon sites are – quite properly – reviewed in both these contributions, it is impossible not to survey the development of Anglo-Saxon archaeology over the last forty years without discussing the enormously important and influential work carried out in the field of rural settlement and urban archaeology. To avoid overlap and repetition, the following section concentrates on certain broader topics which the new work on all kinds of Anglo-Saxon habitation site is producing.

As the case of Sutton Hoo demonstrates, one of the most important ways of extending our understanding of the period is not by simply excavating individual sites, but by integrating this work into a survey of the surrounding area. Thus, at Sutton Hoo, current survey work in the vicinity has produced evidence of two early Anglo-Saxon settlements within a mile of the royal cemetery, while in the wider context of East Anglia as a whole this royal centre and its satellites are now being studied in relation to the origins of towns such as Ipswich (Suffolk) and market-places, such as Barham, near Ipswich, which demonstrate the acceleration of wealth and commerce within the kingdom in the later seventh and eighth centuries.

While not all area surveys are so ambitious in scope, elsewhere in the country intensive study of a locality is focusing the picture of rural settlement and its development. This is seen very clearly in the work at Wharram Percy (E. Yorkshire) (see chapter 5), and in the seventh–fifteenth-century manorial complex at Raunds.[23] The Anglo-Saxon village at Raunds is seen to have expanded from two seventh-century sunken-featured huts to four timber buildings in a ditched enclosure in the middle Saxon period, culminating in a major reorganisation in the tenth and eleventh centuries, which included the construction of a central aisled hall, with a church and its associated cemetery; the latter has yielded valuable information about the population. By the end of the Anglo-Saxon period it seems likely that the village had manorial status, and the excavators plan to test the nature of the excavated settlement against the more fully documented manor site of Burystead in the immediate vicinity, along with fieldwalking in the area to establish the early and middle Saxon settlement pattern. Through such patient and meticulous interrogation of a landscape and its features, a detailed picture of the nature and growth of a settlement can be built up.

For the more fugitive habitation sites of the early phases of Anglo-Saxon settlement the insights provided by extended investigations have been considerable. At Mucking (Essex), for example, excavation of a complex prehistoric and Roman site, dramatically revealed by aerial photography, provided as a bonus a remarkable complex of an Anglo-Saxon settlement of over 213 structures dating from the fifth to the eighth centuries (70). These were accompanied by two contemporary Anglo-Saxon cemeteries. Bone survived very badly in the local acid soil conditions, so that there is no scope for demographical studies; but the interrelationship of artefacts – particularly pottery – found in the houses and workshops as well as in the graves enables cemeteries and

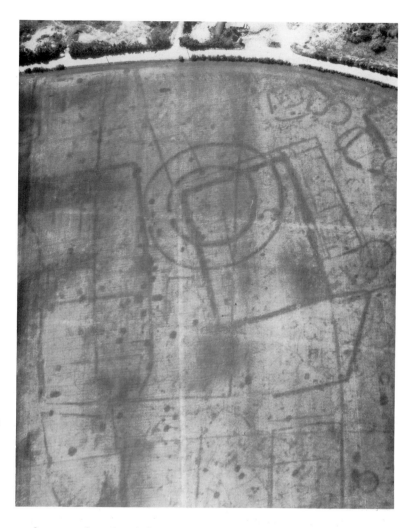

70 Crop marks of an Anglo-Saxon village and cemeteries at Mucking (Essex), seen from the air. The complex rectangular and circular ditches are of Roman and earlier date: the Anglo-Saxon huts and graves show up as specks and dots overlying the bolder traces of earlier occupation.

settlement to be related chronologically, and for some hypotheses about the functioning of the community to be made. For instance, the rich finds of late Roman military material from both graves and houses suggest that it probably had its origins as a Germanic federate garrison. The intensive early Roman fortifications on the site and its strategic location give support to this; Mucking lies on a high, bleak and windy gravel ridge above the Thames, commanding the river approaches to London. The notable proportion of weapon burials in the sixth century suggests that the community possibly retained its military standing, and certainly its prosperity, an impression which is reinforced by the extensive industrial activity on the site – pottery-making, textile manufacture, metalworking in precious metals, iron and lead. It remains nevertheless a matter for debate – as with a number of sites on fairly inhospitable upland locations – as to whether occupation was genuinely permanent or intermittent, dependent on a settlement on the more sheltered and fertile lower slopes. It could have been seasonal, for instance or used as a retreat in times of trouble; or it could have been used primarily for industrial rather than domestic activity.

Indeed, the great increase in the numbers of rural settlements explored since 1945 has transformed – and complicated – our notions of Anglo-Saxon rural life beyond all measure, and nowhere more than in our conception of where a village or large farm might be sited in the landscape. The old view that the earliest Anglo-Saxon villages were established on the heavier soils of valley floors, which their ploughs could exploit more efficiently than those of their Romano–British predecessors, can no longer be held. Though undoubtedly many later Saxon villages do underly modern ones, a significant number of sites occupy apparently less favourable marginal land, for example on hilltops, like Chalton (Hampshire), or on unfavourable soils, like Mucking. Here the recently discovered fact that Roman land use and settlement was much denser than had previously been thought must have conditioned how the early Anglo-Saxons fitted into the landscape. Similar factors operated throughout the Saxon period. Some settlements, such as the middle to late Saxon period homesteads at Gauber High Pasture, Ribblehead (W. Yorkshire) and Simy Folds (N. Yorkshire) are at altitudes high enough to have made life moderately unattractive during a Pennine winter (even allowing for early medieval climatic improvement), and so may have been used on a seasonal basis only.

The internal organisation of settlements has also provided revelations about the hierarchy and status of particular communities. West Stow (Suffolk), for example, provided a contrast between sixty-seven partly industrial, dugout buildings (known in current jargon as sunken-featured buildings, or SFBs) and the more elaborate post-built halls.[24] These possibly represent some three to four families and their attendant slaves. The farm buildings at Chalton (Hampshire) give some indication of having been constructed around a central courtyard area.[25] The large tenth-century hall at Netherton (Hampshire), with its associated subsidiary buildings, seems to prefigure the later medieval manor house on the site.[26] Other sites are more enigmatic. At Cowdery's Down (Hampshire), a sixth- and seventh-century site has produced impressive evidence for elaborate timber building at an unexpectedly early date for such architectural sophistication (71–73). Ground-plans of timber buildings permit the construction of a variety of hypothetical super-structures, but there can be no doubt that on any scale some of the buildings at Cowdery's Down represented considerable status, both in terms of architectural sophistication and in the sheer deployment of resources. The amount of timber used and earth shifted are prodigious, showing that these buildings must have been commissioned and used by people of high status.[27] It has also been suggested that the internal organisation of the site supports this: in each of the three successive phases of the settlement a major focal structure is positioned outside enclosed compounds which housed some, but not all, of the other buildings. While some of the buildings may be ancillary buildings with agricultural or other functions, the careful planning of the rest of the site

71 Interpretative ground-plan of building c 12 at the Anglo-Saxon settlement at Cowdery's Down (Hampshire), showing positions of posts and wall timbers which survived as 'ghosts' in the soil.

72 Reconstruction of the building shown in 71, showing one kind of elaborate superstructure which could have been constructed on the heavy wall timbers.

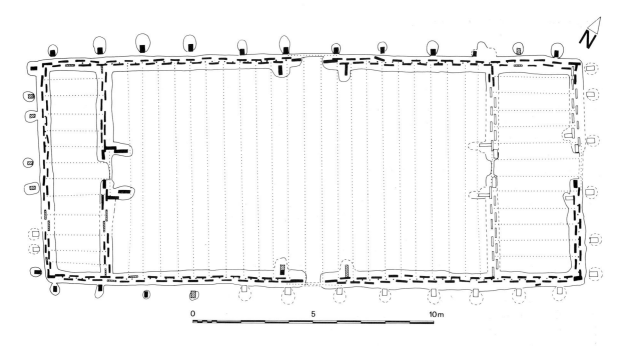

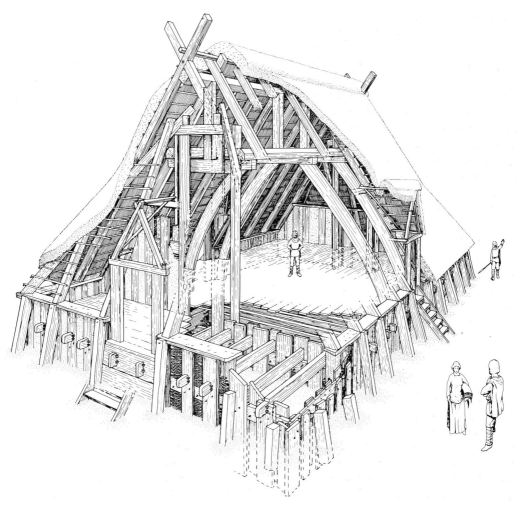

73 Alternative reconstruction drawings of the exterior of the building shown in 71 and 72, to illustrate the broad range of forms which can be produced from the same evidence.

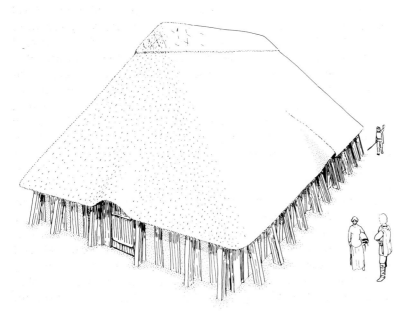

suggests some kind of division according to social units. This interpretation gains support from the spectacular absence of finds, which is paralleled in some other high-status sites like Chalton. There are a number of possible explanations for this, but the most plausible, in view of the sophisticated nature of some of the buildings, is that the site was indeed primarily an aristocratic one, rather than an operational farm. It is also possible that in a society where it is recorded that kings moved around from residence to residence, other élite classes may also have done so, leading to intermittent occupation of the site. Even so, the occupants must have been unusually efficient in disposing of their domestic rubbish, particularly food bones.

But if our ideas about aristocratic life in Anglo-Saxon times are being steadily expanded by such discoveries, our understanding of royal residences has extended by leaps and bounds. More than seven Anglo-Saxon palace sites have now been identified, of which three have been excavated: the palace of the early seventh-century Northumbrian kings at Yeavering (north Northumberland),[28] Alfred's palace at Cheddar (Somerset),[29] and the recently published successive timber and stone halls discovered in the centre of present-day Northampton.[30] At Yeavering and Cheddar, discussed in specific detail below, the royal halls were excavated in a whole complex of other domestic, agricultural and ceremonial buildings, which enabled the excavators to reconstruct overall images of the sites at critical stages in their lives (74). The meticulous techniques of archaeological dissection and recording put into practice on area excavation at Yeavering in the 1950s and early 1960s set standards for a whole generation of excavations of fugitive timber structures. Successive timber halls of a distinctive scale and pattern, some with annexes at each end, were discovered, as well as evidence for some kind of assembly place, seemingly related to the *cuneus*, or wedge of banked seats, of a Roman amphitheatre. Royal authority clearly knew how to exert itself through imposing structures such as this. Yeavering lies at a remote and dramatic site, on a broad and fertile valley floor hemmed in by substantial hills, but aerial photography, and excavation at Milfield and Thirlings in the near neighbourhood have shown that, though remote by modern standards, the lower stretches of this Northumbrian valley were fairly well populated by Anglo-Saxons in the seventh century, a picture reinforced by survey and documentary study of the Anglian settlement of the Tweed basin immediately to the north.[31] This was a fertile and well-controlled landscape, which could contribute substantially to the economic power base of the Anglo-Saxon kings of Northumbria.

The context of the Northampton palace site is much more enigmatic, since we lack the specific documentary evidence which exists for Yeavering. However, the excavated ground-plan of the first building on the site, in the centre of modern Northampton, is so close in scale and structure to the timber halls identified on the royal sites at Yeavering and Milfield (Northumberland) and to others known from aerial photography, that it must be regarded as belonging to this series; it measures

29.4 × 8.35 m (96.5 × 27.5 ft) compared with 30 × 9 m (98.5 × 29.5 ft) and 25 × 7 m (82 × 23 ft) for buildings at Yeavering. A radiocarbon date in the eighth century confirms the close chronological relationship of the Northampton timber hall with the seventh-century Northumbrian sites. Even more telling is the discovery, unique in Britain so far, of the foundations of a massive stone hall, 37.5 m × 11.5 m (123 × 37.5 ft), which immediately succeeds the timber hall on the same site and alignment. Radiocarbon dates for this structure suggest that it was built in the late eighth or early ninth century. At a time when all other

74 Reconstruction drawing of the Northumbrian royal palace complex at Yeavering (Northumberland), showing it as it might have appeared during the reign of Edwin (616–32). The amphitheatre (in the background) and large enclosure (partly visible in the foreground) were public works constructed for communal use. After B. Hope-Taylor

secular building, no matter how grand, was constructed in wood, the presence of a stone hall on such a scale instantly invites comparison with the great stone palaces of the Carolingian empire. These would have been familiar to the Anglo-Saxon royal envoys and high-level ecclesiastics who are known to have visited the Carolingian courts, and thus form a very likely source of inspiration for an Anglo-Saxon royal palace. The Northampton stone building provides concrete (in more than one sense, see below p. 149) illustration of this documentary evidence for contacts between Anglo-Saxon and Carolingian courts in the later eighth century. Its precise historical context is less clear, though it most surely illustrates the wealth and power at the command of the Anglo-Saxon kingdom of Mercia at this period.

The siting of the Northampton palace also highlights another important factor which has come more sharply into focus due to the excavations of recent years. This is the question of the origins of medieval towns (see chapter 5). Though Northampton was a thriving town by the end of the late Saxon period, it has no Roman predecessor and there is no indication that the two palaces were at the time of their construction in any sense in an urban setting. They are, however, apparently aligned on the same axis as another contemporary stone-built structure running westwards under the present St Peter's church, and thus at present archaeologically inaccessible. This was almost certainly an Anglo-Saxon minster church, built in conjunction with the palace site as part of a centre of ecclesiastical and secular authority; again, this is a phenomenon very much on Continental lines, and one with parallels elsewhere in England at Gloucester, Winchester, London, York and Canterbury. It seems increasingly likely that from such beginnings a regional administrative centre could develop.

The final area illuminated by rural and urban settlement studies which must be mentioned here is the thorny question of continuity – in this case, continuity between the formal collapse of Roman administration in the early fifth century and the establishment of Anglo-Saxon settlement – an issue which lies right at the heart of all the traditional politico-historical concerns of Anglo-Saxon specialists. It is a notoriously difficult area in which to arrive at any kind of consensus, not least when, as at present, scholars find it difficult even to accept as reliable any of the conventional documentary dates for the Anglo-Saxon takeover of Roman Britain. No doubt the process was more haphazard and slower than conventional wisdom allowed, and in certain areas of the country new evidence, and the reassessment of old, is suggesting that the continuity of building techniques and of individual site usage and even of regional control[32] is much more widespread than was once imagined. The rural settlement at Catholme (Staffordshire) in the Midlands shows a planned farmstead growing and developing over three to four centuries, with a complex sequence of enclosed timber long-houses dating back at least to the early sixth century.[33] Given the area's relative isolation from the primary targets of Anglo-Saxon settlement, it seems perfectly possible that local Romano-British building traditions were simply maintained by the indigenous local population, which slowly became Anglo-Saxonised rather than slaughtered or exiled. The Anglo-Saxon village at West Stow was also clearly slotted into a gap in a landscape – the Lark Valley – already extensively exploited by the Romano-Britons. The nearby Roman town at Icklingham was, however, in serious decline by the early fifth century and the nature of the Roman material found at West Stow strongly suggests that it was the result of scavenging in the semi-deserted town, rather than the product of exchange with a viable community.[34] The incomers ably exploited a situation of existing economic decline, gradually absorbing the native population. The whole question of ethnicity as seen in the buried populations of the cemeteries, and their artefacts, is a question which is too specialised to enter into here. Nevertheless, as the above has sketched, the evidence seems to suggest that on a significant number of rural sites there was evidence of extended contact between the native and immigrant communities.

Towns

As has already been suggested, the enormous activity in urban excavation and associated documentary research which has taken place since 1945, and especially in the last twenty years, has dramatically increased our knowledge of the development of towns in the Anglo-Saxon period. As with the rural settlements, no single model can be made to account for the variety of town types as they developed in the Anglo-Saxon period. The excavations have, therefore, been accompanied by considerable theoretical discussion on the nature and development of towns. Particularly important has been the contribution of Martin Biddle, who in a crucial series of papers, surveys and excavations has re-drawn the boundaries of the subject.[35] From his work at Winchester, and from that carried out on other major town sites such as Southampton and York, it is clear that there are at least three broadly different types of Anglo-Saxon town: early administrative centres, coastal or riverine commercial stations, and the deliberately founded fortified towns known as *burhs*. Of course, these functions can all overlap to some degree, and towns can alter their nature over a period. But the general distinctions are worth looking at more closely.

Canterbury and Winchester, for example, both functioned in the middle Anglo-Saxon period not as commercial towns, but as royal and ecclesiastical centres, administrative functions which are perhaps still reflected today in their modern status as bishoprics and county towns. Trade and industrial activities were focused in nearby coastal and riverine towns – at Southampton in Winchester's case, and Fordwich on the River Stour, where Canterbury was concerned. Many of these royal and ecclesiastical centres developed from Romano-British towns, though there are exceptions, as we have already seen at Northampton, which was clearly an administrative centre by the eighth century but has no Roman antecedent. There is growing evidence to suggest that in many of these former Roman towns Anglo-Saxons made deliberate use of Roman administrative buildings, which still survived as standing structures. At York, for example, the evidence indicates that the first Anglo-Saxon minster was constructed within the Roman military headquarters; at Winchester the Anglo-Saxon palace was sited in the forum area, and the Old Minster (founded in AD 648) was built alongside it and adjacent to the south range of the forum. At Lincoln a major Anglo-Saxon ecclesiastical site was established in the Roman forum, and at Gloucester the late Anglo-Saxon royal palace at Kingsholm was constructed in the first-century Roman fort, later a Roman cemetery. On this evidence, from the later sixth and seventh centuries, Anglo-Saxons were clearly making use of pre-existing Roman administrative structures, adapting them for major royal and ecclesiastical functions.

Such adaptations, whether consciously re-invoking Roman authority or not, do not, however, constitute the continuation or renewal of urban life. It is one of the important confirmatory insights gained from the post-War researches into urban development that organised political, economic and social activity – everything that made a town urban – gradually ceased in these Roman towns during the fifth century. Some, like Silchester or Wroxeter died altogether; others like Verulamium, shifted location. For others, among them Canterbury, Winchester, Gloucester and Lincoln, urban decay was emphatic enough to give rise to the accumulation of a dark, sterile, humic deposit over much of the town, clear evidence that active urban life had ceased and the busy streets had silted up and grown over. However, this is not to say that some form of reduced use and even occupation, however tenuous, did not continue: the occurrence of fifth- and sixth-century Germanic pottery and Visigothic coins at Canterbury, for instance, suggests that Anglo-Saxons were at least intermittently present in parts of the town. They were probably cultivating rural holdings and grazing animals. Documentary references also show that at least one church was available for Christian worship when, later in the sixth century, the Kentish King Ethelbert's Frankish queen Bertha wished to practise her Christian faith; and it is surely significant that when St Augustine's Christian mission arrived in Kent in AD 597 Canterbury itself became the focus of religious activity and the seat of the bishopric.

Something similar seems to have taken place at York, Lincoln, Winchester and Gloucester during the same period. At Canterbury the results of recent archaeological excavation have overwhelmingly confirmed that it was, however, only at the very end of the sixth century that systematic settlement was resumed in the former Roman town – presumably as part of the renewed royal and religious activities. The seventh-century Anglo-Saxons in Canterbury lived on a fairly modest scale, and there is no evidence of industrial activity other than the kind of cottage crafts, weaving and so on, one would encounter on any rural site. Canterbury and other such administrative centres may have been inhabited, but they were not, in the middle Saxon period, towns proper.

These were instead the newly founded ports and mercantile centres which began to develop along rivers and on the coast in the middle

Saxon period. Recent excavations have made a great contribution to our knowledge of early Anglo-Saxon economic growth at sites such as Ipswich or *Hamwih*, the Anglo-Saxon port at Southampton (Hampshire).[36] Finds of quantities of imported goods, such as pottery from the Rhineland or from western France and coins, testify to the vigorous trading activities which began in both places during the seventh century. Alongside this went the development of local crafts and industry, such as the pottery manufactory which developed in the Cox Lane area at Ipswich at this time, trading its wares over a considerable area of eastern England. *Hamwih* came to occupy about thirty hectares (74 acres) – small perhaps by Continental standards, but impressive in terms of middle Saxon England. The goods traded are, of course, only partly visible in the archaeological record. The well-fired Frankish pots found at *Hamwih* were imported not just as commodities in themselves, but for the contents they carried: wine and foodstuffs. Frankish vessel glass also indicates luxury trade, which was no doubt reciprocated with Anglo-Saxon textiles, slaves and hunting dogs, as the historical sources record. *Hamwih* must have been the kingdom of Wessex's trading outlet to the Continent, successor to an early, Kentish-dominated trading station on the Isle of Wight. In the same way, Ipswich seems to have been established under royal control from the East Anglian kings, whose wealth and political clout was symbolised in the royal graveyard at Sutton Hoo. In this way, too, the rich body of information available from these recent and current town excavations is contributing to our ideas about the contemporary political consolidations and expansions, which are known from documentary sources.

The boom in post-War urban excavations has also brought other information on the devopment of Anglo-Saxon towns to light. We can now see that the growth of many towns was accelerated in the ninth and tenth centuries, as evidence of an increase in craft activities and more specialised and controlled activities such as coin production shows. Evidence of large-scale replanning is also to be found at a number of places. Northampton, for instance, expanded from its original royal and ecclesiastical base at this time into an active commercial centre, engaged in metalworking, bone- and antler-carving and pottery manufacture, and, by the mid-tenth century at latest, had a mint (75). The impetus for all this was probably the Scandinavian presence in the community in the late ninth century, a known stimulus to urban expansion at other centres such as Lincoln, York and, as recent work is suggesting, perhaps at Ipswich also.[37] In the early tenth century there is certainly good evidence in the neatly laid-out street frontages of the Anglo-Scandinavian towns of York and Lincoln for formal planning, and the abundant documentary and archaeological information from Winchester suggests systematic large-scale planning during the reign of Alfred.[38]

York may stand as an example of the wealth of information which these late Saxon, fully fledged towns are beginning to yield – not only about building types and street layouts, or crafts and industry, but

75 Northampton: a reconstruction drawing of part of the tenth-century town. After J. H. Williams

about many aspects of daily life, health, diet and even entertainment.[39] We know that early in the tenth century the heart of Viking York, on the well-known Coppergate site, was laid out afresh, with new tenement boundaries of post-and-withy fences, and the construction of buildings on what is now the modern Coppergate street frontage. Such a radical reorganisation suggests some kind of centralised, municipal decision, which is supported by the issue of an anonymous York coinage which first appears at this time. The new property divisions were to endure with scarcely any variation for the next thousand years. The buildings, constructed of posts and wattle panels, coated over all with concrete-like daub, were occupied by specialist craftsmen and traders who manufactured their goods in workshops at the rear of the premises and sold them on stalls at the front. Metalworkers and glass-makers were present, as moulds, crucibles and waste material show, and the remarkable discovery on the site of two iron coin dies and three lead trial pieces for testing coin dies show that, as well as producing jewellery, the craftsmen were involved in the minting of royal issues of coins. The working of leather, bone and antlers respectively producing shoes and other goods such as scabbards, and needles, combs and knife-handles, was practised on the site. There was also a wood-turner, making cups, bowls and platters in ash, yew and maple for domestic use (76). Amber and jet were carved into beads, pendants and finger-rings.

The picture of a prosperous society with plenty of surplus cash to

76   Products of a wood-turner's workshop from the Anglo-Scandinavian town of York.

spend which this presents is confirmed by the items of luxury trade found on the Coppergate site; these include large pottery wine containers made in the Rhineland, and, of course, their contents, which were obviously as popular as the Hocks and Rieslings of today. A silk cap provides a fascinating and instructive piece of evidence – a distinctive flaw in the weave is identical to that in a silk fragment found during the excavations of the contemporary town of Lincoln, suggesting that both pieces of textile were cut from the same bale, which was probably offered for sale in both cities. The silk probably came to England from Byzantium; other goods came from even more exotic parts. Fragments of early Chinese pottery found in Anglo-Scandinavian Lincoln support the growing picture of eastern trade in the Viking period, which we know from documentary evidence and from Scandinavian excavations.

The Coppergate excavations have provided abundant evidence for other aspects of daily life, especially diet. Cattle, sheep, goats and pigs were butchered on site, and careful sieving of the excavated soil has produced thousands of fish and bird bones, as well as fruit pips, seeds and nuts. A wide variety of sea and freshwater fish and shell-fish was eaten; domestic chickens and geese and duck appear, as well as more exotic species, such as guillemots and cranes. Hawks and falcons among the detritus suggest that wild-fowling contributed to the diet. Apples, sloes, bilberries, blackberries and raspberries were the most common fruit, while carrots, parsnips, celery and cabbages prevailed amongst vegetables. Dill and coriander were used for flavouring. Cereals include wheat, rye, barley and oats, though significant amounts of the poisonous weed corncockle in some of these deposits must have been responsible for considerable Anglo-Scandinavian stomach-ache. Parasitic infestations too were almost universal in the community; they were mainly roundworms, whose eggs survived in huge numbers in the cess-pits, from which drinking water would have been all too easily contaminated. All was not dyspepsia, however, and gaming pieces, bone whistles, even a set of pan-pipes, hint at the social diversions which alleviated an otherwise uncomfortable life.

The last major category of Anglo-Saxon urban establishment to have been extensively investigated in recent years is the borough (Old English *burh*), or fortified town. Essentially a planned or reorganised town within new or pre-existing defences, it may perhaps have had its origins in early ninth-century Mercia, on the tentative evidence for early fortification and regular planning at Hereford and Tamworth (Staffordshire). Certainly by the later ninth century in Wessex a whole series of planned or replanned towns with regular grids of streets within new or restored fortification were planted throughout the kingdom.[40] This was Alfred's brilliant response to the Danish invasions, designed to guard the main routes through Wessex and to act as refuges for the population. But the towns replanned or founded from scratch at this time were certainly also intended as viable urban centres, bases for co-ordinated economic activity. Towns such as Cricklade (Wiltshire), Wareham (Dorset), Lydford (Devon) and Oxford were all new foundations at this time, all with ditched earth and timber ramparts and regular street layouts – convenient both for the purposes of defence and of organised commercial development. By the end of the tenth century Winchester, one of the *burhs* replanned in Alfred's time, had a high degree of internal specialisation, with specific areas for administrative, commercial and domestic activity. Implantations on such an extensive scale have no Continental parallel and stand as one of the outstanding achievements of the Anglo-Saxon period. That the idea was quickly adopted by other authorities, and kings in Mercia and the Danelaw confirmed its practical value and viability.

The overall information which has steadily accumulated on Anglo-Saxon towns in the last twenty years has been quite staggering in its volume and variety. The work of synthesising and interpreting it all will go on for many years, and ideas will certainly shift and change as the new information is published and assimilated. Already, as we have observed, excavation and documentary research have revealed several different kinds of urban community and patterns of urban development during this fertile and changeful period.

Craft and Technology

As we have already seen at towns such as York and Lincoln, there is abundant and ever-growing evidence for craft and technology in the later Saxon period. Indeed, from the earliest stages of Anglo-Saxon settlement there is plentiful evidence from both habitation sites and cemeteries for the systematic, organised production of pottery and metalwork. The mechanisms whereby such goods were produced and marketed beyond their point of manufacture are less well understood, however, than the means by which they were made, which has been the subject of much recent study and practical experiment. No early Anglo-Saxon workshops have been found to compare with the extensive industrial complex discovered on the sixth–seventh-century Swedish jewellery-working site at Helgö, though it is hard to believe, from the abundance of brooches which survive, that comparable workshops did not exist, producing rather stereotyped metal jewellery on a considerable scale. A very few moulds and dies have been discovered on early settlements and in graves, but the direct evidence for metalworking is small indeed compared with that now accumulating for the later Saxon period. Such activity was not confined to the urban workshops known from York, Lincoln, Northampton and elsewhere, though they undoubtedly represent large-scale commercial production. But the excavations on the tenth-century manorial site at Netherton have brought to light crucibles and mould fragments, as well as metal waste and unfinished or rejected artefacts, testifying to fine metalworking on the site in bronze, gold and silver as well as iron. The extent of the industrial area is, however, small and the debris not intensive, which suggests that work here was intermittent, perhaps seasonal. The estate on which the Netherton settlement lies belonged in the tenth century to a wealthy noblewoman, Wynflæd, in whose will it is mentioned. It seems likely that the archaeological evidence for metalworking represents the activities of visiting craftsmen who carried out repairs and small-scale production work for the estate, perhaps only when the lord (or lady) visited it, or as part of their rounds through all the lord's holdings.

New light has also been shed by excavation and research on a number of other crafts and industrial activities, including, as we have seen from various sites already mentioned, carpentry and wood-turning, bone- and amber-working, and textile manufacture. All these, and other industrial activities, have been usefully surveyed by D.M. Wilson.[41] Two particular finds are worth describing in more detail since they have illuminated in unexpected ways our notions about Anglo-Saxon technology.

The first discovery is that of a horizontal-wheeled watermill at the Mercian urban centre of Tamworth (Staffordshire), where it was possibly part of a palace complex.[42] Radiocarbon dates place it in the eighth century. The wheel rotated horizontally in a wheel-house below, turning, by means of a shaft, the grind-stones in the mill-house above (77). The

77 Reconstruction drawing of an Anglo-Saxon watermill from Tamworth (Staffordshire). After P. A. Rahtz

1. Shaft
2. Millstone
3. Hopper
4. Scooping up the flour

wheel was fed by a chute from the mill-pool, controlled by a sluice gate. The building itself was quite sophisticated, to the extent of apparently having paned windows. Two other Anglo-Saxon mills are also known from the royal estate at Old Windsor (Berkshire). The earlier of these, which dates to the ninth century, was a very sophisticated construction consisting of three parallel vertical wheels driven by water from a great leat dug across a loop of the Thames. Enterprises on this scale aptly illustrate the resources and technological sophistication of major royal estates. Further remarkable confirmation of this comes from Northampton, where five massive mortar-mixers have been discovered immediately adjacent to the eighth-century stone palace described above and the contemporary Anglo-Saxon stone minster, the foundations of which run under the present-day St Peter's church.[43] The mortar-mixers survive as huge congealed discs of concrete, with a central hole for a pivot and concentric groovings where the paddles of the horizontal mixing beam stirred it round (78). Known elsewhere in England so far only at the great monastic centre at Monkwearmouth (Co. Durham),

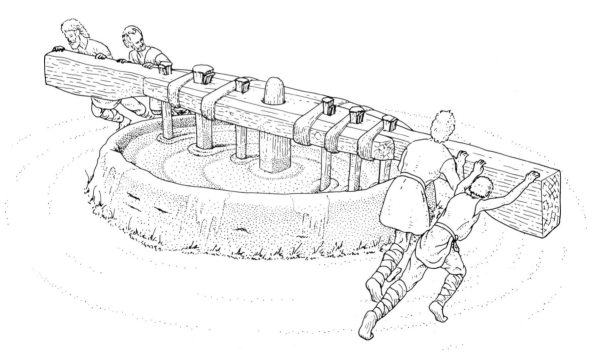

78 Reconstruction of an early ninth-century mortar-mixer in use, one of five found on the palace site at Northampton. After J.H. Williams

they graphically express the technological expertise and developing power and organisation of royal and ecclesiastical enterprise in the middle Saxon period.

Churches and Monasteries

In contrast to cemeteries and settlements, many Anglo-Saxon churches are readily recognisable, and form the most numerous surviving type of field monument from the period. Buildings such as St Laurence's chapel at Bradford-on-Avon, and Brixworth parish church are, in their very different ways, impressive constructions which instantly engage the non-specialist's eye. But recent archaeological work has dramatically demonstrated that what we see is but the merest tip of a large iceberg. The physical remains of some 500 Anglo-Saxon churches have been recorded so far, but it is estimated that there are in fact approximately 4–5,000 identifiable Anglo-Saxon church sites throughout the country.[44] And as with the other forms of archaeological evidence we have looked at, the information yielded by modern systematic programmes of investigation extends far beyond study of the monument itself, illuminating much wider aspects of society at large.

Up until the 1940s, however, the attention given to Anglo-Saxon church sites was, with few exceptions, largely devoted to architectural analysis. Some nineteenth-century investigative work was of very high quality, such as the meticulous survey of the standing structure of St Laurence's chapel at Bradford-on-Avon carried out by J.T. Irvine between the 1860s and 1880s.[45] Others recorded features now obliterated by later destruction or rebuilding; for example, during the clearances and restorations of about 1880–1908 at Hexham Abbey (Northumberland) the resident architect C.C. Hodges made observations and plans of the walls and foundations of St Wilfrid's seventh-century church, a building described by Wilfrid's biographer as unmatched in scale by any other church north of the Alps. By 1925, when Baldwin Brown published the first edition of his volume *Anglo-Saxon Architecture*,[46] a synthetic study based on an accumulation of observations of the subject was possible.

Unfortunately, it was almost another forty years before archaeologists were in a position to augment and build upon these foundations. The destruction of churches in war, which provided the impetus for systematic church investigation in Germany and Denmark, had little effect in England, with the honourable exception of work carried out in the City of London. It was not until the 1960s that the full potential of this rich field of study began to be realised.

A major influence in the revival of Anglo-Saxon church studies was the pioneer work of Joan and Harold Taylor. Their three-volume survey *Anglo-Saxon Architecture*, published in 1965 and 1978, described all known churches with Anglo-Saxon structural remains, and in a series of articles they also dealt with a number of specialised aspects, such as architectural sculpture.[47] Since Joan Taylor's death Professor Taylor's work has continued to inform and inspire much of the work which has so drastically altered our view of the Anglo-Saxon church.

In particular, his advocacy of the technique of 'structural criticism' has shown how standing buildings can be closely and systematically interrogated to reveal how and when they were put together, and – as so often – reshaped many times. The method is essentially one of vertical, above-ground archaeology in which every stone and pebble and mortar line in a fabric is patiently and accurately examined and planned so that as full a record of the structure as possible is obtained.

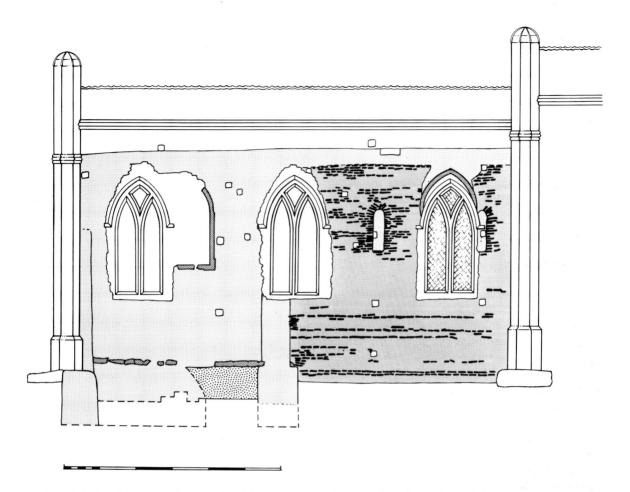

79 Rivenhall Church (Essex): analytical
drawing of the north wall of the Chancel.
Eleventh-century walling is shown in
darker tone; within it reused Roman brick
(black) reveals Anglo-Saxon windows,
now blocked. After W.J. Rodwell and
K. Rodwell.

In this way not only can the chronological building sequence be
understood, but all manner of more intimate information about construction can be obtained: for instance, where and how the scaffolding
was located, how much walling a builder could construct in one
operation, and where the builders called a seasonal halt to the project
during weather too cold for this sort of work.[48] Some major investigative
projects, such as that currently under way at Brixworth Church have
begun by concentrating primarily on this kind of analysis before engaging
in major excavations in the church. Others have embarked on the
excavation of a church which has entirely vanished, as at the Anglo-
Saxon village of Raunds, or combined the two selectively, as at Deerhurst
(Gloucestershire).[49] The approach to church archaeology as it has
developed since the 1960s has shown that the greatest dividends are
obtained from the ideal combination of structural analysis, excavation
both within and without the building, and documentary research. Even
dowsing may play its part in tracing buried foundations, as recent
controlled trials using the technique on church sites in Northumberland
have suggested.[50] The study of a given Anglo-Saxon ecclesiastical
building is part of the history of a community; the ultimate aim is to
elucidate the church, cathedral or monastery wherever possible in its
contemporary context.

Some of the most exciting results in recent years come from seemingly
very unassuming subjects, particularly in the field of the parish church.

In particular, work carried out by Warwick Rodwell successively at Rivenhall and Hadstock (Essex), and more recently at Barton-on-Humber has transformed perception of these buildings. They may stand as examples of the kind of unsuspected wealth of complex information which lurks behind an apparently straightforward exterior (79). At Rivenhall a church supposedly completely rebuilt in 1838–9 was subjected to careful excavation and structural scrutiny between 1971 and 1973.[51] It was soon apparent that an Anglo-Saxon church survived substantially intact behind the layer of nineteenth-century stucco, and that this in turn had had a timber predecessor just to the west of the later stone structure. Actual excavation at Rivenhall had to be limited to the exterior of the church and part of the churchyard, since it remained in active use. At Hadstock, the same team seized the opportunity of making a full-scale internal excavation while the church was closed for reflooring, again in tandem with survey of the standing structure.[52] What had been assumed to be in origin a single-period Anglo-Saxon church was revealed to be Anglo-Saxon work of three periods, including a central timber tower which was replaced in the major third alteration in the eleventh century. A complete programme of internal and external excavation and full-scale structural study of the redundant church at Barton-on-Humber followed and is still in progress.[53] The results of the excavation of 1,326 graves in the adjoining cemetery have already been mentioned. Within the church itself the building sequence and techniques have been minutely observed; for instance, the complete scheme of internal scaffolding can be reconstructed, using the evidence of pole-holes in the floor and putlog holes revealed in the wall where the plaster was stripped off. (Similar traces of timber scaffolding found during the structural study at Brixworth produced radiocarbon dates in the tenth century.) The churchyard also produced evidence of holy wells and a free-standing cross.

The message from these three, though by no means isolated, examples is that it has been possible to reconstruct their development over the centuries and to show that a seemingly simple and straightforward building may conceal a complex history.[54] (The late-Saxon and medieval church of St Paul-in-the-Bail at Lincoln had eighteen building phases.) Equally important has been the business of interpreting the church's place in the landscape and the settlement's history,[55] not only on deserted sites, as at Raunds and Wharram Percy, but in existing villages as at Deerhurst, Brixworth and Repton, and with both minsters and urban churches in towns such as Winchester, York and Wells.

Martin Biddle's pioneering work in Winchester during the 1960s aimed at elucidating the growth of medieval Winchester, and his careful dissecting work on the Anglo-Saxon Old and New Minsters underlying the present Cathedral Green has stressed the importance of understanding the buildings within the ecclesiastical, administrative and economic framework of the environment.[56] Here, in the context of the late Anglo-Saxon royal and ecclesiastical centre, the documentary and archaeological evidence has been meticulously examined to enable

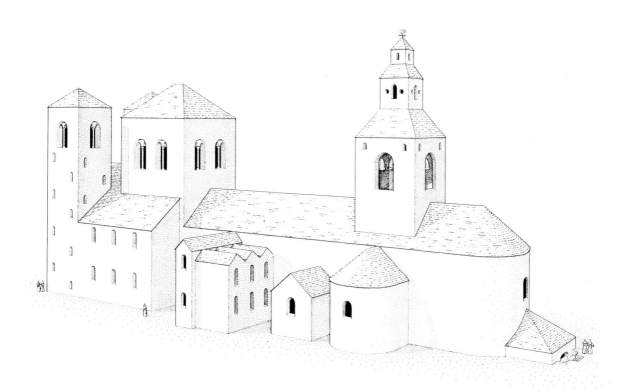

80 The Old Minster, Winchester, as it might have appeared in the time of Cnut (1016–35): a conjectural reconstruction drawing based on the archaeological evidence. After M. Biddle and B. Kjølbye-Biddle

a reconstruction of the later phase of the Old Minster to be made, which graphically reveals the wealth and power of later Saxon Wessex, as demonstrated in its most public works (80). That important information can be obtained even in the most unpromising conditions was revealed by the rescue excavations underneath York Minster. Though severely restricted, they gave remarkable insight: here the headquarters building (*principia*) of the Roman legionary fortress was found to have been at least in part standing well into the tenth century, the present medieval minster being in the middle of the fortress. It appears that its Anglo-Saxon precursor was sited in the courtyard of the *principia*: a classic instance of the continuing use of a site in which power and authority were located.

Other specialised features have also been illuminated by recent investigations, such as the eighth- to ninth-century chapel at the monastic site at Repton; baptismal arrangements; the siting of altars; and the position of focal graves or shrines – all of which may have had effects upon the layout and use of a building. More specifically, it is hoped that future investigations will be able to shed more light on liturgical practice and the use of churches, in conjunction with the documentary sources for such activities.

Anglo-Saxon monasteries have been much less intensively investigated than the contemporary churches. Until Rosemary Cramp's major work at the twin foundation of Wearmouth and Jarrow (Tyne and Wear) in the 1960s and 1970s only two early medieval monastic sites had been extensively excavated: Whitby Abbey (Yorkshire), which had been excavated in the 1920s with shocking negligence and disregard for even the basic practices of recording, and the supposed Celtic monastery at Tintagel (Cornwall), which has subsequently been shown to be a secular site after all. The Wearmouth and Jarrow sites are especially important, since both contain standing churches with substantial portions of Anglo-Saxon masonry and sculpture, and they are exceptionally well documented through the writings of the Venerable Bede, who was a member of the community at Jarrow in the late seventh and early eighth centuries AD.[57] A unique picture has been obtained of life on an early Anglo-Saxon monastic site (81). The dis-

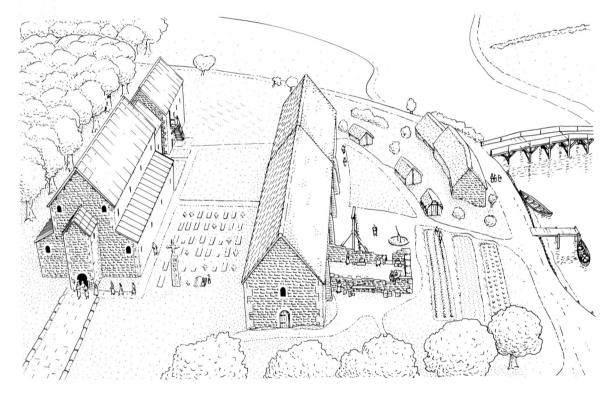

covery, for instance, of coloured window glass, some of it clearly figural, fleshes out Bede's reference to the Frankish glaziers that the monastery's founder, Benedict Biscop, brought over to glaze his new buildings (82). Floors of *opus signinum* (concrete of Roman type containing crushed brick) and painted wall-plaster expand the impression of Mediterranean sophistication. Outside the conventual buildings all kinds of practical activities necessary to the running of the monastery went on: evidence for gardening, fishing and metal- and glass-working has all been discovered during the course of the excavations.

Such domestic and industrial activities were evidently the norm. Their traces were discovered in the abortive excavations at Whitby, and seem to be evident on a middle Saxon site currently under excavation at

81 Reconstruction of the Anglo-Saxon monastery at Jarrow (Tyne and Wear), as it might have looked in the late eighth century, showing the two churches, monastic buildings, the cemetery, workshops and the monks' garden. After reconstruction by R.J. Cramp

82 Conjectural reconstruction of a glass window from the middle Saxon monastery at Jarrow (Tyne and Wear). Window-glass was not used by the early Anglo-Saxons, so Frankish glaziers were brought to Jarrow and Wearmouth in the late seventh century to do the work.

Brandon (Suffolk). This excavation is a splendid case-study in the interpretation of data, since there is no Anglo-Saxon documentary evidence for the site whatsoever; only archaeology can reveal the truth. However, both the location, on what was effectively an island in the Fens, and the finds suggest that the site was of specialised status and had a wealthy and literate community with a high proportion of females. The community was, however, a mixed one and included children. Ultimate assessment must, of course, depend on the completion of excavation, but it looks remarkably like a small but wealthy mixed religious house of the kind we know to have existed in England in the seventh–ninth centuries. Work such as this, and excavations currently under way at the Anglo-Saxon site of Barking Abbey, and at the

Mercian royal and monastic site at Repton, will undoubtedly contribute to our understanding of Anglo-Saxon monastic foundations for some years to come.

Conclusion

Even within the necessary constraints of such a selective survey, it is abundantly clear that the map of Anglo-Saxon England, both literally and intellectually, has been redrawn beyond recognition since 1945. Not only are there simply many more archaeological sites of all kinds known nowadays, but, as we have seen, approaches to the entire spectrum of evidence which they provide have become more various and more sophisticated. A changeful, inventive and complex society is steadily emerging from the Dark Age of archaeological data.

The recent trends towards fully integrated and wide-ranging area studies offer tremendous potential for our understanding of the Anglo-Saxon landscape and how, in the widest sense, people used it. In other words, any given unit – field systems, villages, cemeteries, churches, palaces, towns, and so on – is ideally studied in its context; indeed, the context is the goal. Beyond this ideal, two specific things stand out as particularly urgent needs. The first also lies in the field; it is the need to excavate more waterlogged sites, both for the better-preserved organic artefacts which are largely absent from the Anglo-Saxon archaeological record, and more particularly for the microscopic potential of the deposits – those tiny seeds, pips, plant debris and micro-organisms which help to show, among other things, what the climate was, how the land was used, how people ate, lived, fell sick and died.

The other and perhaps even more important need is for more arm-chair archaeology. Now that Anglo-Saxon archaeology has, as it were, come of age in terms of breadth and sufficiency of data, the need for more overall synthesis becomes more pressing. With it goes a need for a revised philosophy of the subject. Much recent debate has centred around the question of whether Anglo-Saxon archaeology needs to be liberated from what has been described as 'the historical strait-jacket'. As was noted at the outset of this chapter, it was partly the traditional, document-orientated preoccupations of Anglo-Saxon archaeologists that hindered them from observing and recording some of the wider aspects of Anglo-Saxon culture that have since been extracted from the archaeological data. Some have gone so far as to argue that the subject should be treated as one would a prehistoric period, devoid of texts. However, to ignore the evidence of texts when they exist seems as perverse as to allow them to direct one's archaeological judgements. History is a unified discipline: what is required is a new theoretical and methodological framework in which documentary and archaeological evidence are scrupulously assessed in tandem.[58] Scientific rigour is essential but not an end in itself. It is, in the end, a fully rounded picture of a buried society which we seek to piece together. Perhaps it is fitting that in concluding this survey of a still elusive but fascinating period we should return for the last word to that humane and wise student of the past, Sir Thomas Browne, whose preface to *Urne-Buriall* ends with the following, pertinent, thoughts:

> Unto these of our Urnes none here can pretend relation, and can only behold the Reliques of those persons, who in their life giving the Law unto their predecessors, after long obscurity, now lye at their mercies. But remembring the early Civility they brought upon these Countreys, and forgetting long passed mischiefs; we mercifully preserve their bones, and pisse not upon their ashes.

NOTES

1   Throughout this chapter the conventional terms early, middle and late Saxon are used for convenience. Their approximate date ranges are: early Saxon, *c.*400–650; middle Saxon, *c.*650–850; late Saxon, *c.*850–1100

2   Available in a modern edition in Sir Thomas Browne, *Selected Writings* ed. Sir G. Keynes (1970)

3   B. Faussett (ed. C. Roach Smith), *Inventorium Sepulchrale* (1856)

4   J. Douglas, *Nenia Britannica* (1793)

5   J. Kemble 'On Mortuary Urns found at Stade-on-the-Elbe and other parts of Germany', *Archaeologia* 36 (1855), pp. 270–83

6   W.M. Wylie, *Fairford Graves: A Record of Researches in an Anglo-Saxon Burial Place in Gloucestershire* (1852)

7   J.Y. Akerman, *Pagan Saxondom* (1855); Baron J. de Baye, *The Industrial Arts of the Anglo-Saxons* (1893); C. Roach Smith, *Collectanea Antiqua*, vols 1–7 (1840–80)

8   E.T. Leeds, *The Archaeology of the Anglo-Saxon Settlements* (1913); *ibid.*, 'The Distribution of the Angles and Saxons Archaeologically Considered', *Archaeologia* 91 (1945), pp. 1–106; *ibid.*, *Early Anglo-Saxon Archaeology* (1935); *ibid.*, *A Corpus of Early Anglo-Saxon Great Square-headed Brooches* (1949); *ibid.*, 'Denmark and Early England' *Antiquaries Journal* 26 (1946), pp. 22–37

9   N.F. Åberg, *The Anglo-Saxons in England during the early Centuries after the Invasion* (1926)

10   G. Baldwin Brown, *The Arts in Early England*, vols 1–6 (1903–37)

11   J.N.L. Myres, *Anglo-Saxon Pottery and the Settlement of England* (1969); *ibid.*, *A Corpus of Anglo-Saxon Pottery in the Pagan Period* (1977); T.D. Kendrick, *Anglo-Saxon Art to 900 AD* (1938); *ibid.*, *Late Saxon and Viking Art* (1949)

12   T.M. Dickinson, 'The Present State of Anglo-Saxon Cemetery Studies', in P.A. Rahtz, T.M. Dickinson and L. Watts (eds), *Anglo-Saxon Cemeteries 1979*, British Archaeological Reports, British Series 82 (1980), pp. 11–33

13   S.C. Hawkes, 'Finglesham: a Cemetery in East Kent', in J. Campbell (ed.), *The Anglo-Saxons* (1982), pp. 24–25

14   A.C. Hogarth, 'Structural Features in Anglo-Saxon Graves', *Archaeological Journal* 130 (1973), pp. 104–19

15   C.M. Hills, *The Anglo-Saxon Cemetery at Spong Hill, North Elmham: Parts I, II and III*, East Anglian Archaeology Reports 6 (1977), 11 (1981), 21 (1984)

16   C.M. Hills, 'Anglo-Saxon Cemeteries with particular Reference to Spong Hill, Norfolk' in P.A. Rahtz, T.M. Dickinson and L. Watts (eds), *op. cit.* in note 12 above, p. 202; G. Putnam 'Spong Hill Cremations', in the same volume, p. 219. Since these papers were written, estimates of the number of multiple burials at Spong Hill have been revised downwards, but the point remains valid

17   M.L. Faull, 'The Location and Relationship of the Sancton Anglo-Saxon Cemeteries', *Antiquaries Journal* 56 (1976), pp. 227–33

18   For example: C.J. Arnold, 'Wealth and Social Structure: a Matter of Life and Death' and E. Pader 'Material Symbolism and Social Relations in Mortuary Studies', both in P.A. Rahtz, T.M. Dickinson and L. Watts (eds), *op. cit.* in note 12 above, pp. 81–160; L. Alcock 'Quantity or Quality: the Anglian Graves of Bernicia', in V.I. Evison (ed.), *Angles, Saxons and Jutes; Essays Presented to J.N.L. Myres* (1981),

pp. 168–86; S.M. Hirst, *An Anglo-Saxon Inhumation Cemetery at Sewerby, East Yorkshire*, York University Archaeological Publications 4 (1985), pp. 96–102

19   A.L. Meaney, *Anglo-Saxon Amulets and Curing Stones*, British Archaeological Reports, British Series 96 (1981), pp. 61–5

20   S.C. Hawkes 'The Dating and Significance of the Burials in the Polhill Cemetery' in B. Philp (ed.) *Excavations in West Kent 1960–1970* (1973), pp. 195–6; C. Fell 'A *friwif locbore* revisited', *Anglo-Saxon England* 13 (1984), pp. 157–66

21   S.M. Hirst, *op. cit.* in note 18 above, pp. 38–43

22   M.O.H. Carver, *Bulletin of the Sutton Hoo Research Committee*, no. 4 (forthcoming, 1986)

23   G.E. Cadman, 'Raunds 1977–1983: an Excavation Summary', *Medieval Archaeology* 27 (1983), pp. 107–22; G.E. Cadman and G. Foard, 'Raunds: Manorial and Village Origins', in M.L. Faull (ed.), *Studies in Late Anglo-Saxon Settlement* (1984), pp. 81–100

24   S.E. West, *West Stow, The Anglo-Saxon Village*, East Anglian Archaeology Report 24 (1985)

25   P.V. Addyman and D. Leigh, 'The Anglo-Saxon Village at Chalton, Hants', *Medieval Archaeology* 17 (1973), pp. 1–25

26   J.R. Fairbrother, *Faccombe, Netherton: Archaeological and Historical Research*, University of Southampton Thesis 1984 (publication forthcoming, 1986)

27   M. Millett and S. James, 'Excavations at Cowdery's Down, Basingstoke, Hampshire', *Archaeological Journal* 140 (1983), pp. 151–279, esp. p. 247

28   B. Hope-Taylor, *Yeavering, an Anglo-Saxon Centre of Early Northumbria* (1977)

29   P.A. Rahtz, *The Saxon and Medieval Palaces at Cheddar*, British Archaeological Reports, British Series 65 (1979)

30   J. Williams, M. Shaw and V. Denham, *Middle Saxon Palaces at Northampton* (1985)

31   I.M. Smith, 'Patterns of Settlement and Land Use of the late Anglian Period in the Tweed Basin' in M.L. Faull (ed.), *op. cit.* in note 23, pp. 155–76

32   M.G. Welch, *Early Anglo-Saxon Sussex*, British Archaeological Reports, British Series 112 (1983), pp. 217–28

33   S. Losco-Bradley and H.M. Wheeler, 'Anglo-Saxon Settlement in the Trent Valley: some Aspects' in M.L. Faull (ed.), *op. cit.* in note 23, pp. 102–14

34   S.E. West, *op. cit*, in note 24

35   For example: M. Biddle, 'Winchester; the Development of an Early Capital', in H. Jankuhn, W. Schlesinger and H. Steuer (eds), *Vor- und Frühformen der Europäischen Stadt im Mittelalter* (1973), pp. 229–66; *ibid.*, 'The Evolution of Planned Towns: Planned Towns before 1066', in M.W. Barley (ed.), *Plans and Topography of Medieval Towns in England and Wales*, Council for British Archaeology Research Report 14 (1975), pp. 19–31; *ibid.*, 'Towns', in D.M. Wilson (ed.) *The Archaeology of Anglo-Saxon England* (1976), pp. 99–150

36   P.V. Addyman and D.H. Hill, 'Saxon Southampton: a Review of the Evidence', *Proceedings of the Hampshire Field Club and Archaeological Society* 25 (1968), pp. 61–93, 26 (1969), pp. 61–96; P. Holdsworth, *Excavations at Melbourne Street, Southampton, 1971–76*, Council for British Archaeology Research Report 33 (1980)

37   J.H. Williams, 'A Review of Some Aspects of Late Saxon Urban Origins and Development' in M.L. Faull (ed.), *op. cit.* in note 23, pp. 25–34

38   M. Biddle, 'Towns', in D.M. Wilson (ed.), *op. cit.* in note 35

39   R.A. Hall, 'The Topography of Anglo-Scandinavian York', A. MacGregor, 'Industry and Commerce in Anglo-Scandinavian York', H.K. Kenward, 'The Environment of Anglo-Scandinavian York', all in R.A. Hall (ed.), *Viking Age York and the North*, Council for British Archaeology Research Report 27 (1978); R.A. Hall *The Viking Dig: The Excavations at York* (1984)

40   M. Biddle, 'Towns', *op. cit.* in note 38, pp. 124–34

41   D.M. Wilson, 'Craft and Industry', in D.M. Wilson (ed.), *op. cit.* in note 35, pp. 253–80

42   P.A. Rahtz and K. Sheridan, 'A Saxon Watermill in Bolebridge Street, Tamworth', *Transactions of the South Staffordshire Archaeological and Historical Society* 13

(1971–2), pp. 9–16; P. A. Rahtz and D. Bullough, 'The Parts of an Anglo-Saxon Mill', *Anglo-Saxon England* 6 (1977), pp. 15–38

43 J. H. Williams, *op. cit.* in note 30, pp. 21–6, 36–7

44 W. J. Rodwell, *The Archaeology of The English Church* (1981); R. Morris, *The Church in British Archaeology*, Council for British Archaeology Research Report 47 (1983), pp. 1–11; W. J. Rodwell, 'Churches in The Landscape', in M. L. Faull (ed.), *op. cit.* in note 23, pp. 1–23

45 H. M. Taylor, 'J. T. Irvine's Work at Bradford-on-Avon', *Archaeological Journal* 129 (1972), pp. 89–118

46 G. Baldwin Brown, *The Arts in Early England: II Anglo-Saxon Architecture* (1925)

47 H. M. Taylor and J. Taylor, *Anglo-Saxon Architecture*, vols I and II (1965); H. M. Taylor, *Anglo-Saxon Architecture* III (1978)

48 For example: W. J. Rodwell, *The Archaeology of the English Church* (1981), fig. 58

49 P. A. Rahtz, *Excavations at St. Mary's Church, Deerhurst*, Council for British Archaeology Research Report 15 (1976); D. S. Sutherland and D. Parsons, 'The Petrological Contribution to the Survey of All Saints Church, Brixworth, Northamptonshire: an Interim Study', *Journal of the British Archaeological Association* 137 (1984), pp. 45–64

50 For example: H. D. Briggs, E. Cambridge and R. Bailey, 'A new Approach to Church Archaeology, II: Dowsing and Excavations at Ponteland and St Oswald's, Durham', *Archaeologia Aeliana* 5th series, 13 (1985), pp. 133–46

51 W. J. and K. A. Rodwell, 'Excavations at Rivenhall Church, Essex: an Interim Report', *Antiquaries Journal* 53 (1973), pp. 219–31

52 W. J. Rodwell, 'The Archaeological Investigation of Hadstock Church, Essex: an Interim Report' *Antiquaries Journal* 56 (1976), pp. 55–71

53 W. J. and K. A. Rodwell, 'St Peter's Church, Barton-upon-Humber. Excavation and Structural Study, 1978–81', *Antiquaries Journal* 62 (1982), pp. 283–315

54 For example: R. Morris, *op. cit.* in note 44, fig. 24

55 W. J. Rodwell, 'Churches in the Landscape', in M. L. Faull (ed.), *op. cit.* in note 23, pp. 1–23

56 M. Biddle, 'Excavations at Winchester', interim reports in *Antiquaries Journal* 44–50 (1964–70), 52 (1972), 53 (1973)

57 R. J. Cramp, 'Excavations at the Saxon Monastic Sites of Wearmouth and Jarrow, Co. Durham', *Medieval Archaeology* 13 (1969), pp. 21–66; R. J. Cramp, 'Monastic Sites' in D. M. Wilson (ed.), *op. cit.* in note 35, pp. 201–52

58 T. M. Dickinson, 'Anglo-Saxon Archaeology: Twenty-Five Years on', in D. A. Hinton (ed.), *Twenty-Five Years of Medieval Archaeology* (1983), pp. 33–43

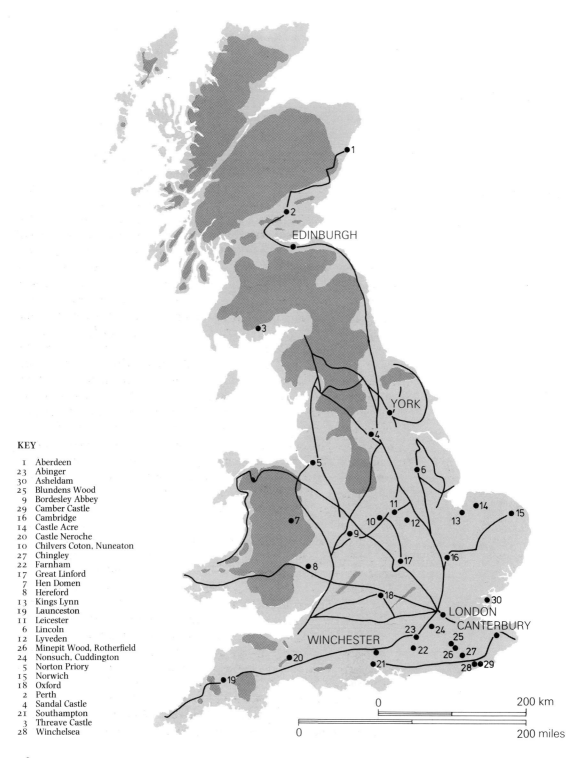

4 Technology, Towns, Castles and Churches AD 1100–1600

The development of medieval archaeology

83 Map showing the location of sites mentioned in the text.

The visible monuments of the Middle Ages in Britain are impressive, and it is through them rather than via museum displays or archaeological excavations that most people are introduced to the period. The grandeur of the castles of Edward I in North Wales, and the seclusion of the Cistercian monasteries, or the developing architecture of a major church can all inspire the imagination to form an impression of what life was like in the Middle Ages. Literary sources, the *Canterbury Tales* or the *Paston letters*, can provide another introduction. The diversity and human interest of many of the alternative sources of evidence for the Middle Ages may make archaeology, and particularly evidence produced from excavation, appear at first sight dry and unexciting. However, the excitement of archaeology lies in discovery, and it is here that excavation can reveal to us aspects of the Middle Ages that would not have been thought possible thirty or forty years ago, giving insights into activities on which documents are silent. Unlike the prehistorian, the medieval archaeologist has to relate discoveries to a pre-existing historical framework, and the richness of alternative sources of evidence creates both problems and opportunities for understanding of medieval and post-medieval Britain. Documentary sources, contemporary works of history, government and legal documents such as taxation returns and charters, and the extensive evidence for goods and their prices obtainable from account rolls have given historians a vast range of evidence on which to build conceptions of the medieval period. Yet it is now realised that the understanding of medieval society derived from documents can be enhanced by the evidence provided by material remains.

The history of medieval archaeology has not yet been written. The study of ecclesiastical remains of the Middle Ages attracted antiquaries in the seventeenth and eighteenth centuries, and it flourished especially as part of the heightened interest in medieval architecture during the nineteenth century. Although it was primarily monastic sites and objects such as tiles that attracted attention, other antiquities, amongst them pottery and metalwork, began to be collected, for example by Charles Roach Smith, whose collection of objects found in the rebuilding of London in the 1840s is now in the British Museum. The first person to apply the idea of scientific recording to the archaeology of a medieval building and its finds was General Pitt-Rivers, who examined the hunting lodge known as King John's House at Tollard Royal (Wiltshire) in 1890. He commented: 'It is true that medieval relics have not the same importance as those of prehistoric times, in which they generally afford the only reliable evidence of time. In dealing with historic buildings, they are only accessory to the main object of our researches. Nevertheless, there are conditions in which they afford the only evidence available even in medieval times, and a more thorough knowledge of them than we possess would be desirable'.[1] It was not until some fifty years later that Ward Perkins, in compiling the London Museum Medieval Catalogue, provided a broad survey of medieval artefacts, ranging from weapons and horse decorations to domestic and agricultural objects. He noted the problems that affect the medieval archaeologist and which do not arise in earlier periods. These are the continuous occupation of sites such as towns and villages, fine craftsmanship which distracts attention from the systematic study of everyday objects and, with the triumph of Christianity, the effective suppression of the practice of burying objects with the dead. On the other hand, he drew attention to the wealth of comparative material in the form of contemporary illustrations, particularly in manuscripts, sculpture and brasses, which, 'while they do not override the need for excavation and typological study, do supply an additional method of approach, which is of the first importance'. Despite all this, medieval archaeology remained undeveloped as a subject until the last thirty years – even in the 1960s urban excavators were ignoring all the upper levels of sites in order to excavate those of the Roman period. The major survey of archaeology in Britain published in 1932 by Kendrick and Hawkes ended with the Anglo-Saxons, and until recently the subject of archaeology as taught in many universities concluded with the Vikings.[2]

Work in and around Oxford in the years immediately before the Second World War showed how excavations could add to our knowledge of rural sites (such as the deserted medieval village of Seacourt) and how, by the careful collection and recording of pottery from medieval wells (as on the site that was to be the New Bodleian Library in Oxford), a sequence of pottery development could be established.[3] Although post-War urban archaeology has important roots in the investigations made after the war damage in London and other cities, it was the erasing of medieval street patterns and buildings by urban redevelopments from the late 1950s onwards that provided the major opportunity for the growth of medieval archaeology. The excavations at Norwich, for example, in the Barn Road and St Benedict's Gates area in the late 1940s and early 1950s showed how excavation could provide evidence for the late Saxon development of the town, the medieval defences, and the type of pottery and glass used on the site up to the post-medieval period.[4]

The Society for Medieval Archaeology was founded in 1957, and its early officers played a notable part in the development of the subject in the next thirty years. An important early article was 'Monuments or muniments? The interrelation of material remains and documentary sources' by W. A. Pantin.[5] This far-sighted discussion considered college buildings, priests' houses, inns and town houses, and stressed the need to combine the study of buildings and of the documentary sources to arrive at an understanding of their use. Pantin ended with a plea for the study of the occupation and use of areas or groups of houses, for example, the original location of merchants' and professional houses and their subsequent spread to the suburbs. His approach was important, since he saw that archaeology could provide evidence for the way in which people had lived not only from excavations, but from documents and from the analysis of the history of buildings.

Approaches to medieval archaeology

As much of the work in this field has been derived from rescue archaeology and not from any planned programme of research, the choice of the sites excavated has been largely arbitrary. But it is worth reflecting on the changes over the last forty years in the approach to the information that archaeology can provide about medieval society. There are remarkably few general statements of the underlying ideas behind the study of medieval archaeology. The Council for British Archaeology Survey of Field Research published in 1948 went only up to the seventh century AD. One of the earliest general statements of the opportunities available to medieval archaeology was made in 1948 in the *Archaeological News Letter*. Rupert Bruce-Mitford, foreseeing the developments in the study of both village and town sites and writing as a museum curator, gave particular emphasis to the study of medieval pottery, tiles and other objects. He noted that humble traces of ordinary life and habitation have much to tell us about elements of society infrequently mentioned in the documents of the period.[6] An important new concept was developed by E.M. Jope in a study of the regional cultures of medieval Britain published in 1956. His attempt to see medieval society in terms of social anthropology is perhaps one of the most illuminating ways of analysing archaeological evidence. Observing that medieval Britain was a complex society stratified according to social, economic and intellectual distinctions, with a continual relationship between groups, he commented that medieval Britain with its abundant documentary sources gives the archaeologist the opportunity to combine the exploration of the intangible, such as the use of language or social behaviour, with the material aspects of the life of communities, and to inquire to what extent any of these can be assembled into regional cultures. His principal conclusion was that since regional cultures do not emerge clearly in conjunction with patterns of medieval pottery distribution, this should dictate caution in postulating prehistoric cultures in terms of pottery distribution.[7]

Since 1978 three general surveys have appeared outlining the contribution that archaeology has made to knowledge about the period after the Norman Conquest of 1066. Each of these discusses the results provided by archaeology at much greater length than is possible here. The special feature of Colin Platt's *Medieval England* (1978) is his chronological analysis of the social conditions of medieval life. The survey ranges from the Anglo-Norman settlement, through the economic growth of the thirteenth century, the setback through over-population and plague in the fourteenth century, the combination of conspicuous consumption and improved living conditions in the fifteenth century, and finally to the changes in society with developing technologies, social unrest and new fortifications of the Tudor period. This chronological approach enables Platt to relate documentary sources and archaeology, often with great insight, as for instance when he moves from the discussion of the decline in public order in the early fourteenth century to one possible effect of violence and social change: the increasing popularity of moated sites during the same period.

Two general surveys, Helen Clarke's *The Archaeology of Medieval England* (1984) and John Steane's *The Archaeology of Medieval England and Wales* (1985), assess the contribution of archaeology to individual themes, such as the countryside, castles, churches and monasteries, towns, industries and crafts. This approach attempts to show that archaeology's contribution must be seen as something independent, and not merely illustrative of a history based on documentary evidence. Clarke concentrates particularly on analysing the contribution of excavation in different areas, while Steane's approach is essentially that of an archaeologist with experience of field survey, concerned with the impact of man on the urban and rural landscape. His book concentrates on the technological aspects of the creation of landscapes, construction of buildings and manufacture of objects.

All three approaches concentrate on the archaeological evidence provided for the social life of medieval people. It is curious, however, that the work of the French social historians, known as the '*Annales*' school from their periodical, has until recently had so little effect on the development of medieval archaeology. The work of Marc Bloch, for example, who combined an appreciation of topography and the actual practices of medieval farming with a sociological approach, developed a new understanding of the social relationships in French feudal and rural society.[8] More recently Fernand Braudel, in *Capitalism and Material Life 1400–1800* (1977), has analysed the patterns of material life in Western Europe. He stresses how a pattern of repetitive economic action forms the background to nascent capitalism, as it developed from 1400 to 1800, and shows how the daily round of producing necessities – food, drink, buildings, clothing – provided the basis for the development of economic growth and inequality, which led to the increase of trade, communication and industry that in turn promoted the changes in society up to the French Revolution. It is a fundamentally materialist approach, and as such it could provide an inspiration for the creation of hypotheses that could be explored by both medieval and post-medieval archaeology. One way in which this historical approach has been related to archaeology is in environmental archaeology, where the increasing recovery of animal and bird remains, fish bones and cereal seeds gives more information on the diet, not only of the more prosperous inhabitants of castles and monasteries, but also the poorer people of the villages. The study of environmental evidence is of recent growth and it has not received the same attention as the study of architecture or objects. There are limitations in the conclusions that can be drawn from, say, the evidence of animal bones: they tell us little about the rate of consumption or, particularly in an urban site, the social class of the consumer. Nevertheless, the growing interest in different types of archaeological evidence provides an opportunity for a greater understanding of the past.

This brief and personal survey of the achievements of non-rural archaeology of the period after 1066 will review some of the evidence provided mainly by excavations relating to the sources of energy, such as wind and water power, to the crafts and industries based on these sources, and to the exchange of goods through trade and the development of towns. The archaeology of structures such as castles, churches and monasteries which represented medieval display will also be considered. Finally, some of the evidence provided by archaeology for the development from medieval to post-medieval Britain will be discussed.

Sources of energy (wind and water power)

Before the Industrial Revolution nearly all energy was derived from either animals or men. It is this fact that gives the development of techniques to exploit the inanimate forces of wind and water such importance. The effect of new technology on social change in the early medieval period was analysed in 1962 by Lynn White in a book whose appearance was hailed as 'providing a synthesis or overall picture into which the comparatively trivial objects of material culture could be fitted'.[9] He identified three main agents of change. The first was the use of the stirrup, which gave greater importance to the mounted warrior. The second was the introduction of new ploughing techniques, and the third was the development of mechanical power through the use of both watermills and windmills.

Our knowledge of these has been enlarged by the excavation of watermills and windmills. The first European windmills, which appeared in England and Normandy at the end of the twelfth century, were post mills. The sails were mounted on a horizontal axis fixed to a post which had to be turned to face the wind, so that the mill required substantial foundations of wood set in the earth. At Great Linford (Buckinghamshire) excavation has revealed the cross-shaped wooden foundations of a later medieval mill set in a low mound. The reconstruction (84) is based on archaeological evidence and drawings of mills in manuscript illuminations.[10]

Windmills were used almost solely for grinding corn, but it is the use of the water-wheel for other industries that gives it a particularly significant role in the development of technology. Domesday Book, compiled in 1086, records the existence of a large number of watermills spread right across the country. These may have been driven by the water hitting a wheel placed either horizontally or vertically in the stream. The Saxon watermill at Tamworth, for example, had a horizontal

water-wheel (see 77), and it is possible that some of those indicated in Domesday Book may have been of this type.[11] On the other hand, all the watermills belonging to the post-Conquest period which have been excavated are of the vertical type. A number of excavations have revealed the complex wooden structure of the channels through which the water passed and the pits in which the wheels were set. One of the most illuminating recent excavations of a medieval mill was of that at the Cistercian Abbey of Bordesley (Worcestershire), where remarkable alterations to the landscape made by the Abbey, and in particular the change in the course of the River Arrow, have been studied in detail. On the edge of the site a triangular pond was created, with a mill at one corner. Here the leat, wheel-pit and mill building have been excavated (85). The mill building enclosed at least two hearths and a large posthole packed with tiles that may have been a foundation for an anvil. The tail-race was an extremely sophisticated structure, and the flow of water was controlled by sluices. While the head-race remained unaltered during the life of the mill, the wheel-pit and the tail-race were rebuilt at least once.

Most of the mills referred to in Domesday Book were presumably for grinding corn, but it is clear that the Bordesley mill and also one excavated at Chingley, on the Kentish lands of Boxley Abbey, were used for metalworking. From documentary sources we know that watermills were used in Europe for ironworking as well as cloth-fulling from the

84 A reconstruction of a fourteenth-century post mill excavated at Great Linford (Buckinghamshire). The reconstruction of the upper structure is based on early-fourteenth-century manuscripts.

twelfth century. At Chingley excavation has provided the earliest instance in England of a hammer forge used in ironworking. The use of water power in cloth-fulling, however, so far lacks any archaeological illustration, despite the notable work by Professor E. Carus Wilson on the importance of the fulling-mill in the development of the English textile industry.[12] She argued that cloth-making was located in the country rather than in towns because of the availability of water power to drive fulling-mills.

Medieval crafts and industry were described in 1927 by L.F. Salzman, using the documentary evidence.[13] Archaeology has added new information on almost all the crafts he described by the excavation of production sites and the study and analysis of medieval objects. A wide-ranging survey of this new information is provided by the articles and bibliography of the 1981 Council for British Archaeology research report.[14] Although there are many areas in which archaeology has increased our understanding of medieval industry, this chapter will concentrate on the iron and pottery industries.

Iron was fundamental to the expansion of the economy in the twelfth and thirteenth centuries, since it was a basic material in the manufacture of agricultural tools, fittings for buildings, wagons and ships, and military equipment. Iron ore was extracted, roasted and then

85　The excavation of the fourteenth-century mill at Bordesley Abbey. From the pond at the top of the picture the water was channelled through the mill turning a wheel to supply power to the building indicated by the pebble foundations on the right.

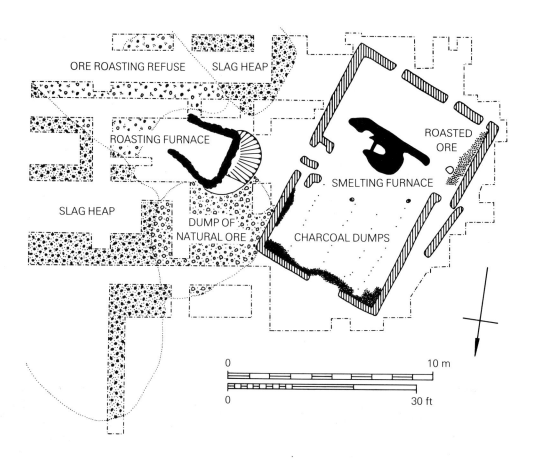

ORE ROASTING REFUSE SLAG HEAP

ROASTED ORE

ROASTING FURNACE

SMELTING FURNACE

SLAG HEAP

DUMP OF NATURAL ORE

CHARCOAL DUMPS

0   10 m

0   30 ft

smelted. The smelting process separated the impurities from the ore, producing a lump of iron (called the bloom) and waste material (the slag). Some impurities remained; these had to be removed by hammering. The metal was then heated and forged (hammered) to the required shape. A complete and undisturbed ironworking site of the fourteenth and fifteenth centuries was excavated in Minepit Wood, Rotherfield (Sussex). The roasting hearth was a clay platform bordered by a low stone kerb; the stone-built smelting furnace was covered by a substantial timber house or shelter (86). The bellows were behind the furnace, supported on the timber structure or the stonework, and were operated through an aperture in the wall of the furnace.

Although Rotherfield provides valuable indications of the techniques employed and an opportunity to study the efficiency of smelting by analysis of the slags, it is striking that it was, however, a small-scale operation. The only set of accounts existing for a smelting furnace is for that on the lands of the Clare family at Tudeley, Tonbridge (Kent) for the period 1329–54, during which the estimated level of output varied from 1.52 to 3.16 tonnes a year. The water-wheel was introduced into iron manufacture to drive both the bellows – thus increasing the capacity of the bloomery – and the hammers. At Chingley a timber wheel-race was surmounted by a massive frame, now assumed to be the foun-

86 Plan of the fourteenth-century ironworking site at Minepit Wood, Rotherfield (Sussex). Iron was first roasted in the roasting furnace and then smelted in a covered furnace on the right. After J.H. Money

dations of a hammer, and so at this site there may have been a forge utilising iron produced in bloomeries without water-power operated in the same manner as Rotherfield. At Chingley there is an archaeological illustration from later in the sixteenth century of the change to the use of the blast furnace. In such a furnace with a high shaft the correct mixture of ore and charcoal could produce iron carbide, which, having a lower melting point than bloomery iron, could form as a liquid and be cast. Documentary evidence indicates that the Chingley furnace was built between 1558 and 1565 and was in decay by 1588. The plan (87) shows the main elements – the culvert in which the wheel-pit was situated, the bellows sited inside a bellows house, and the pillar of the furnace which contained both the blowing arch towards the bellows

87 Plan of the ironworking furnace at Chingley (Kent) showing the positions of the culvert, wheel pit, bellows and hearth. The water-wheel was used to drive the bellows. After D.W. Crossley

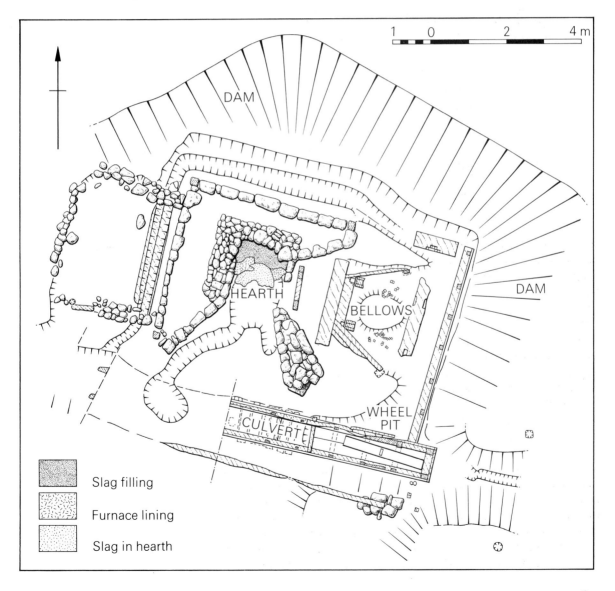

and the casting arch towards the casting floor. All this archaeological evidence for the medieval iron industry has been discovered in the last forty years.

Tile and pottery kilns were discovered and recorded in the nineteenth century and in the first half of the twentieth century. By 1949 only twenty-seven medieval pottery kiln sites were known, but now there are about eight times that number. These vary from single kilns to groups of kilns associated with one particular industry. At Chilvers Coton, near Nuneaton (Warwickshire), some forty-two kilns and associated features have been excavated. The major archaeological contribution to the study of medieval pottery has been the excavation, not only of the kiln, but also the area surrounding it. Large area excavations at sites such as Lyveden (Northamptonshire), Nuneaton and Olney Hyde (Buckinghamshire) have shown the quantity of information that can be obtained about the different stages of manufacture. At Lyveden (88) the puddling pits for mixing the clay, the potter's workshop (with its associated tools) and the drying sheds were found, and these enabled the excavator to give a picture of the whole process from the digging of the clay to the firing of the pot. So many pottery kilns have now been discovered that the development from single flue to double flue kilns

88 Photo of the thirteenth–fourteeth-century potter's complex at Lyveden (Northamptonshire). The rectangular building in the centre (cut diagonally by a modern field drain) is the potter's workshop. It has a lean-to clay store at the rear, and a path leads from the door on the left-hand side to the multi-flued kiln.

and finally to multi-flue kilns can be worked out. With other industries, such as glass, very few production sites have been found. One of the most notable is that at Blundens Wood (Surrey). The site revealed three furnaces dating to about 1330. The main barrel-vaulted furnace had two benches on which the crucibles stood, and was probably used for melting. The two small furnaces were probably used for fritting and annealing (89). It is not, however, excavation alone that has produced new information: it is also the scientific examination of the products.[15]

One of the most fruitful ways of attributing medieval pottery is by defining the clay source in terms of any geological inclusions in the clay that can be specifically identified. One of the most impressive recent studies of a pottery industry is by Alan Vince.[16] From an analysis of the clay by thin section he has been able to describe the distribution of pottery produced in the Malvern area of Worcestershire. He has shown that the twelfth-century distribution lay within a 32-kilometre (20-mile) radius of Malvern, but that this distribution considerably expanded in the thirteenth century and that in the fifteenth century the proportion of Malvernian wares to others found in the area significantly increased. The definition of distribution areas has led to an examination of the distribution systems for pottery. Stephen Moorhouse, in a detailed

89 A reconstruction of the glass-working site excavated at Blundens Wood (Surrey).

analysis of the documentary sources, has reviewed, not only the physical nature of the English road system in the Middle Ages, but also the use of markets and fairs as distribution agents and the effect on the supply of medieval pottery of tenurial influence, monastic property, and even travelling households. He concludes that the documents suggest that 'while the mass of the population obtained their pots at the local market in small numbers, the various landlord classes had a much greater variety of options open to them, not only as to how they obtained their pots initially, and the quantity purchased, but also how they were moved around when in use'.[17]

Towns

Although medieval England was largely agricultural, knowledge of the medieval town is important for understanding medieval society. It was a focus of trade, a place for specialised craft and industry, a source for the generation of wealth and an indicator of social differentiation. Urban excavation was initially concerned primarily with Roman remains, and it was only after the end of the Second World War that excavations in London gave equal attention to all periods from Roman to medieval. The excavations in Norwich in the late 1940s were specifically aimed at finding evidence for the late Saxon occupation and defences. Early finds in Norwich were analysed by producing a distribution map which plotted finds against their topographical and historical background, thus providing evidence for the occupation of certain areas.[18] Similar maps, made in the 1950s and 1960s for Norwich, Oxford, York and Cambridge, provided an initial basis for understanding the archaeology of these towns.[19] In 1968 Martin Biddle published an important survey of the problems and methods of archaeological research in towns. After analysing the documentary and geographical approaches, he notes the use of the distribution map set against the physical geography and man-made structures 'to trace the growing and changing pattern of a town over the whole period of its existence', and then draws attention to two uses of archaeological excavations. Either these could aim to solve a particular problem (such as the nature of the merchant house in Southampton), or they could analyse the character of a particular area of a town over a period of time.[20] Both approaches have been followed with impressive results. Biddle's article characterised the increasing attention being focused on the problems of rescue and urban archaeology, caused by the growing threat of redevelopment. The effect of this was summed up by the Council for British Archaeology's volume, the *Erosion of History*, published in 1972. Of the many subsequent surveys of the archaeological potential of English towns and cities the fullest was perhaps *The Future of London's Past* by M. Biddle and D. Hudson. The main general summary of all the work carried out in English towns is by John Schofield and David Palliser, *Recent Archaeological work in English Towns*, published in 1981. Since then many volumes on individual towns have added so much to the information available that there is a major problem to be solved in elucidating the assessing the contribution of archaeology to the history of the medieval town. There is only space here to provide one or two indications of the type of evidence that has been added.

The increased study of the documentary evidence for life in the medieval town is of considerable importance. From the twelfth century onwards there is a vast amount of evidence, such as descriptions of property, rentals and deeds, from which scholars can create a picture of the medieval town. Surveys based on such material have been published for both Oxford and Angevin Canterbury.[21] The recent survey of Winchester based on the Winton Domesday, itself a combination of two lists of property in the town made in 1110 and 1148, provides the earliest and most detailed description of an English or European town of the Middle Ages.[22] This tells us of the ownership of property, density of occupation and relative wealth of different areas, enabling changes to be charted in the social structure, land holdings and trades of the late Saxon *burh*, the Anglo-Norman city, and the town in the region of Stephen (1135–54). Winchester changed from the capital of Wessex to a great provincial town that formed the administrative capital of the Kingdom in the eleventh century; its status declined with the removal of royal administration in the twelfth century.

Within Winchester the Brooks Street site demonstrates the considerable contribution that archaeology can make to urban history. Here the changes in the use of this part of Winchester, where there were two churches and several houses, have been revealed from the eleventh century to the end of the Middle Ages. The plan of the site in the early fourteenth century shows, in front of the houses, workshops that were used by fullers and dyers in cloth-finishing. Behind the living quarters were yards used for stretching out the cloth to dry. North of St Mary's church there was a row of four cottages, possibly a speculative development for occupation by the manual workers who worked in cloth-finishing. Before the twelfth century the occupation was less dense, and by the mid-fifteenth century the site was an unoccupied open space.

Archaeology can also provide evidence relating to the nature of housing. It is notable how the recording of standing structures, often, alas, shortly before their demolition, has increased our knowledge of the medieval town. The destruction of the Clarendon Hotel in Oxford in 1956 was an early opportunity for recording both the above-ground structure and the underground archaeology.[23] The work of W. A. Pantin on town houses and merchants' houses has been followed by many studies of medieval buildings, notably at King's Lynn, where both excavations and the recording of standing buildings have added enormously to our understanding of this important medieval port.[24]

One of the major developments in housing in the medieval town is the change from wood to stone. This change takes place at different times according to the inhabitants' prosperity and the building materials locally available. The range of evidence for housing that can be provided by archaeology may be illustrated by two reconstructions. The thirteenth-century house at 42 St Paul's Street, Aberdeen (90) illustrates the

smaller building of thirteenth-century Scottish burghs. Sited away from the frontage, it may tentatively be interpreted as a house and workshop of one of the poorer inhabitants and craftsmen – the majority of the urban population. The post-and-wattle walls are made of willow, which was probably clad with daub, mud or dung. The reconstruction of the roof supposes a ridge held on posts outside the main structure and shows it covered with thatch on a wattle base. It would have had vents at the apex of the gable walls for the smoke to emerge.

This house may be contrasted with a twelfth- or thirteenth-century house excavated on the corner of Flaxengate and Grantham Street in Lincoln, a prosperous area inhabited by several Jews. Here the houses were solidly built and were probably continued in stone up to the eaves. The excavations revealed a complex of stone buildings that developed from the twelfth-century house, which was later extended by an adjoining hall range to the west and finally a further two-storeyed wing added on the north side. The reconstruction (91) gives an impression of how the foundations discovered in excavation can be elucidated by the comparative study of standing buildings.

90 A reconstruction drawing of the thirteenth-century house excavated at 42 St Paul's Street, Aberdeen. The post-and-wattle walls are of willow and the thatched roof was supported on posts outside the main structure. After G. Smith

Waterfront archaeology has provided a new understanding of a different aspect of the medieval town. A good example is at London, in Trig Lane, where a succession of revetments dated by dendrochronology between about 1140 and about 1460 have been found, some surviving up to two metres (5 ft) high. Due to the very good conditions for the preservation of organic material, they provide many groups of dated collections of objects, mostly from medieval crafts in leather, bone and textiles. It is suggested that the purpose of the Trig Lane revetments (92) was to prevent silting and to provide quay frontage for small boats.

Individual sites in towns, however clear the stratification, can only give a limited indication of the development of the whole town. It is here that topographical interpretation including the study of both archaeology and documents, can clarify the whole picture. At Hereford the

91 A reconstruction drawing showing how the foundations discovered during excavation at the corner of Flaxengate and Grantham Street in Lincoln can be interpreted as a twelfth-century house with an adjoining hall range to the west and a further two-storeyed wing on the north side. After S.R. Jones

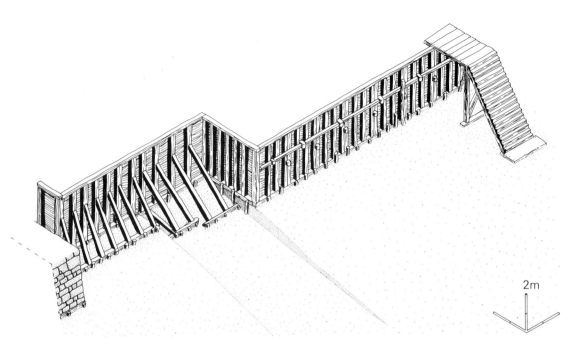

92 A reconstruction of the waterfront at Trig Lane, London, in the mid-fourteenth century. The stone wall, back-braced and front-braced revetments are all contemporary. After G. Milne

93 Aerial photograph of New Winchelsea (Sussex), a new town founded by Edward I (1272–1307). A grid of streets containing thirty-nine quarters was laid out on the site.

94 Plans of the successive stages of development of the town of Hereford. After Ron Shoesmith

investigation of the defences has been related to the growth of the town. It was the intersection of trade routes at the site of an easy crossing of the River Wye that provided the stimulus for the initial foundation of the town: the Saxon defences were entered by gateways on the line of the principal approach. To the north of the Saxon town the great market of Hereford was resited shortly after the Norman Conquest.

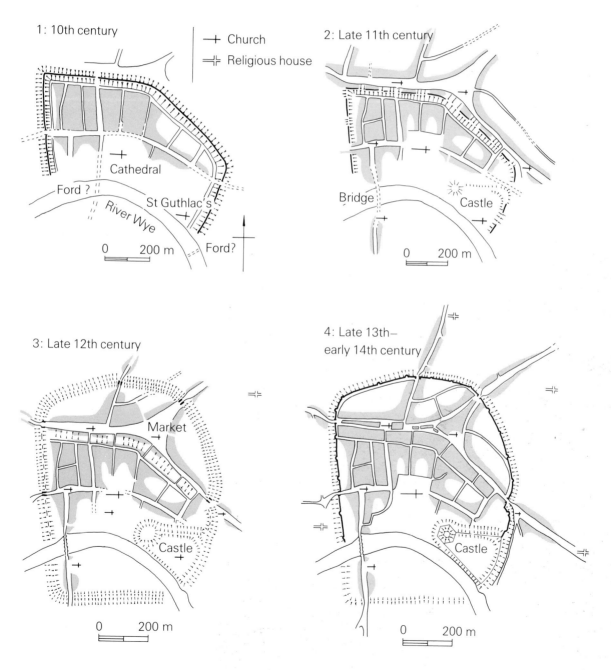

1: 10th century

—┼— Church
═╬═ Religious house

Cathedral
Ford ?
River Wye
St Guthlac's
0   200 m   Ford?

2: Late 11th century

Bridge   Castle
0   200 m

3: Late 12th century

Market
Castle
0   200 m

4: Late 13th– early 14th century

Castle
0   200 m

Gradually the housing spread out along the line of the streets that converged on the market. The plans of the town (94) show how the defences at first enclosed a limited area, but later included a larger area, with the market-place. The chequerboard street pattern of Winchelsea (Sussex), one of the new towns created by Edward I (1272–1307), is shown in 93, demonstrating how aerial photography can aid topographical interpretation. For such new towns Maurice Beresford has shown in his wide survey how a combination of historical geography and economic history can enable us to interpret the physical remains of such towns to illustrate the effect of population increase, and sometimes the failure of too optimistic an endeavour.[25]

Castles

Excavation has done more to improve our understanding of post-Conquest castles for the period immediately after 1066 than for the later Middle Ages, although great progress has been made for the latter period by studying the documentation for the building, under the direction of Edward I, of the great Welsh castles such as Carnarfon, Conwy and Harlech (Gwynedd). For the late eleventh and twelfth centuries excavations of castles have revealed a more complex picture than was previously apprehended.

The motte and bailey is generally thought to be a Norman introduction into England. It consisted of a mound surmounted by a tower of either stone or wood, the whole surrounded by an enclosure. At Abinger (Surrey) careful examination of the top of the mound revealed holes which originally held posts providing the support for a central wooden tower and a palisade strengthened by bracing posts on the inside which protected the edge of the mound. The archaeological evidence has been interpreted in a reconstruction (95), using the illustrations in the Bayeux Tapestry as a possible model (96). The structure illustrated at Abinger is likely to date to the mid-twelfth century, some seventy years later than the Tapestry, although it did replace an earlier structure of similar form. In 1086 Abinger was a small part of a large estate belonging to William Fitz Ansculf which was later divided, and so the motte was probably built by a later tenant, Robert of Abinger or his son, some time in the 1090s or 1100s.

One of the most interesting discoveries has been the demonstration that sometimes the stone or wood tower was founded on the original ground surface and the motte raised around the lower parts of this tower as part of the same operation. At South Mimms (Hertfordshire) a castle built by Geoffrey de Mandeville, a leading baron in the reign of Stephen (1135–54), possessed a massive timber-framed tower which had the motte piled up around its base. The motte itself was probably covered with a revetment of timber so that the external appearance would have been of a wooden tower above the wooden revetment. At Farnham (Surrey) a castle built in the 1140s by Henry of Blois, Bishop of Winchester, the stone tower was constructed together with the motte, which was bound to the tower by a masonry flange.

95 Reconstruction of a twelfth-century motte surmounted by a wooden tower at Abinger (Surrey). This reconstruction is based on the excavated postholes (*below*) and illustrations of motte-and-bailey castles in the Bayeux Tapestry (see 96). After B. Hope-Taylor

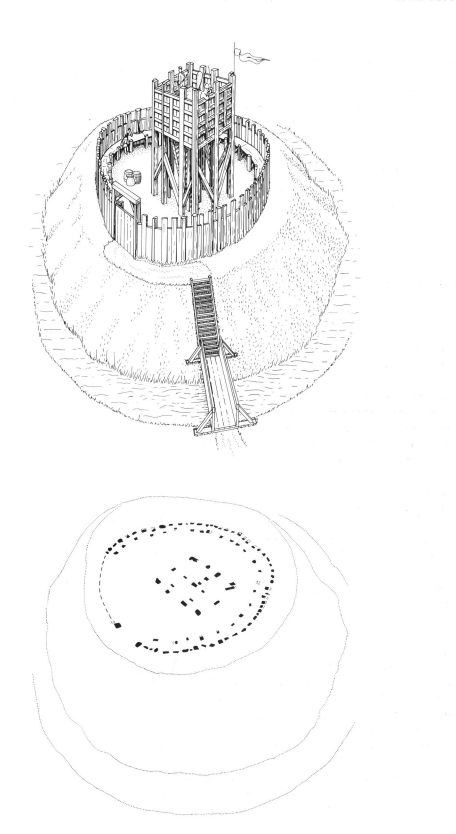

AD DOL: ET·CONAN: FV

The study of the origins of the castle has provoked considerable controversy, particularly over the nature of castles in the eleventh century. This controversy led to a sustained programme of research on early castles, sponsored by the Royal Archaeological Institute, which resulted in support being given to five excavations on castle sites at Hastings (Kent), Baile Hill (York), Sulgrave (Northamptonshire), Bramber (Sussex) and Hen Domen (Powys). The principal general result was to show that 'castles are by their nature extremely complex structures and their surviving earthworks deceptively simple'.[26] The exact origins of the motte and bailey are still obscure, but it may be that the idea of a high tower was an important factor in their development. The popularity of the motte and bailey in England after the Conquest has been seen as a result of a number of diverse influences, such as the division between the tower and forecourt that occurred in the Rhine-

96 The motte-and-bailey castle at Dol, in north-western France, under attack, as seen in the Bayeux Tapestry probably embroidered in England about 1075.

land, the timber towers of Normandy and Anjou, and the Anglo-Saxon fortified enclosure frequently termed the 'ring work'.

It is the fortified enclosure that has received greatest attention in the last twenty years. The 'ring work' is a ditch with a bank behind, probably supporting a palisade; the defences of Goltho (Lincolnshire) (see p. 210) provide a good example of the type. A striking example of a ring work fortification converted to a motte and bailey was found during excavations at Castle Neroche (Somerset). Here in 1067–9 Robert of Mortain ordered the strengthening of the defences by the creation of an enclosure; pottery with rim forms characteristic of Northern France was found in the enclosure. Later a motte was built over part of it and the rest used as a bailey. Thus it was not the motte and bailey that was built first at Castle Neroche by the Normans, but the ring work. Archaeology has here shown that there is a more complex pattern than might have been deduced from using a single non-archaeological source such as the Bayeux Tapestry.

A castle combines the functions of both fortress and residence. Excavation of the interior of castles has revealed new evidence for the way in which early castles were occupied. At Launceston (Cornwall) excavations have provided considerable evidence for buildings in the bailey, and at Castle Acre (Norfolk) a remarkable sequence of construction in the late eleventh and twelfth centuries has been uncovered. Castle Acre was the centre of the Norfolk estate of the Warenne Earls of Surrey, who ranked among the greatest magnates of Anglo-Norman England. William de Warenne, the first Earl of Surrey, had fought with William I at Hastings and was the builder of at least two castles, at Reigate (Surrey) and Lewes (E. Sussex). The aerial photograph of Castle Acre (97) shows the present castle sited in the south-east quarter of the town. The evolution of structures on the site in the eleventh and twelfth centuries is shown by the four drawings (98). The first stone building was a two-storey country house with a ground-floor entrance. Surrounded by a ditch and bank, probably topped with a palisade, it was first approached through a timber gate. This was replaced in stone in the second phase, though defensive considerations were still subordinate to domestic convenience. The third drawing shows how the country house was extensively modified internally for conversion to a keep. The perimeter bank was heightened and the curtain wall built on top of the bank. The last drawing shows how the emphasis on defence moved from the keep to the curtain wall. Initially it was intended to build the keep on both halves of the house. In fact, it was only built on the northern half, while the southern half was demolished. On the outside the perimeter wall was raised and a second curtain wall built directly on top of the first. Initially the castle was probably regarded by the Warennes as the headquarters for their Norfolk estates, a place to be lived in periodically by the Earl and his family. The deteriorating political situation of the 1130s caused nobles to look to their defences, and it is then that the conversion of Castle Acre to a keep began, although the initial scheme was too ambitious and a smaller scheme eventually adopted. The end of the direct male line, with the death of William de Warenne on crusade in 1147, may have provided the reason for the abandonment of major works in the upper ward of the castle. It is interesting to note that the finds from the upper ward – such as the high proportion of gilded metalwork or even the butchery on the food bones – point to the wealth of the inhabitants.

The excavations at Castle Acre concentrated on the upper ward. At

97 Aerial photograph of Castle Acre, showing the earthworks of the castle and the town.

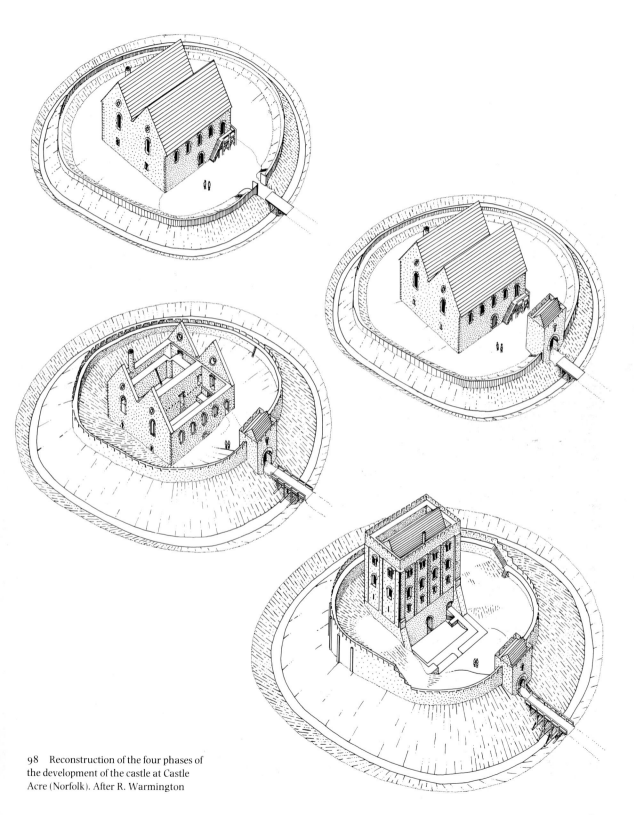

98   Reconstruction of the four phases of
the development of the castle at Castle
Acre (Norfolk). After R. Warmington

other castle excavations details of the buildings in the interior of the bailey have been revealed, most notably by the painstaking excavation of Hen Domen (Powys), a castle belonging to Roger de Montgomery. Here the impression of the bailey as an empty space was contradicted by the detection of buildings, such as a timber fighting platform around the bailey perimeter, a chapel, rectangular structures and a timber tower in the interior.

Excavators at both Castle Acre and Hen Domen concentrated on a small part of the site. The only castle that has been thoroughly excavated is Sandal Castle (Yorkshire) which also belonged to the Warenne family. Here the whole of the $2\frac{1}{2}$-hectare (6-acre) site was excavated with an unparalleled degree of thoroughness between 1964 and 1973;

99 Sandal Castle.
Below plan of the earthworks and the stone fortifications added during the second half of the thirteenth century.
Below left aerial photograph of the excavations, showing the barbican in the foreground and the keep behind.

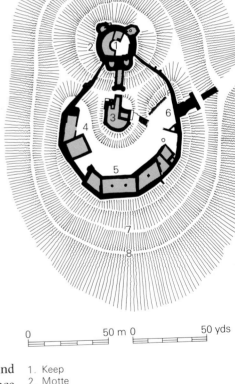

| 0 | 50 m | 0 | 50 yds |

1. Keep
2. Motte
3. Barbican
4. Kitchen
5. Great Hall
6. Gatehouse
7. Outer moat
8. Outer defences

the scale of the project can be seen from the view of the keep and barbican (99). The motte was originally built of wood, and the sequence of its conversion from wood to stone probably began in the late twelfth century. However, the major part of the change took place between 1240 and 1270 during the time of John de Warenne, 7th Earl of Surrey, who played a prominent political and military role under Edward I. The stone keep was approached by a steep passage between the two drum towers. To reach these any attacker would have to cross a bridge to the barbican tower set in the bailey, the foundations of which are visible in the photograph. Within the barbican the attacker would have to pass gates and portcullises and make a right-angled turn before reaching the bridge across to the drum towers. The barbican tower at Sandal is an unusual feature in English military architecture and may have been influenced by work for the French king Philip III (1270–85) at the

100 Drawing of Sandal Castle in 1562, which gives an impression of the appearance of the upper stories of the barbican, the bridge and the towers on both the base and the top of the keep.

Louvre and by the Lion Tower erected for Edward I (1272–1307) at the Tower of London.

Churches and monasteries

The archaeology of monastic sites attracted much interest in the nineteenth century. In the last forty years, although there has been some notable work on monastic sites, it is the study of the English church that has provided one of the most rapidly developing areas of medieval archaeology. Churches have always attracted attention for their architecture, but the approach of archaeology has been to scrutinise and record the fabric in far greater detail than hitherto. Archaeology pays greater attention to the previous use of the site by the examination of earlier buildings underneath or alongside the church, since the recovery of the total structural history may require investigations beyond the present fabric. Archaeology can also provide evidence for liturgical arrangements – for instance, vanished screens may be represented by postholes, or beam slots and patterns of wear in the floor may suggest the position of focal points, such as venerated graves or altars. The setting of the church in the landscape has also attracted study, especially the relationship with field systems or neighbouring structures, such as the manor house, motte or roadways. The recording of the churchyard, of the shape and the pattern of burials within it, can also provide additional information for the understanding of the whole history of a church and its local community.

Although there were some notable excavations on ecclesiastical sites in the 1950s and 1960s, more recently two factors have helped to focus attention in this area. Firstly, the two great campaigns of archaeological excavation at Winchester Cathedral and at York Minster have given us valuable and copious information on these great ecclesiastical centres. At Winchester the plan of the Old Minster was revealed beside the Norman cathedral (see p.152). At York the plan of the Norman cathedral built by Archbishop Thomas of Bayeux shortly after 1069 has been recovered in excavations conducted in combination with the programme for strengthening the foundations of the Minster. The Norman cathedral had an aisleless nave, transepts with single eastern apses, and a long chancel ending in an apse. The second factor in the expansion of church archaeology is the impetus provided by the problem of dealing with surplus ecclesiastical buildings. The Pastoral Measure of 1968 presented the option that redundant churches should either be converted to another use or demolished. This led to the application of the principles of modern archaeological investigation to 'ordinary' churches.

There have been many investigations of such churches that have added much to our understanding of parish churches. An example is the church at Asheldam (Essex) which was declared redundant in 1975. In 1923 the church was described as having been wholly rebuilt in the fourteenth century, the tower being later in date than the rest of the building. The excavations revealed, however, differing phases of development (101). While the plan of the nave is based on that of an earlier twelfth-century church, there were changes at both the east and the west ends. The apse was replaced by a square-ended chancel, which was itself subsequently replaced. At the west end the thirteenth-century tower was demolished and the present tower built in the mid-fourteenth century. The investigations at Asheldam show how much can be learned of a church's history from an exhaustive study of the upstanding fabric at the same time as excavation below ground.

In contrast to the very considerable expansion of archaeological research on churches, relatively little work has been done on monastic sites. Here again, the same use of the techniques of meticulous examination of the archaeological layers and the concentration of effort on the areas away from the church and cloister has led to greater emphasis on the relationship of the site and landscape. One of the largest monastic excavations has been undertaken at Norton Priory (Cheshire), a modest priory of Augustinian canons, sited near the present new town of Runcorn (102). The need to examine the whole site before opening it to the public led to the largest excavation to modern standards on any monastic site in Britain. The church was of cruciform design with a short tower under which the canons' choir was situated. The cloisters

11th–12th century

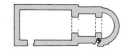

13th century

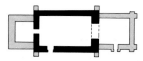

Late 13th century–early 14th century

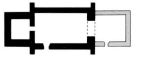

Early 14th century

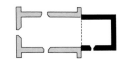

Mid-14th century

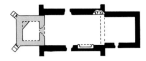

Mid–late 14th century

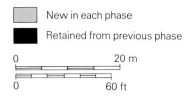

New in each phase

Retained from previous phase

0   20 m

0   60 ft

101   Plan of the successive stages of development of the church at Asheldam (Essex), from the twelfth to the mid-fourteenth century, revealing a more complex series of stages of development than previously suspected. After W. Rodwell

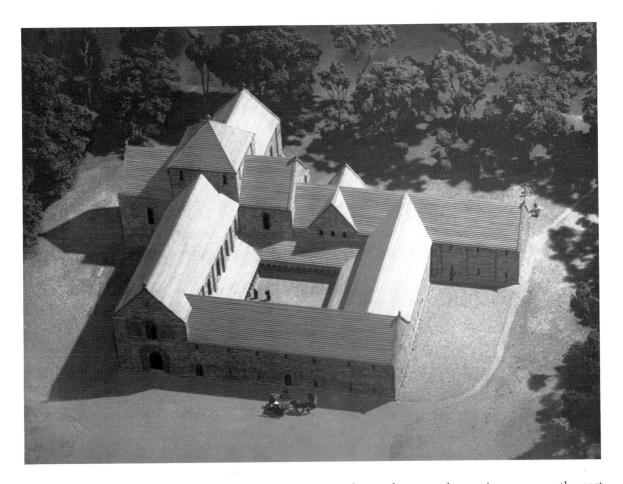

102 Photograph of the model based on the excavated ground-plan of Norton Priory (Cheshire), a small Augustinian priory sited near Runcorn. It shows the first stone buildings of the priory as they would have been seen in the second half of the twelfth century.

linked the dormitory, chapter house and warming room on the east with the refectory on the south and the accommodation for the Prior on the west. Unusually, here the timber buildings, that were constructed before the masonry buildings, were found. The former were impressive, with large oak posts and wattle-and-daub walls. They were found away from the main area of church and cloister and they are an example of the type of new discovery that can be made by the excavation of areas away from the monastic centre. Finds such as the tile kiln or the ditches for the water supply indicate how this new approach to monastic archaeology can illuminate the economy of the monastery. Excavations at Bordesley Abbey (Worcestershire), a Cistercian house near Redditch, have revealed much information about the abbey's industrial area (see p.166); they have also shown how much detail about the life of the inhabitants of this type of monastic house can be illuminated by high-quality area excavations, meticulous recording and comprehensive surveying. An example of such detail is represented by the changes in position of the choir stalls, indicated by variation in the position of the stone base of the stalls, which were moved from the crossing to the first bay of the western arm of the church.

Owing to increasing urban development and consequent rescue archaeology, the Friars, whose houses were often established in towns, have had considerable attention in the last twenty years. Lawrence Butler has recently surveyed the archaeological work on these orders.[27] Of the 60 Franciscan houses, 15 have been excavated. Excavations have also been carried out at 22 of the 53 Dominican houses, 7 of 38 Carmelite houses and 6 of the 34 Austin houses. Although many excavations were on a small scale, some, such as those at Oxford, Bristol and Leicester, have been of major areas. The excavation of the Austin Friars site at Leicester shows not only how detail of the structures can be recreated, but also how the finds, and in particular the environmental evidence, can be used to give a picture of the friars' domestic life, particularly their diet, which cannot be gained from the written records.

Excavation has considerably increased our knowledge of burials. The rich burial of the Archbishop of York, Walter de Gray (died 1255),

103 Reconstruction of the domestic and farm buildings at the preceptory of the Knights Templar at South Witham (Lincolnshire). Set about a courtyard they include a gatehouse on the north, barns on the west, a domestic area with hall, chapel, and kitchen in the south and a workshop area to the east. After P. Mayes

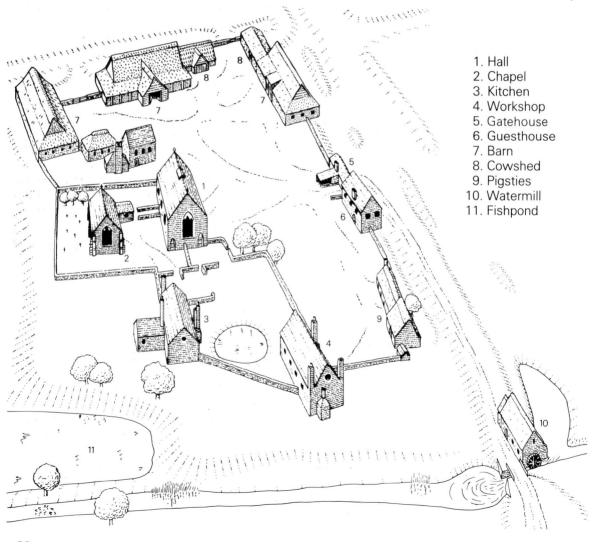

1. Hall
2. Chapel
3. Kitchen
4. Workshop
5. Gatehouse
6. Guesthouse
7. Barn
8. Cowshed
9. Pigsties
10. Watermill
11. Fishpond

reflects the importance of a distinguished prelate, with his richly decorated pastoral staff, chalice, paten and ring.[28] The burials of a small and poor urban parish church, such as St Helen on the Walls, Aldwark (York), can offer much information about the physical characteristics of medieval people.[29] Here over a thousand skeletons were analysed. There appears to have been a low life-expectancy: the excavation indicated that 27 per cent of the local population died as children and only 9 per cent lived beyond the age of 60. Osteoarthritis and dental decay were frequent, while the number of skeletons showing evidence of wounds (eighteen) is extremely small. One of the points of greatest interest is that there is a marked change in skull type between the Saxon and medieval groups. This change is supported by excavations at other graveyards and is the most puzzling feature of the physical change in early medieval population. It seems unlikely that it can have had anything to do with the Scandinavian or Norman invasions, but the reasons for this change are unknown. Perhaps the next forty years of medieval archaeology will answer this question.

The discovery that some sites, such as Grove Priory (Bedfordshire), changed from secular to religious use, points to the danger of too simple a division between these two spheres. The total excavation of the preceptory of the Knights Templar at South Witham (Lincolnshire), for example, has shown how a religious site can also illustrate agricultural history. This site, on poor marginal clay land, was completely deserted after it was handed over to the Hospitallers in 1324. In the centre of the site were the domestic quarters, the hall, chapel and kitchen. Surrounding these, around the outer farm buildings, were barns for storage and housing for animals. On the stream was a mill (103). The value of the excavation at South Witham is that it has revealed not only a complete example of a Templar preceptory but also a complete farm layout of the thirteenth century. This shows how a complete area excavation can reveal the use and the development of the whole site.

Post-medieval Britain

The problems of assessing how archaeology has enhanced our knowledge of post-medieval Britain are even more acute than for the earlier period. In the former, to a greater extent, the mass of information from alternative sources – standing buildings, documentary records and even views and plans of buildings – tends to make archaeology an ancillary rather than an all-embracing activity. Indeed, at the launch of the Society for Post-Medieval Archaeology in 1967, it was stated that in the eighteenth century 'the publication of (or survival of) trade pattern books and architectural plans, and the parallel work of the encyclopaedists in France removes from archaeology much of the value in supplying information otherwise incapable of or difficult of recovery'.[30]

The Society for Post-Medieval Archaeology arose from the study of the post-medieval ceramics found in increasing numbers in the excavations of the 1960s. It is excavation that has shed most light on post-medieval sites, in contrast with industrial archaeology, where above-ground recording of standing factories and mills has always received pride of place. Hence two types of site – fortifications and palaces – taken from the whole field of post-medieval archaeology will serve as illustrations.

The decline of the medieval castle was not a simple result of the introduction of gunpowder and artillery in the fourteenth century. For some two hundred years after the introduction of artillery into Britain the main effect on castle architecture was the insertion of gunports into towers and walls constructed as before. Although the history of the castle in Scotland is rather different from that of the English castle, the manner in which new work incorporated guns has been demonstrated by the excavations at Threave Castle (Galloway). Here, to strengthen the castle's resistance to artillery bombardment, a stone-built artillery work was constructed around a fourteenth-century tower house. The work consisted of three three-storey towers linked by walls. The two lower storeys of each tower were provided with gunports. Both numismatic and dendrochronological evidence have combined to show that the entire artillery work and its enclosing ditch were constructed in about 1450 at the time of William, 8th Earl of Douglas.[31]

It was not until the sixteenth century that fortresses were constructed which were exclusively for military use and which did not combine the two functions of defence and residence as the castle had done. One of the most important series of coastal fortifications in England was that undertaken by Henry VIII in 1538–9 when faced with the threat of invasion (105). This was described by B.H.St John O'Neil as 'the one scheme of comprehensive coastal defence ever attempted in England before modern times'.[32] The fortresses were designed for the mounting of cannon and were centrally planned. Of the many built, the one which best illustrates how intensive archaeological and documentary investigation can increase our understanding is Camber Castle (W. Sussex), set on a shingle ridge guarding the open water which then existed between Rye and Winchelsea. Three main periods of construction were revealed (104). During the first period, 1512–14, the central tower was built by Sir Edward Guldeford. In the second, in 1539–40, an elaborate concentric structure was erected, which consisted of four bastions backed by stirrup-shaped towers linked to each other by an eight-sided curtain. These four bastions were replaced in the third period, 1542–3, by four massive semicircular bastions linked by their own curtain. It was an immensely strong fortress, and the combination of archaeological excavation and documentary analysis has shown how the complex history of the structure can be disentangled and related to the political and military development of the period.[33]

Archaeology has provided an additional source of evidence for reconstructing the history of royal palaces in the sixteenth century. These palaces, accumulated by Henry VIII from many sources – such as the dissolved monasteries or the King's own subjects – are one aspect of what has been called the 'Age of Plunder'. Excavation has provided

Phase I
1512–14

Phase II-IIIa
1540–3

Phase IIIb
1542–3

104   Reconstruction of the three main periods of construction of Camber Castle (Sussex). After M. Biddle

105   A design for an artillery fort on the Kent coast, c. 1539. This gives an impression of how a contemporary would have seen a castle such as Camber.

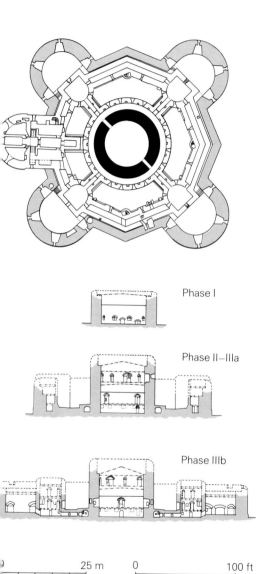

Phase I

Phase II–IIIa

Phase IIIb

25 m   0   100 ft

plans or partial plans of several of the Tudor royal palaces, notably Baynards Castle, Bridewell, Greenwich and Whitehall (all in London), and Oatlands (Surrey). In most cases archaeology can only reveal the ground-plan and not the nature of the architecture above. The most important excavation in this field a study took place on the site of the long-demolished palace began by Henry VIII in 1538 at Cuddington (Surrey), which was to be named Nonsuch. Here not only was the plan revealed (106), but also important evidence for the decoration of the

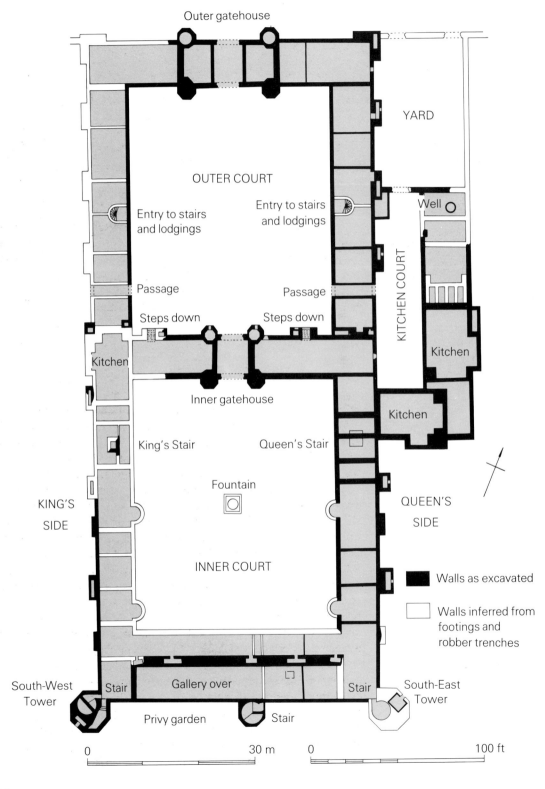

Outer gatehouse

OUTER COURT

YARD

Entry to stairs
and lodgings

Entry to stairs
and lodgings

Well

KITCHEN COURT

Passage

Passage

Steps down

Steps down

Kitchen

Kitchen

Inner gatehouse

King's Stair

Queen's Stair

Kitchen

Fountain

KING'S
SIDE

QUEEN'S
SIDE

INNER COURT

■ Walls as excavated

□ Walls inferred from
footings and
robber trenches

South-West
Tower

Stair

Gallery over

Stair

South-East
Tower

Privy garden

Stair

0   30 m

0   100 ft

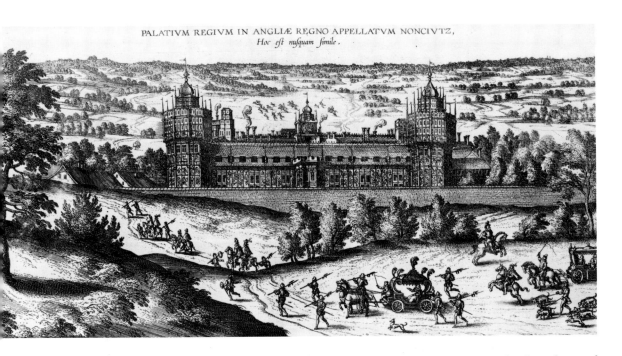

PALATIVM REGIVM IN ANGLIÆ REGNO APPELLATVM NONCIVTZ,
Hoc eſt nuſquam ſimile .

107 Engraving, dated 1582, of the south front of Nonsuch Palace after a drawing by Joris Hoefnagel made in 1568.

106 Plan of the palace of Henry VIII at Nonsuch (Surrey), as revealed by excavation. It consisted of two courts, the outer court to the north stone-faced with a brick core, the inner court stone-faced on the ground floor and timber-faced with slate on the two upper storeys. After M. Biddle

upper storeys. The palace consisted of two courtyards of nearly equal size. The outer courtyard, approached from the north through a three-storey gatehouse, was faced with stone. An inner gatehouse led to the inner court, which was decorated with moulded stucco and carved and gilded sheets of black slate showing human and animal figures, fruit and flower swags, and royal badges, including the Garter. The work on the slate was executed by Nicholas Bellin of Modena, an Italian sculptor who had worked at the French royal palace of Fontainebleau. The distinctly Renaissance style of the slate fragments is clearly related to the stuccos at Fontainebleau and permits a brilliant interpretation of archaeological discoveries in terms of both the documentary record and the art-historical relationships of the period. The architecture of the building is known from pictorial representations, which include the drawing of the south front by Joris Hoefnagel, dated 1568 (107). It is interesting to compare this drawing with the excavated plan, since we can now see that, in order to represent the grandeur and impressiveness of the building, Hoefnagel has shown the towers as being too wide in relation to the total width of the front. Archaeology has here provided us with the actual size of the building and the opportunity of comparing it with the way in which it was seen by a contemporary.

The grandiose and luxurious accommodation provided in the royal palaces was far above that enjoyed by the rest of the population, but one of the most interesting features of the sixteenth century is the increasing purchasing power of important sections of the landowning and farming families and their improved standards of comfort in buildings and furnishing, particularly the use of glass in windows of many more houses. A considerable increase in the scale of glass-making has been traced after 1567 when Jean Carré, an Antwerp merchant, was awarded a licence by the City of London for the manufacture of window glass. The successful introduction of Lorrain craftsmen to make glass in the Weald of Kent led to an expansion of the industry into areas such as Hampshire, Gloucestershire, Staffordshire and, ultimately, into Lancashire and Yorkshire. The technology that lay behind this influx of immigrant craftsmen has been revealed in a number of excavations of glass-working sites, notably at Abbots Bromley (Staffordshire) and also at Rosedale (Yorkshire).[34]

Glass-making is only one of the industries where archaeology can demonstrate the physical reality behind the economic and social development that took place in the sixteenth and seventeenth centuries. While some industries expanded by the adoption of innovative techniques, others, like the leather-working industry, functioned in the same manner as they had in the Middle Ages. Some innovations, such as those introduced like the textile industries (known as the 'New Draperies') by immigrants from the Low Countries, have left few traces in the archaeological record; others, like the introduction of the blast furnace, can be illustrated archaeologically – for example, at Chingley (Kent) (see p. 169). These excavations of the industrial production sites of the sixteenth century give us an insight into the nature and development of the production of goods that led to the increasing division of labour, and so to an increasingly capitalist society. Post-medieval archaeology, by exploring the relationship between the means of production and the demands of fashion in satisfying the needs of housing, food and clothing, can expand our comprehension of the past.

The wide range of examples given above – mills, towns, castles, churches and palaces – has, it is hoped, shown how it is necessary for archaeology to be related to all the sources of history, and how work carried out in the past forty years has demonstrated that even in a well-documented period the excavation and study of physical remains have a vital role to play in developing our understanding of the past. Although we see the past from the viewpoint of today, we can, by the study of both documents and physical remains, begin to understand, not only what happened, but also how our predecessors saw themselves.

NOTES

1   Lieut.-Gen. Pitt-Rivers, *King John's House, Tollard Royal, Wilts.* (1890), p.13

2   T.D. Kendrick and C.F.C. Hawkes, *Archaeology in England and Wales 1914–1931* (1932)

3   M. Biddle, 'The deserted medieval village of Seacourt, Berkshire', *Oxoniensia*, XXVI–XXVII (1961–2), pp.70–201; R.L.S. Bruce-Mitford, 'The Archaeology of the Site of the Bodleian Extension in Broad St., Oxford', *Oxoniensia*, IV (1939), pp.89–146

4   J.G. Hurst and J. Golson, 'Excavation at St Benedict's Gates, Norwich 1951 and 1953', *Norfolk Archaeology*, XXXI, pt 1 (1955), pp.1–112

5   *Medieval Archaeology*, II (1958), pp.158–68

6   R.L.S. Bruce-Mitford, 'Medieval Archaeology', *Archaeological News Letter*, No. 6 (October 1948), pp. 1–4

7   E.M. Jope, 'Regional cultures of medieval Britain', in I.L. Foster and L. Alcock (eds), *Culture and Environment, Studies presented to Sir Cyril Fox* (1968)

8   M. Bloch, *French Rural History* (1966) and *Feudal Society* (1962)

9   L. White, *Medieval Technology and Social Change* (1962). See also the review by M.W. Thompson, *Medieval Archaeology*, VIII (1964), pp. 314–15

10 R.J. Zeepfat, 'Post Mills and Archaeology', *Current Archaeology*, 71 (1971), pp. 375–7

11 P. Rahtz, 'Medieval Milling', in D.W. Crossley (ed.) *Medieval Industry CBA Research Report*, 40 (1981), pp. 1–15

12 E.M. Carus Wilson, 'An industrial revolution of the 13th century', *Economic History Review*, II (1941), pp. 39–60

13 L.F. Salzmann, *Medieval Industry* (1927)

14 D.W. Crossley (ed.), *Medieval Industry CBA Research Report*, 40 (1981)

15 E.S. Wood, 'A medieval glass house at Blundens Wood, Hambledon, Surrey', *Surrey Arch. Collections*, 62 (1965), pp. 54–79

16 A.G. Vince, 'The medieval and post-medieval ceramic industry of the Malvern region: the study of its wares and its distribution' in D.P.S. Peacock (ed.), *Pottery and Early Commerce* (1977), pp. 257–305

17 S. Moorhouse, 'Documentary evidence and its potential for understanding the inland movement of medieval pottery', *Medieval Ceramics*, 7 (1983), pp. 45–88

18 E.M. Jope, 'Excavations in the City of Norwich, 1948', *Norfolk Archaeology*, XXX (1952), pp. 287–322

19 The plan for Oxford is published by E.M. Jope, 'Saxon Oxford and its region', in D.B. Harden (ed.) *Dark Age Britain* (1956), pp. 234–58

20 M. Biddle 'Archaeology and the History of British Towns', *Antiquity*, 42 (1968), pp. 109–16

21 For Oxford see H.E. Salter *Survey of Oxford* (1960 and 1969) and for Canterbury see William Urry *Canterbury under the Angevin Kings* (1967)

22 F. Barlow, M. Biddle, O. van Feilitzen and D.J. Keene, *Winchester in the Early Middle Ages: an edition and discussion of the Winton Domesday* (1980); and also for later medieval Winchester see D. Keene *Survey of Medieval Winchester* (1985)

23 E.M. Jope and W.A. Pantin, 'The Clarendon Hotel, Oxford', *Oxoniensia* XXIII (1958), pp. 1–129

24 For King's Lynn see H. Clarke and A. Carter *Excavations in King's Lynn 1963–70* (1977)

25 M.W. Beresford, *New Towns of the Middle Ages* (1967)

26 A.D. Saunders, 'Five Castle Excavations', *Archaeological Journal*, 134 (1977), p. 5

27 L. Butler, 'Houses of the mendicant orders in Britain: recent archaeological work', in P.V. Addyman and V.E. Black (eds.), *Archaeological Papers from York presented to M.W. Barley* (1984), pp. 124–36

28 H.G. Ramm, 'The tombs of Archbishop Walter de Gray and Geoffrey Ludham', in *Archaeologia*, CIII (1971)

29 Jean D. Dawes and J.R. Magilton, *The cemetery of St. Helen on the Walls Aldvark* (1980)

30 Editorial in *Post-Medieval Archaeology* I (1967), p. 2

31 G.L. Good and C.J. Tabraham, 'Excavations at Threave Castle, Galloway 1974–8', *Medieval Archaeology*, XXV (1981), pp. 90–140

32 B.H. St John O'Neil, *Castles and Cannon* (1960), p. 43

33 For Camber see H.M. Colvin (ed.), *History of the King's Works*, IV: 1485–1660 (1982), pp. 415–47

34 D. Crossley, 'Glassmaking at Bagots Park, Staffordshire, in the 16th century', *Post Medieval Archaeology*, I (1967), pp. 44–83; D.W. Crossley and A. Aberg, 'Sixteenth century glass making in Yorkshire: excavations at furnaces at Hutton and Rosedale, North Riding, 1968–71', *Post Medieval Archaeology*, VI (1972), pp. 107–59

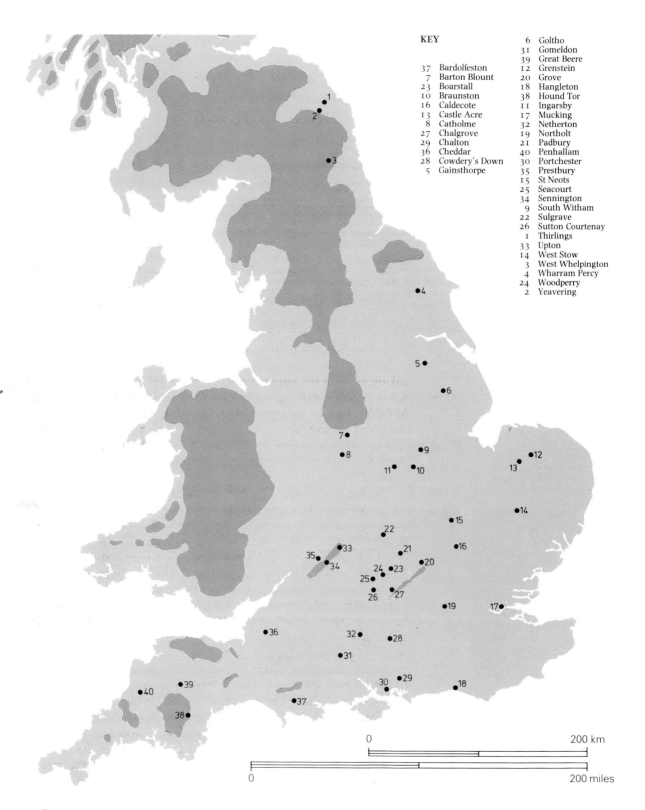

KEY

37	Bardolfeston	6	Goltho
7	Barton Blount	31	Gomeldon
23	Boarstall	39	Great Beere
10	Braunston	12	Grenstein
16	Caldecote	20	Grove
13	Castle Acre	18	Hangleton
8	Catholme	38	Hound Tor
27	Chalgrove	11	Ingarsby
29	Chalton	17	Mucking
36	Cheddar	32	Netherton
28	Cowdery's Down	19	Northolt
5	Gainsthorpe	21	Padbury
		40	Penhallam
		30	Portchester
		35	Prestbury
		15	St Neots
		25	Seacourt
		34	Sennington
		9	South Witham
		22	Sulgrave
		26	Sutton Courtenay
		1	Thirlings
		33	Upton
		14	West Stow
		3	West Whelpington
		4	Wharram Percy
		24	Woodperry
		2	Yeavering

0   200 km

0   200 miles

5 The Medieval Countryside

Early Work

108   Map showing the location of sites mentioned in the text.

The changing pattern of medieval rural settlement has many manifestations, but the best known is undoubtedly the deserted medieval village. Many hundreds of English villages were deserted in the closing years of the Middle Ages: their study in the last forty years has been one of the main sources of the new ideas on the origins and development of rural settlement as a whole. So it is interesting to commence by looking back and considering briefly the history of the study of deserted medieval villages: it is a story of waxing and waning scholarly interest, of false dawns and fresh insights.

Early historians recorded the major economic changes which were taking place in the fifteenth century which led to these desertions: a major retreat from marginal land followed the halving of the population in the fourteenth-century plagues. Meanwhile, the rising wool industry made it more profitable for landowners to put whole parishes down to grass for sheep rearing: such an enterprise could be run from a single farm, rather than several where a number of families would cultivate the land for crops.

John Rous at the end of the fifteenth century recorded desertions, particularly in Warwickshire, and produced the first list of deserted medieval villages for a whole county. Antiquarians in the sixteenth–eighteenth centuries did not simply study documents: they carried out fieldwork, observed and published details of changes to standing buildings. They also noted foundations and earthworks of ruined buildings. Camden, in the sixteenth century, and Stukeley in the eighteenth, published details of crop marks caused by the variation in the growth of crops over buried features. From the sixteenth century the drawing-up by landowners of large-scale estate plans provides us with a detailed record of some contemporary village layouts. Not only do these plans enable subsequent changes to be examined by comparison with present-day maps, but they also often provide a record of land use patterns that were already defunct. On a broader basis the development of smaller-scale county maps in the seventeenth century enabled the wider landscape to be recorded, for example the parks. It was Dugdale, in his *Antiquities of Warwickshire* in 1656, who produced the first county distribution map of deserted medieval villages, by showing the sites of depopulated places, each marked on the map by a symbol in the form of a diamond. Most antiquarian accounts were, however, descriptive, and the first plan of the earthworks of a deserted medieval village – Dalton (Lancashire) – was not made until 1774.

It was only in the middle of the nineteenth century, with the great upsurge of archaeology, triggered partly by the many discoveries made during the construction of the railways, that national and county archaeological societies were formed. Members of these, besides taking part in excursions to standing medieval buildings, carried out the first medieval rural fieldwork and excavations. Oxfordshire took the lead in this with the work of Stephen Stone, who excavated the first Anglo-Saxon huts, some of which were found by quarrying and others observed as crop marks in the 1850s. In the 1840s John Wilson, at Oxford University, had excavated a medieval village for the first time, at Woodperry (Oxfordshire). He recorded medieval foundations and described and illustrated pottery and small finds. The early volumes of the *Archaeological Journal* in the third quarter of the nineteenth century were full of records of pottery, small finds and other items illustrating daily life found on similar excavations. In the early 1850s surveyors from the Ordnance Survey in some areas, especially Yorkshire, were, as a matter of course, making plans of earthworks, including those of deserted medieval villages. All seemed, therefore, set fair for the development of the study and excavation of medieval rural sites. But interests seemed to change. While prehistorians and Romanists went on to excavate a wide range of sites in the late nineteenth and early twentieth centuries, medievalists diverted their work from the study of how ordinary people lived to concentrate on the study of churches, monasteries and major secular buildings. While Pitt-Rivers characteristically included medieval sites in his pioneer excavations, these were not village sites, and in the seventy-five years before the Second World War there was but a handful of excavations of medieval peasant houses, and these seemed to arouse little interest. The initiation of the *Victoria County History* at the close of the nineteenth century, together with the surveys of Hadrian Allcroft in his *Earthwork of England* in 1908, led to the recording of some deserted medieval village earthworks. Crawford's important early work in aerial photography included the publication in 1924 of the first aerial photograph of a deserted medieval village, that of Gainsthorpe in Lincolnshire (109). None of this, however, led to any significant results at a time when historians were sitting in their libraries, either ignoring or casting doubt on the existence of deserted medieval villages.

It was in the 1930s that the situation was changed dramatically: interestingly enough the leaders were a number of young graduates from Oxford, which had led the abortive start eighty years before. The new initiative had been started in the 1920s in Oxford, by E.T. Leeds, who was watching and recording the Anglo-Saxon settlement at Sutton Courtenay (Oxfordshire). In the late 1930s, Martyn Jope excavated a medieval peasant house at Great Beere (Devon) and Rupert Bruce-Mitford started excavations on the deserted medieval village of Seacourt

109 Vertical aerial photograph showing the earthworks of a stone-built deserted medieval village at Gainsthorpe (Lincolnshire). Rectangular enclosures are visible with a network of roads between. In each enclosure the rectangular earthworks cover the foundations of peasant houses. In many cases not only may doorways be seen but also partitions between rooms. Compare with 130.

(Oxfordshire), just west of Oxford. Their interests were wider than peasant houses, as Bruce-Mitford also initiated urban excavation in Oxford, while Jope was studying medieval pottery following the work of Gerald Dunning in the earlier 1930s. The work of another Oxford graduate, John Ward Perkins, on small finds, resulted in the London Museum *Medieval Catalogue* published in 1940. Meanwhile, amateur archaeologists in the 1920s and 1930s had continued the earlier antiquarian tradition of studying total landscapes. Their comprehensive studies, extending from prehistoric times to modern folklife, included the collection of medieval artefacts from many a ploughed field. Three of the most notable of these amateurs were Ethel Rudkin in Lincolnshire, Helen O'Neil in Gloucestershire – who started excavations at the medieval village of Sennington and the manor of Prestbury – and Tony Brewster, who not only carried out extensive fieldwork in Yorkshire, but also took aerial photographs and carried out some of the earliest experimental archaeology on pottery production. Again, everything seemed ready, in 1939, for a renaissance in medieval archaeology, extending the range of studies from high-status buildings to the life of the medieval peasant. However, the Second World War intervened and put back work for a further ten years.

In the same way that medieval rural settlement was low in priority or interest on any archaeological programme during the first half of the twentieth century, medieval historians, although working on manorial documents, were looking at events too much from the national point of view and not taking account of local conditions; Tawney's advice that 'history needs not more books but more boots' was not heeded. As long ago as 1883 Seebohm had published a plan of the constituent parts of the open field system at Hitchin (Hertfordshire), while Loggan's seventeenth-century views of the unenclosed fields of Cambridge must have been on many college walls. Others reproduced early maps, but even the Orwins in their pioneer study, *The Open Fields* (1938), reproducing the 1635 map of Laxton (Nottinghamshire) seem never to have considered looking on the ground for the archaeological evidence of the open fields they wrote about. Even Tawney's own exhortation did not lead him to carry out archaeological fieldwork, but rather to tramp the Cotswolds looking at the surviving buildings in wool-market towns and cloth-making villages. It is baffling how the well-known historical and archaeological facts of changing medieval rural settlement, which were taken for granted in the seventeenth and eighteenth centuries, were ignored by Victorian and later historians, who remained isolated in their libraries for nearly a hundred years. As late as 1949 Clapham, in his *Concise Economic History of Great Britain*, could state that 'deserted villages are singularly rare in England'. Both archaeologists and historians seem to have been equally blinkered in their outlook and their appreciation of these earthworks, which demonstrate the changing pattern of British medieval rural settlement and which must be more extensive than those of any other period.

During the Second World War medieval rural settlement research was stirring on both the historical and archaeological fronts. Two young economic historians, William Hoskins and Maurice Beresford, were at the same time taking history out into the field and trying to establish the nature of the medieval landscape by comparing maps and documents with the evidence on the ground. The release of the hundreds of thousands of vertical aerial photographs taken immediately after the War enabled whole landscapes to be appreciated in a way that was not at first possible for Hoskins and Beresford, walking over the ground and painfully building up the picture field by field on foot. A series of articles by both authors during the 1940s and early 1950s culminated in Beresford's *Lost Villages of England* (1954) and *History on the Ground* (1957), and Hoskins's *Making of the English Landscape* (1955); these set off the expansion of local landscape history research which has made so much impact on the study of medieval rural settlement over the last forty years.

On the archaeological side it was from Cambridge that the main impetus came in the 1940s. Here, M.M. Postan, together with Eileen

Power and John Saltmarsh, had been the main influences in introducing Beresford to landscape studies in the early 1940s. In the 1930s the German archaeologist Gerhard Bersu introduced the technique of open area excavation to Britain with his prehistoric excavation at Little Woodbury (see p. 54). Most of the earlier work had been based on the excavation of square boxes with baulks between them, as developed by Mortimer Wheeler for substantial Roman and other structures. While he was interned in the Isle of Man during the War, Bersu excavated a complex Viking settlement at Vowlam, which showed how scanty were the remains that medieval structures might leave in the soil, as a consequence of their timber rather than stone construction. Bersu's technique was to excavate the whole site as a single area. Axel Steensberg in Denmark during the 1940s, also employed open area excavation to elucidate such slight traces.

In 1948 Postan called a meeting of historians and archaeologists to discuss the possibilities of excavating medieval peasant houses: the aim was to find out more about how the medieval peasant lived and if possible obtain evidence for Postan's theory of the expansion and contraction of settlement in the medieval period. At this time the early archaeological work of the Oxford graduates in the 1930s was not being followed up and some very unsatisfactory work was in progress. From the historical side, both Hoskins and Beresford attempted trial trenches on deserted village sites, but were deterred by the fact that they were dealing with Midland clay sites: as there had been no stone available for building, these houses had not had stone walls and so there were few structures to see and the results were very disappointing. At the same time archaeologists were applying the Wheeler box or trench system on sites where, even if there were stone foundations, the slight traces could not be interpreted from such techniques. At Cambridge there had been no tradition of medieval archaeology, so the invitation of Steensberg to Postan's 1948 seminar was crucial in suggesting a programme which should include open area excavation of medieval rural sites.

In 1951, Jack Golson, who had been one of Postan's history students, began work on the deserted villages of Lincolnshire. John Hurst, also a Cambridge graduate, studied medieval pottery in East Anglia. In 1952 they made contact with Beresford, who had started trial excavations at Wharram Percy (Yorkshire). In view of the promising results, the Deserted Medieval Village Research Group was founded there in August 1952, with the aim of investigating medieval rural settlement in a multidisciplinary way. An excavation started in 1953 on one of the peasant house sites at Wharram Percy led to the main research project of the Group, this is still in progress today and is described below. At the same time the Deserted Medieval Village Research Group encouraged people from different academic disciplines to work together on common problems all over Britain. At Wharram Percy the project has developed over the last thirty years from the investigation of a single medieval peasant house to the thorough study of two parishes, comprising six townships, in an attempt to build up the complete landscape history of the area. This now absorbs the interests of over one hundred specialists in many fields. It is through this type of research, in which not only are settlement patterns examined from different points of view but the various specialists work together as a team rather than as individuals, that the study of medieval rural settlement has made such large strides in the last forty years.

Main developments of the last forty years

The main factors which have led to fundamental changes in our ideas as to how ordinary medieval people lived are threefold: the vast increase in fieldwork both on the ground and from the air, the more sophisticated and larger-scale open area excavations, and the bringing to bear of modern scientific techniques. Similar work on the prehistoric and Roman periods has fundamentally changed our whole conception of the background to the medieval period, especially in the Anglo-Saxon centuries before the Norman Conquest. Scientific advances have had a major impact on our knowledge of the medieval period. Results from new methods of dating have extended our knowledge of settlement and woodland clearance in Britain back several thousand years before the medieval period and make it impossible to envisage the early Anglo-Saxon settlers battling their way through, and clearing, the virgin forests which fifty years ago were thought to have covered most of Saxon Britain.

As fieldwork on the ground has got under way all over the country, it has demonstrated most remarkably that prehistoric and Roman settlement was not only ten times more extensive than previously thought, but that it extended over the supposedly intractable claylands, as well as the well-drained gravels and chalk areas. At the same time the continually expanding use of aerial photography has shown that large areas of Britain are not only thickly sown with archaeological sites, but are in fact underlain by whole archaeological landscapes, so that most of Britain is one great palimpsest, recording several thousand years of intensive exploitation of the environment. Although the woodland clearance has not been continuous and there were many advances and retreats, just as in the medieval period itself, the effect was that at the peak of the Roman occupation there was probably as much land farmed as in the eighteenth century, while the population was much larger than at any point in medieval times. So it is from this baseline that medieval rural settlement should be viewed.

Our advances in knowledge have not been due simply to increased interest, but are also the result of fundamental economic changes in our society, of the same type which led to the changes in settlement patterns in the medieval period. Many medieval sites, after they were deserted, were put down to grass, so their earthworks remained undamaged during the sixteenth- and seventeenth-century period of intensive sheep farming. With the introduction of improved farming techniques in the late eighteenth century, there was a major return to arable, which, despite various setbacks in the late Victorian period, led to the destruction of many sites. But the vast increase of ploughing after the Second World War, particularly intensified in the 1950s and 1960s, with the introduction of the bulldozer which could level a site in a few hours, led to the destruction of whole landscapes; with threats from other forms of development, that acted as a catalyst to both fieldwork and excavation. It is most unfortunate that so much has been destroyed, but there is little doubt that without this opportunity to investigate large areas which have had a long period of occupation and have hitherto been concealed beneath the grass-grown earthworks of the later medieval period, settlement studies would not have advanced so far.

This is particularly true of excavation. While fieldwork is a fairly simple and cheap operation, excavation is a costly business. Research funds have always been limited in Britain, and if the results of excavation on unthreatened sites only were available, we would know very little on a national basis about medieval rural settlement. The government response to this damage to the archaeological heritage resulted in an increasing number of rescue excavations in the 1950s and 1960s, paid for by the then Ministry of Works. While much earlier excavation was haphazard, or depended on the whim of individual archaeologists in certain parts of the country only, the universal nature of the threats of the last forty years has enabled a programme of excavation to take place on selected sites, supplemented all over the country, especially in the 1960s, by a limited number of research excavations. In the early 1970s regular archaeological units were established in most parts of the country to carry out rescue excavations. The trend now is towards fewer but larger-scale excavations, as, despite the continuing threats from agriculture, building developments, mineral operations and new roads, the present financial situation precludes any major expansion of work. Many of the major rural excavation projects of the 1980s have, however, been helped by Manpower Services Commission schemes, which provide the labour for excavations, while the core finance is provided by English Heritage, the successor of the Ministry of Works, the Ministry of Public Buildings and Works, and the Department of the Environment.

This interest and activity have led to a large amount of fieldwork and many hundreds of excavations, which have resulted in medieval rural settlement being looked at in a way quite different from that usual before the Second World War. Medieval archaeology, such as it was, was then still almost entirely concerned with the activities of the upper classes. Work was concentrated on the architecture of churches, monastic sites, castles and manor houses. Excavation was almost entirely concerned with the elucidation of these sites, and more specifically with the main structures of the living quarters of manor houses and monastic cloisters. Little attention was paid to the attached agricultural buildings which formed the economic unit, much less to their place in the wider village economy. Villages and peasant houses were usually thought of as being represented by pretty pictures of Cotswold or Northamptonshire stone houses or the timber-built villages of south-east England. In the few cases where village layout was considered, both historians and geographers had compared present-day plans with earlier maps and found the plans and layouts to be the same as they were in the sixteenth century. Although there was no evidence, as there were no earlier plans or extensive excavation of villages, this idea of the medieval village was projected backwards in time, and so it was thought that many villages had been laid out to the plan that we now see by Anglo-Saxon settlers, who expanded existing settlements and added new ones as their population grew, clearing new areas out of the extensive woodland and wastes. This picture was encouraged by historians, who often wrote about an ideal medieval village of the thirteenth century based on evidence from the Midlands. Geographers wrote about the Saxon origins of green villages, and economic historians thought that they could reconstruct the medieval landscape as though it was a simple developing sequence.

The most fundamental result of the last forty years' work on medieval rural settlement has been to show that the story of its development is not a straightforward one; still less has the picture been static since early medieval times. The whole situation is very complex, and a great deal still has to be worked out in detail. In the first place, few, if any, medieval settlements were built on virgin land which had not previously been cultivated, though the cultivation might have been organised from different centres in prehistoric and Roman times. From the evidence of earlier settlements under so-called primary medieval woodland it is clear that many of the later forests had regenerated over previously occupied land or were actually the result of reafforestation. With the collapse of Roman administration in Britain in the fifth century, and a considerable drop in population, much land must have gone out of cultivation and reverted to woodland and scrub: this would have been relatively easy to recolonise as the population increased throughout the Saxon period.

Excavation and fieldwork evidence suggests that these early Anglo-Saxon settlements were not nucleated villages, that is, with their houses set close together, but largely comprised scattered farms and small hamlets, very much continuing the pattern of prehistoric and Roman settlement. Nearly all such early Anglo-Saxon settlements which have been investigated seem to have been abandoned in the middle Saxon period, often in the eighth and ninth century. This appears to have been a major period of change, when small settlements first became nucleated into larger villages, which may then have acquired a church with a burial ground and regular common fields. Whether these nucleated villages represent the expansion of certain of the earlier small hamlets, or whether they were originally larger centres which now attracted the population of the surrounding farms and hamlets through seigneurial control or initiative or through the agreement of the peasant community, is a hard question to follow up. It is difficult to carry out excavations in surviving villages, where so much of the ground is covered by buildings or where the archaeological evidence has been destroyed by intensive human activity over many hundreds of years. There is evidence that nucleation was a process which continued from late Saxon times into the medieval period and that no particular time can be laid down for these fundamental changes in medieval settlement patterns. There are also many areas of England, for example, the west and in East Anglia, where scattered settlements survive and nucleation never occurred.

Whatever their origin, many of these newly created villages were planned in a regular pattern, while others grew from several centres which merged to form haphazard plans. Another major discovery to result from work during the last forty years is that once these villages were formed they by no means remained static. This might be expected in very general terms, in view of the increasing population and prosperity of the twelfth and thirteenth centuries, followed by the vast reduction in population after the fourteenth-century plagues which led to considerable contraction of settlement. This can best be demonstrated by the excavation of many of the villages which were deserted for various reasons during the post-Conquest period. While some villages remain fixed in their layouts, with the enclosures retaining the same land use, others show changes of land use within individual enclosures (124) or more fundamental changes in layout of the whole village (110).

Moreover, excavations have shown that almost all Anglo-Saxon peasant houses were built of timber, or some other insubstantial material, even when the settlement was in a stone area. The change to stone-

110 Plan of the surviving earthworks of the deserted medieval village at Bardolfeston (Dorset), showing an early layout of rectangular enclosures forming an L-shaped plan (examples marked A). No house sites are visible, as they are likely to have been built of timber, which has decayed, leaving no traces above ground. This early plan is overlaid by a late medieval regular street village laid right across the earlier enclosures, comprising a straight street (stippled) with, on each side, the rectangular earthworks covering the stone foundations of peasant houses (examples marked B). After Royal Commission on Historical Monuments (England)

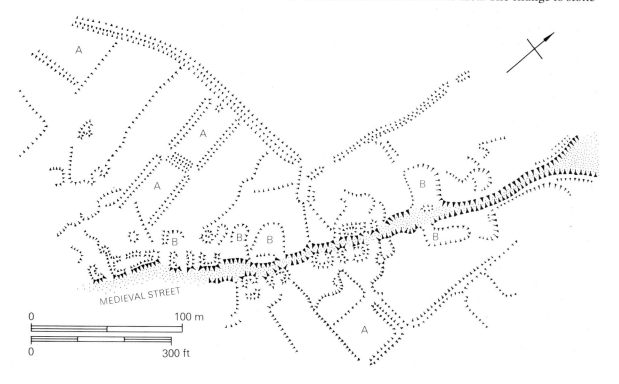

MEDIEVAL STREET

0   100 m

0   300 ft

built peasant houses took place only in the twelfth and thirteenth centuries and then only where stone was readily available. In clay and other areas peasant houses continued to be built of timber or earth mixed with straw. These houses seem often to have been of flimsy construction, and they had to be rebuilt frequently. It is for this reason that no medieval peasant houses survive today. Most, 'medieval cottages' are in fact of the sixteenth century or later; the only exceptions were the more substantial houses of yeomen farmers. When medieval peasant houses were rebuilt, they were often erected on quite a different site, or on a new alignment overlapping with the earlier building. The reasons for these changes are still obscure. Documentary evidence suggests that the lord often provided building materials and that the peasant had some expectation of his descendants retaining the same property. At the same time there must have been building skills available in most villages. Nevertheless, the archaeological evidence suggests generally that the medieval peasant had no incentive to construct a house to last for several generations, and built very much in a rough do-it-yourself manner.

The main impact of post-War excavation and fieldwork, therefore, has been to suggest that the story of medieval rural settlement is much more complex than had ever been imagined from the documentary evidence, thus demonstrating how much archaeology has to add to the general historical picture. It is, in fact, strange that the medieval village should have been considered as static, for there has always been change. This had long been appreciated for the prehistoric and Roman periods, where the same expansion, contraction and general changes occur. During the last five hundred years that tendency has continued, with many alterations of plan or position of villages, reflecting perhaps a new road, an eighteenth-century park, or the Industrial Revolution. Many farms were scattered again over parishes as a result of the Enclosure Movement, while in the present century there has been much infilling and replanning of villages, as well as decay. The changes apparent in the record of medieval rural settlement should therefore not be looked upon as anything special, but as part of the general pattern of change which has been continuous during the last five thousand years of human settlement in Britain.

Saxon Settlements

The general picture, as conceived before the Second World War, was that the typical Saxon village comprised a series of flimsy huts, with the rectangular floor sunk below ground level and covered by a simple tent-like thatched roof on a ridge-pole. Thirty-three such features were found by Leeds in his excavations during gravel-working at Sutton Courtenay (Oxfordshire) between 1921 and 1937. A limited number of excavations in other parts of the country also frequently produced isolated sunken huts. Sutton Courtenay was dated to the early Saxon period, but as similar huts were found by Fred Tebbut in a late Saxon context at St Neots (Cambridgeshire), it seemed natural to assume that this was the typical Saxon peasant house from the end of Roman Britain to the Norman Conquest. Finds from these structures included rough handmade Saxon pottery and a large number of circular loom weights, from which it was deduced that weaving was a major preoccupation of the Saxon peasant.

After the Second World War there was a fundamental change in views, sparked off by the open area excavations on the Continent. These clearly demonstrated that in addition to huts partly dug into the ground, there were also much larger timber-built structures which were the living quarters, while the associated sunken huts were mainly used for working purposes, often weaving. It was Ralegh Radford who set the stage for the transfer of this idea to Britain, drawing attention in 1957 to the Continental evidence and suggesting that sites like Sutton Courtenay also had major timber buildings between the sunken huts. A number of excavations took place during the 1960s which, by opening up large areas, showed that a typical Saxon settlement site in England indeed comprised substantial timber buildings at ground level, as well as sunken huts. Earlier work had concentrated on the obvious sunken huts, with no attempt to dig areas around them to put them in context. At some sites conditions were hardly conducive to identifying postholes, which represent the only surviving remains in the ground of timber buildings. At Sutton Courtenay, for example, Leeds watched while the gravel was being extracted and so was only able to recognise larger features by the dark stains they left in the soil.

The picture has now been considerably filled out, with a series of large and small excavations in many parts of the country not only demonstrating the universal presence of substantial timber buildings on every site, with or without sunken huts, but producing a hierarchy of sites from royal palaces through aristocratic residences to peasant farms, hamlets and villages. In the 1950s the classic site was a Northumbrian royal palace of the seventh century at Yeavering, where different coloured marks in the soil, forming the outlines of a series of rectangular superimposed buildings, were recorded from the air in an impressive series of photographs. When the topsoil was taken off, the complex marks left by the decayed timber structures were immediately apparent (111). A painstaking open area excavation followed, the different colours and textures of the soils enabling the evidence to be interpreted as a very complex sequence of halls and other major timber buildings, which were of a substantial character and reflected well the poetic descriptions of a Saxon hall found in *Beowulf*.

In the 1960s a late Saxon palace was excavated in Wessex at Cheddar (Somerset). This showed a long sequence of royal buildings from the ninth century through to the post-Conquest period. The reconstructions (112) show how Cheddar might have looked in the ninth century and in the second period in the tenth and eleventh centuries. In each period the site was dominated by a large hall with a series of smaller associated buldings. At Yeavering the halls were rebuilt in different positions on the same general alignment, but at

111 Excavation in progress at the seventh-century royal palace of the kings of Northumbria at Yeavering (Northumberland). After the removal of the shallow topsoil, dark marks appeared in the ground; these were caused by the later filling of trenches and holes dug for the timber uprights and walls of the main hall. The large number of these features represent constant rebuilding as the timber uprights decayed, and demonstrate the complexity of interpreting archaeological features to draw reconstructions such as 112 and 113. Compare with 114.

Cheddar the ninth- and tenth-century halls were not only built in different positions, but also on quite different alignments, a feature that was common throughout the medieval period whether the building was a palace, manor house or peasant house. During the last twenty years other similar Saxon palace sites have been observed by aerial photography in Northumbria, Mercia and Wessex, and some of them partially excavated to confirm their date. A picture has now been built up of a large number of these major Saxon royal sites dotted about the country. At this time there was no fixed royal centre: the kings progressed round their territories, spending some time at each residence attending to royal business and, more particularly, living off the land, as this was more economical than having produce transported to a single place.

At the same time as these major royal sites were being identified, a large number of sites of peasant status were located and excavated, but for a long time intermediate settlements of aristocratic status were not found. This lacuna was filled in the 1970s with the excavation of the manor site of Goltho (Lincolnshire). Underneath the early medieval hall was found an impressive sequence of buildings which were clearly of high status and which must have been the centre from which the estate was run in the Saxon period. The reconstructions (113) show the site as

112 (*Right*) Reconstructions of the royal palace of the kings of Wessex at Cheddar (Somerset).

Above In the ninth century, at the time of King Alfred, there was a long timber-built hall, with two smaller domestic buildings, set in an enclosure with a light fence on two sides and ditch on the left for draining away rain water.

Below In the tenth century the palace was completely rearranged, with a new timber-built hall in a different position at right angles to the old hall. A chapel was built across the site of the hall. The tripartite building in the foreground has been interpreted as a fowl house. The enclosure was still not defended but was defined by a simple fence and drainage ditch as before, but with a possible flagpole by the entrance. The palace was set by itself at the foot of the Mendips in good hunting country.

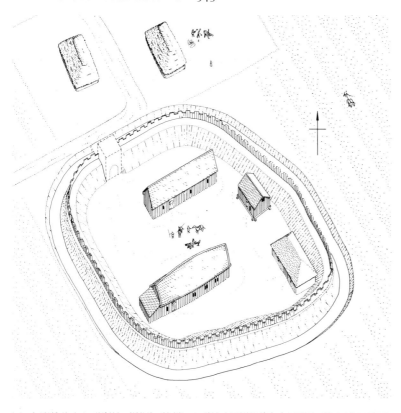

113 Reconstructions of the aristocratic complex at Goltho (Lincolnshire). After G.M.T. Beresford (Medieval Village Research Group)

Top In the ninth century there was a timber-built hall (foreground) with two associated buildings to the right; behind was a large workshop for weaving. Unlike Cheddar (112), the enclosure was defended by an earth rampart with a timber palisade. In the foreground the land was cultivated, behind were the associated peasant houses of the village.

Bottom In the late eleventh century the site was replanned as a motte-and-bailey castle with a defended gate, a tower on a mound (motte) and a hall in the enclosure (bailey).

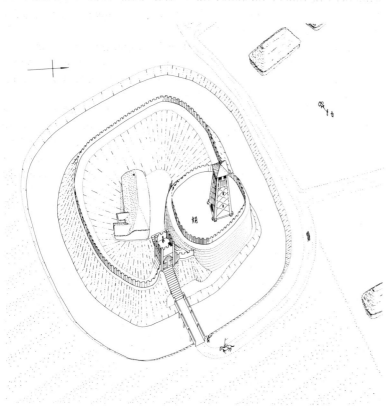

it may have looked in the ninth century and in the late eleventh century. The ninth-century buildings comprised a solidly built hall with close-set vertical timbers, together with a series of associated buildings. What was surprising and unusual was to find that these were not only set in an enclosure but that the enclosure was apparently defended. This was presumably a precaution necessitated by the Viking invasions in the east of England: there was no attempt by Alfred to defend his palace of similar date at Cheddar.

In the eleventh century Goltho developed into a typical small motte-and-bailey castle, comprising a substantial banked enclosure, a motte with a watch tower, and a separate hall inside the enclosure. The large entrance gateway was a major feature. It is interesting to compare eleventh-century Goltho with the contemporary Castle Acre (Norfolk), where there was a partly defended country house (98); the more troubled times of the twelfth century, however, led to the building of a substantial castle at Castle Acre. The character of many of these sites, therefore, does not reflect any standard country-wide chronological sequences of different types of building structure and layout, but is rather the effect of local conditions at the time. In other parts of the country Saxon aristocratic residences have proved elusive, and there are only a very few examples so far discovered, for example, at Portchester (Hampshire), and Sulgrave (Northamptonshire) where in addition to sequences of timber buildings there were some stone structures. In general, however, domestic stone buildings were unusual, stone usually being reserved for some churches.

The numerous Anglo-Saxon sunken huts and timber buildings on sites of peasant status which have now been excavated are more usually chance discoveries made during development works or found as a later phase on a prehistoric site. A planned programme of excavation of such sites is scarcely possible in view of the scant traces which they have left behind above ground: they had none of the ditches and banks whose earthworks led to the discovery of many deserted medieval village sites. In addition, as many of them were abandoned and the sites later cultivated, not only have they left no visible traces, but the archaeological evidence is largely destroyed. Floors are rarely present, and only the postholes and other major features which have been dug into the natural subsoil have survived.

The timber-built Saxon peasant houses were constructed by digging either individual holes for rows of single posts or a trench, which might have spaced posts or close-set timbers (114). A wide range of these building techniques was employed – but unless the conditions are very good – as at Yeavering and Cowdery's Down (Hampshire) – the evidence is often too slight to decide conclusively whether the walls were built of timber or whether wattle-and-daub infill was used between the uprights. It is therefore hard enough to reconstruct the walls of a building, and almost impossible to say what the roof was like. Anglo-Saxon peasant house plans are fairly simple, and there is often little evidence for the use of the various rooms, or even buildings, in view of the fact that few

114   The seventh-century settlement at Chalton (Hampshire). The photograph shows the holes in the ground made by the timber structures, after the clearance of the dark soil (compare 111). The rectangular buildings are clearly visible, showing two different building techniques: rows of individual holes for upright posts and trenches in which rows of posts were put.

floors or other features survive. There is no evidence for animals and people living under the same roof, as in the Saxon homelands on the Continent, so it has been suggested that the peasant houses of the Saxon period may owe more to the native Romano-British tradition than to an introduced type.

Many hundreds of sunken huts have now been excavated, but archaeological opinion is still divided as to whether they should be reconstructed as flimsy tent-like structures, in which people worked on the sunken floors, or whether the sunken areas were perhaps floored over, leaving an air or storage space below, and with a fairly substantial structure on top. The sunken floor may be a very deceptive guide to the size and status of the building, as side walls may have been placed on horizontal beams on the ground surface, leaving no archaeological trace; on these beams a substantial timber-frame could have been constructed, and this may have covered a larger area than the sunken floor itself. This brings to the fore the limitations of archaeological interpretation. It is very easy to reconstruct sunken huts in a number of different ways. There is no doubt, from the presence on a few sites of a hearth at an upper level which then collapsed into the sunken part of the hut, that some sunken huts were clearly floored over. In other cases the fill of the sunken area suggests that the bottom was not used; the difficulty of retaining the sides, especially on sandy sites, and the lack of evidence for trampled floors, support this interpretation. On the other hand, some sunken huts seem to have had steps down or signs that they were lived in. It is, therefore, likely that the hole dug in the ground

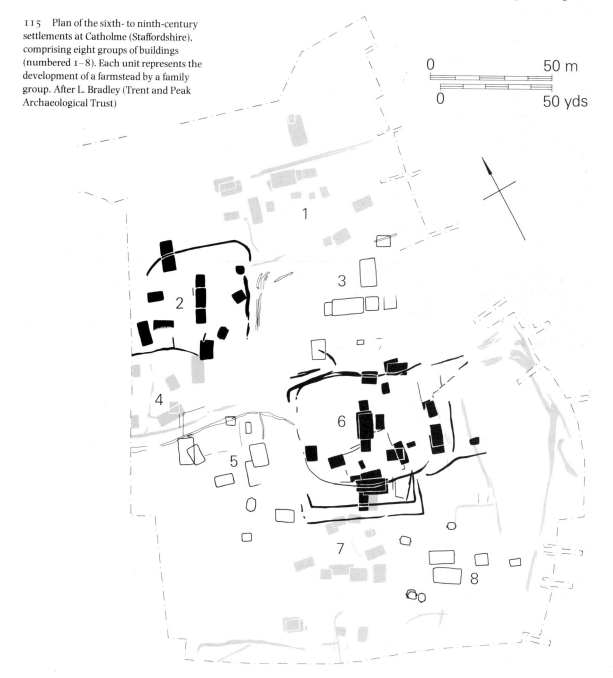

115   Plan of the sixth- to ninth-century settlements at Catholme (Staffordshire), comprising eight groups of buildings (numbered 1–8). Each unit represents the development of a farmstead by a family group. After L. Bradley (Trent and Peak Archaeological Trust)

0   50 m

0   50 yds

served a whole range of functions, and it is dangerous to group all these features under one heading. When more of the major sites which produced a large number of sunken huts have been published it may be easier to form a more considered view.

A number of Anglo-Saxon settlements have been excavated on a larger scale: Chalton and Cowdery's Down (Hampshire), Mucking (Essex) and West Stow (Suffolk), several in Oxfordshire, Catholme (Staffordshire) and Thirlings (Northumberland). These lie in most of the Saxon kingdoms: Wessex, East Anglia, Mercia and Northumbria. As only two of these sites have so far been fully published it is too early to make a final assessment, but no general picture emerges of regional or chronological differences. At West Stow there were several timber buildings with associated sunken huts, though it is hard to determine how many were in use at the same time. There were no clear divisions between the various properties, as seems also to have been the case at Mucking. In contrast at Chalton (114) the buildings were grouped in regular patterns apparently forming courtyard farms separated by fences. Construction was with both individual postholes and continuous trenches, but there were hardly any sunken huts. At Catholme the pattern is of a series of individual farms as at West Stow, but these are set in definite enclosed areas (115), and the development of the settlement over the course of time has been plotted. Cowdery's Down was also organised in a series of regular enclosures (116), but as usual the purpose of the various buildings was hard to determine, so it is uncertain how many farming units may have been involved.

116 Reconstruction of the seventh-century settlement at Cowdery's Down (Hampshire). Ten timber-built structures were found, but as the floor levels did not survive it is hard to interpret the functions of the different buildings. It is therefore uncertain if there was one large farm, with ancillary buildings in two enclosures, or a hamlet of three separate farming units. After M. Millett (Hampshire County Museum Services).

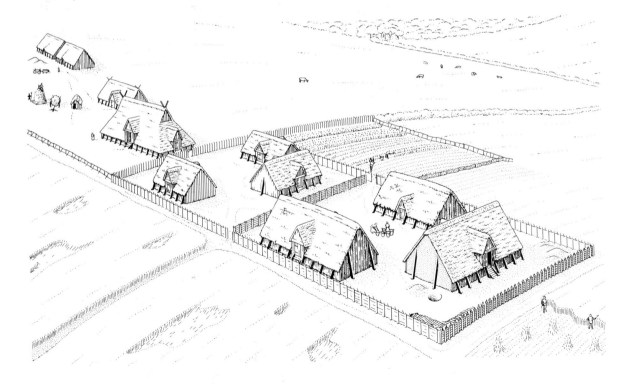

In general, the picture on Saxon peasant sites is not one of large nucleated settlements. All the major sites so far excavated have either comprised a very few units or been scattered in an open layout over considerable distances. The sites are often on hilltops, as at Chalton, Cowdery's Down and Mucking, or in quite isolated positions which were abandoned in the later Saxon period, when larger nucleated villages seem to have been formed.

The Wharram Research Project

Wharram Percy is a deserted medieval village situated on the chalk Wolds of Yorkshire between York and Scarborough. In the early medieval period there were two landowners, the Percies and the Chamberlains, but in 1254 the Percies acquired the whole village. There had been about thirty households, but these were reduced to sixteen in the fifteenth century. From this time the village was gradually depopulated by the Hiltons who had acquired it from the Percies. This was a result of the changing economic conditions, which favoured sheep rearing for wool over the villagers' arable farming. As the last stone houses crumbled away, they left a series of rectangular earthworks set in regular enclosures along the village streets (117). Out of many possible sites, Wharram

117 Oblique aerial photograph of Wharram Percy (East Yorkshire) from the north, showing the earthworks of the deserted village. In the foreground is the north manor (see the plan, 121), and the rectangular earthworks of the fifteenth-century peasant houses with the ruined parish church can be seen in the background.

was chosen as the main research project of the Deserted Medieval Village Research Group in the 1950s, and excavations have continued ever since for up to a month's season each July. These have involved over a hundred specialists in a multidisciplinary study of the whole village and its context.

The general layout of the village was determined by a series of prehistoric and Romano-British earthworks, the remains of some four thousand years of occupation before the scattered Anglo-Saxon farms were nucleated into a village in late Saxon times. This village was planned, with two regular rows of houses set in enclosures on the plateau to the west and on the terrace above the stream. At the north end there was a head row, comprising a manor house and a row of peasant houses. In the middle of the west row there was a second manor house. In the east row, besides the peasant houses, there was a church, a parsonage and a millpond. Excavations over the years have investigated all the major aspects of the village – the church, churchyard and parsonage, the millpond, manor house and two sample peasant enclosures. The present state of the site with its ruined church and reconstructed pond may be seen in 118.

The complete excavation of the church of St Martin (119) showed a very complex development from a small late Saxon church for the personal use of the lord to a large church with nave, chancel, two aisles

118 The ruined parish church and the reconstructed late medieval fishpond at Wharram Percy, as they appear today, from a viewpoint similar to that of the interpretation drawing (120). The main village houses were up on the plateau to the left.

119 General view during excavation of the nave of the parish church at Wharram Percy, seen from the east. In the foreground are the chalk foundations and the few remaining sandstone blocks of the first tenth-century stone church, enclosing postholes of an earlier timber church. The centre and far end are much disturbed by later burials. On the right can be seen a nineteenth-century lead coffin and brick vault.

and chapels which served the five townships of Wharram Percy parish. The church had been unused since 1949, so it was possible to carry out this work, which otherwise would have been very difficult. As it became ruined it was possible to investigate archaeologically the standing fabric in the same way as the excavated foundations, so that the structure could be examined and interpreted as a whole both above and below ground. The reconstruction drawing of the village (120) shows the church at its greatest extent in the fifteenth century. After the desertion of Wharram about 1500, the two aisles were demolished and the chancel was shortened, but the church survived in use to serve the

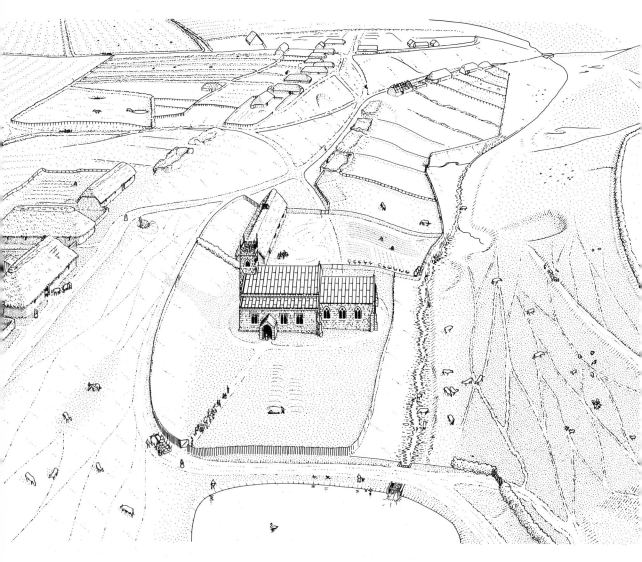

neighbouring villages of Towthorpe, Raisthorpe and Thixendale through the sixteenth and seventeenth centuries, and Thixendale alone during the eighteenth and nineteenth centuries, until a new church was opened at Thixendale in 1870. The church, as the only standing medieval structure, demonstrates the building activities of many of the medieval lords. It also epitomises the expansion and contraction of settlement in the area, as the scattered farms became nucleated to form villages and then reverted to fewer and smaller settlements in the post-medieval period. The disuse of the churchyard also enabled two sample areas to be excavated to the north and west of the church: from these areas, and from graves found in and around the church itself, about a thousand burials were excavated and examined. These are producing important evidence for the physical characteristics, the mortality, diseases and nutrition of a medieval rural population, which can be

120 A reconstruction of how the medieval village of Wharram Percy may have looked in the fifteenth century, combining the evidence of the surviving earthworks with that gained from thirty years of excavation. In the valley were (in the foreground) a fishpond, the parish church and parsonage, and beyond a row of peasant houses in their separate enclosures. On the plateau (to the left) there was a parallel row of houses with (in the background) the site of Percy (north) manor house (121). The hillsides were used for grazing, with the ridge and furrow of the open field system on the higher ground beyond. After Medieval Village Research Group

compared with similar assemblages from urban excavations. As well as the unmarked peasant burials which were laid out in the churchyard in regular rows, three late Saxon aristocratic burials have been found, with simple stone grave covers, while slabs which covered the burials of medieval lords and priests have been found incorporated into the church fabric. Two of the burials were of priests with associated chalice and paten.

The post-medieval parsonage, which survived until the early nineteenth century when Wharram Percy was amalgamated with Wharram le Street, was to the north of the churchyard: its excavation provided close correlations between the surviving foundations and a description in an eighteenth-century survey. The late medieval parsonage was built further to the west and is in process of excavation. The remains of what may be two earlier parsonages have been found to the north and south of the church. It therefore appears that, not only was the parsonage rebuilt many times, but that this was done on a different site each time. At one point in the fourteenth century the parsonage seems to have been built over part of the earlier churchyard, which had itself spread over an earlier parsonage site. It might have been expected that in the same way as the church was rebuilt on the same site the parsonage would have at least remained within a single plot. It was quite a surprise to find, not only that its site was quite fluid, but also that the churchyard boundary was not fixed.

To the south of the churchyard there was the pond, the dam of which was breached in the nineteenth century. A complete excavation of the dam area showed that in the early medieval period there was a water mill here for grinding corn, with an associated millpond. Though the actual mill building had been destroyed, large fragments of millstone were found. In the fourteenth century the mill was abandoned and the pond was made into a fishpond, with a more substantial dam (see 120). More significant for the history of the village, however, has been the environmental work. The investigation of this type of evidence, particularly from waterlogged sites, has been a major advance of recent years. Unfortunately, many rural sites like Wharram, which is on well-drained chalk, are not suitable for environmental work, in such conditions the archaeologist has to rely on the slighter evidence obtained from shells and carbonised grains. On the valley floor at Wharram, however, where the underlying clay has led to waterlogged conditions, all the items which usually decay on a dry site have survived, especially wood and leather. In addition, there are many animal and plant remains which permit the reconstruction of an early medieval landscape, with few trees and mixed arable and pastoral farming. The wooden and leather objects help to fill gaps in the information obtained from dry parts of the site, where only pottery, metal and bone survive.

The north manor comprises a complex series of earthworks in a large enclosure, quite different from those which contain simple peasant house earthworks. No excavation has taken place on the earthworks, but they have been surveyed in some detail and an attempt has been

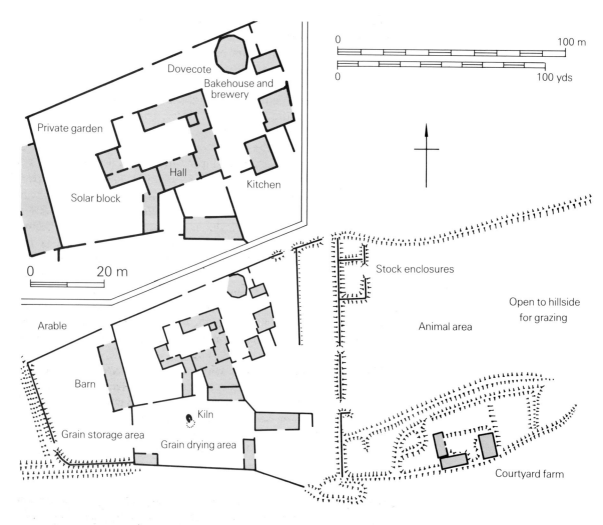

Dovecote

Bakehouse and
brewery

Private garden

Hall

Solar block

Kitchen

0   20 m

Arable

Barn

Kiln

Grain storage area

Grain drying area

0   100 m

0   100 yds

Stock enclosures

Open to hillside
for grazing

Animal area

Courtyard farm

made to interpret them and divide the manorial site into its component parts (121). The central enclosure includes the main buildings, which must have been the living area of the lord of the manor and servants' quarters. In the middle was the hall, with a raised area at the west end where the lord sat. At the west of the hall a series of buildings would have provided the private accommodation (called the solar, or camera, block). Another enclosed area further to the west might have been the private manorial garden, as there was no access to the western enclosure from this eastern side. To the east of the hall would have been the kitchen and other domestic offices and farm buildings, including the brewery and bakehouse, perhaps indicated by a small raised rectangular structure which may have been an oven. In the north-east corner of the central enclosure a circular structure may have been a dovecote, which, together with the fishpond, would have added variety to the medieval diet.

To the west of the central enclosure is the large earthwork of a

121   Plan of the earthworks of the Percy (north) manor house at Wharram Percy. No excavation has taken place, but an attempt has been made to interpret the remains and divide them into their component parts. The main living area was in the centre and the farming activities in associated enclosures. Compare with an excavated example at Chalgrove (132). After Medieval Village Research Group

building 30.5 metres (100 ft) long running north–south. This would have been a barn. In the yard to the south of the central block the one area which has been excavated produced a corn-drying or malting kiln. The west and south enclosures were, therefore, apparently used for grain storage and preparation, sensibly separated for safety in the case of fire. Between the central block and the east enclosure was a track giving access from the village to the fields. The big eastern enclosure contains, in its north-west corner, two large structures which would have been hard to roof; these may, therefore, have been animal pounds. As the enclosure is not separated from the valley on its east side it is likely to have been an animal-grazing area, possibly part of the park mentioned in a fourteenth-century document. The courtyard farm in the south-east corner, which overlies an earlier row of peasant houses, may have been the centre from which the estate was run in the fifteenth century, at a time when there were no resident lords. The actual manorial remains seem to date from the twelfth and thirteenth centuries, when the Percies, who gave their name to the village, owned it. Although there is no doubt that any future excavation would reveal a much more complex situation than that now suggested, simple fieldwork and survey, as used here, can form the basis for a preliminary interpretation of almost any site, based on excavated and surviving structures elsewhere.

The southern manor house, which was unexpectedly found under later peasant houses, has been excavated and a cellar found. This was set in a quarry dug 3 metres (10 ft) into the ground which had provided the chalk building-stone for the cellar, and also for a ground floor structure (see 124), measuring 12 metres by 6 (40 ft × 20 ft). The room above the cellar would have been the camera, the private accommodation for the lord. The walls were still standing several feet high in places

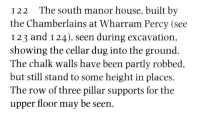

122   The south manor house, built by the Chamberlains at Wharram Percy (see 123 and 124), seen during excavation, showing the cellar dug into the ground. The chalk walls have been partly robbed, but still stand to some height in places. The row of three pillar supports for the upper floor may be seen.

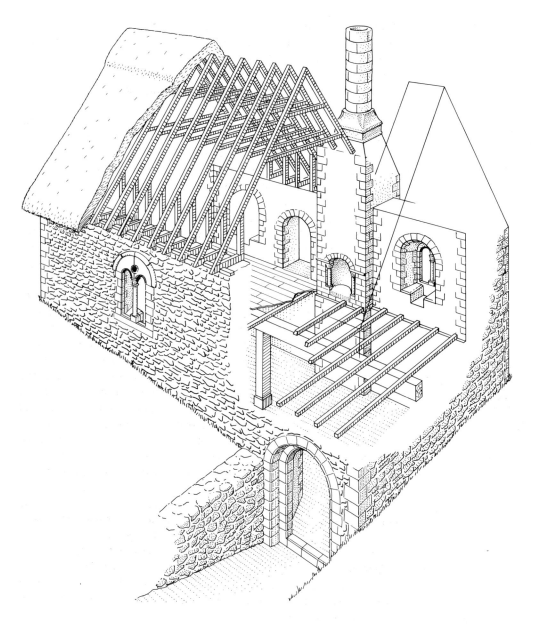

(122). The doorway, with a ramp down to it was found, together with the foundation of a fireplace for the main room, which would have been on the upper floor at ground level. Amongst the rubble infill were found many fragments of carved sandstone from doors, windows and the fireplace, which enabled a reconstruction drawing to be made (123), showing how this building may have looked in the twelfth century, when it was built by the Chamberlains. The surroundings have been much destroyed by later quarrying, but it is likely that beside this stone block was a timber-built hall, together with other buildings, though apparently not on the same scale as the Percy manor house. Excavations

123 A reconstruction of how the twelfth-century Chamberlain (south) manor house at Wharram Percy, may have looked. Its cellar walls were found beneath peasant houses (see 124). It was built of chalk rubble quarried from the site, with doorways, windows and fireplace of sandstone brought from quarries several miles away. The main room, open to the roof, was the living accommodation, with storage in the cellar beneath. After J. Thorn (Medieval Village Research Group)

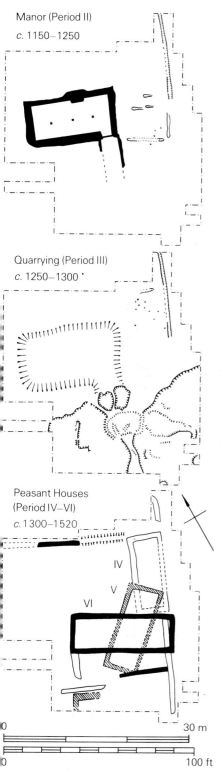

Manor (Period II)
c. 1150–1250

Quarrying (Period III)
c. 1250–1300

Peasant Houses
(Period IV–VI)
c. 1300–1520

IV

V

VI

0   30 m

0   100 ft

to the south-west have revealed a large pit dug into the chalk which may have been for cold storage for food. Next to this was a circular foundation which may have been connected with the storage of grain. Any excavation of the north manor may, therefore, quite possibly also produce additional features of this type, greatly increasing the interest of the main buildings visible as earthworks.

A major effort of the research project at Wharram was the excavation, over twenty seasons in the 1950s and 1960s, of two peasant enclosures in an attempt to find out more about the medieval peasant house and how its occupants lived. Both produced many surprises. The first was the more remarkable, as underneath the latest peasant houses was found the south manor house described above. This represented a fundamental change in land use which was quite unexpected, as it had been assumed that the main components of the village would at least be static, whatever changes there might be within them. There were three main types of medieval use of this enclosure (124). In the twelfth century it was occupied by the Chamberlain manor house, which was abandoned after 1254 when the Percies acquired the whole village. In the second half of the thirteenth century the manor house walls were robbed for building-stone and the rest of the area was quarried for chalk. Then, in the fourteenth and fifteenth centuries, the enclosure was developed for peasant houses; this must have been a major operation, as it necessitated the infilling of the quarries and the levelling of the ground. It is puzzling that this effort should have been expended at a time when the village population ought to have been declining and peasant houses going out of use. It may be that it was the consequence of a major fourteenth-century replanning, which may have involved the clearance of the peasant houses east of the north manor to make the fourteenth-century park and possibly the courtyard farm; the peasants may have had to be rehoused on the south manor site. So, although the regular Wharram village plan remained, there was at the same time constant change in many of the individual components within the basic framework, comprising quite fundamental changes of land use of the manors and parsónages as well as the lesser peasant houses.

During the fourteenth and fifteenth centuries the peasant house was rebuilt at least three times (see 124). It was first built on a north–south axis (Period IV), parallel with the road to the east of the enclosure, on

124   Three plans showing the constant changes in land use, and building position, in a single enclosure at Wharram Percy between the twelfth and fifteenth centuries. Following Anglo-Saxon aristocratic occupation a short distance to the west, a stone manor house (see 122 and 123) was built in Period II in the twelfth century. In Period III, after the manor house was abandoned, the area was used for quarrying. In the fourteenth and fifteenth centuries there was a sequence of peasant houses, which were constantly repaired and rebuilt on quite different alignments until the village was deserted about 1500. After Medieval Village Research Group

solid chalk where quarrying had not taken place; this was presumably at a time when the quarry fills had not yet been consolidated. It was then rebuilt further south at an oblique angle (Period v), overlapping the south end of the earlier house. Finally the house was rebuilt at right angles to the road at the eastern side of the enclosure (Period vi). This was the first major demonstration in England in the 1950s of the constant rebuilding of peasant houses on new alignments, a feature soon to be found commonly elsewhere over much of Britain.

The second peasant enclosure excavated was on the plateau west of the church, where there was a sequence of peasant houses from the twelfth to the fifteenth centuries. The first houses were built of timber, which left few traces other than postholes, from which it was difficult to reconstruct individual buildings. These were then followed by several houses built on different positions and with different alignments, as in the first area; in both areas the stone foundations were built of chalk quarried from the enclosures themselves. This demonstrated the change-over, even on a site where building-stone was readily available, from the earlier tradition of Saxon timber-built peasant houses to the later medieval stone-built house: only where local building-stone was not available did the timber tradition continue.

The earlier houses in this second area were simple small one- or two-roomed structures, but in the fourteenth and fifteenth centuries larger houses of long-house type (125) were built. The main feature of the long-house was that the people and animals all lived under the same roof in one long building. There was a passageway with opposing doorways between the two parts of the house but no partition. The upper part of the long-house comprised a living room with a central hearth, partitioned off from an unheated room which may have been

125 A fifteenth-century long-house: a cut-away drawing of what a medieval long-house may have looked like. The walls and thatched roof would have been simply constructed to enclose a single rectangular area in which both people and animals lived, with no division between the two. The hearth was in the middle of the floor of the living area. The details of construction and furnishing are based on the small finds and other evidence from excavations at Wharram Percy. After Medieval Village Research Group

used for sleeping or as a dairy. In the lower part the cattle were tethered in two rows with their heads to the side walls, a central drain ran off manure. As with Saxon houses, it is often hard to reconstruct the walls, which varied from solid stone to rough timbering and clay walls, often with some timber support. The roofs would often have been constructed simply with rough poles rather than carpentered timber.

The small finds from the excavation give several important clues to house construction, furnishing and daily life both in the house and in the fields. The presence of hinges, locks and keys for doors, chests and caskets shows that there must have been solid lockable doors and that the peasants locked away their possessions in chests and also had smaller caskets for valuables or trinkets. Hinges and hasps show that the windows had wooden shutters. One of the main facts demonstrated about daily life was that the peasant houses were kept swept out and clean; the rubbish was dumped onto heaps and then carted away to manure the fields, not buried in rubbish pits. Hardly any rubbish pits were found in the enclosures at Wharram, but much pottery was found spread over the open fields. The only finds were therefore from rubbish which was left behind and trodden into the ground. The copper-alloy and iron objects throw interesting additional light on daily life, including dress, recreation, spinning and, together with the pottery, food preparation and cooking. The wide range of animal bones shows the various types of animals kept and their uses, including traction, meat, hides, dairy products and wool. Most of the sites excavated produced large quantities of horse bones, some showing marks resulting from the use of the horses for traction; this indicates that much of the medieval ploughing on the light chalk soils at Wharram was done by horses, and not by the traditional oxen of the clay Midlands.

Other objects found provide evidence for local industry and markets. Smithing was carried out with coal brought sixty kilometres (nearly 40 miles) from West Yorkshire: other trades are shown by tools for stone, wood and leatherworking. The coarse cooking pottery came from kilns nearby in the Vale of Pickering, but finer jugs were acquired from York and Scarborough, while sea fish had to come thirty-two kilometres (20 miles) from the coast. The attempt to reconstruct what Wharram may have looked like in the fifteenth century, using the evidence of the surviving earthworks and results of the excavations on various parts of the site (120), may be compared with Wharram from a similar viewpoint today (118), with the reconstructed fishpond in the foreground and the ruined church behind. In contrast is a plan of a fifteenth-century village, Boarstall (Buckinghamshire), as it was envisaged by contemporary people (126). This plan illustrates the main features of a medieval village, with its moated manor house with a gatetower, church and peasant houses, and open fields with blocks of ridge and furrow in different directions; the surrounding wastes in this wooded country may be contrasted with the full exploitation for farming of the Wharram landscape on the Yorkshire Wolds and compared with the uncultivated areas and park land round Braunston in Leicestershire (127).

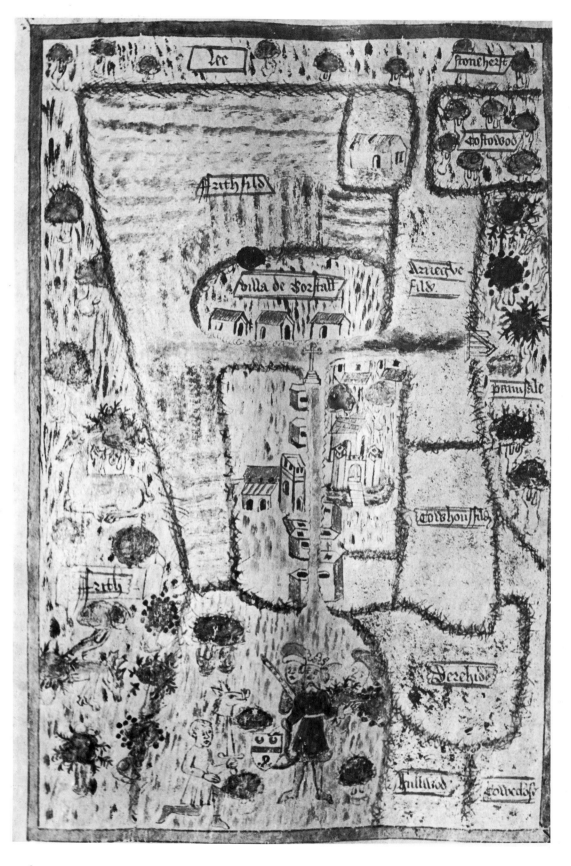

226

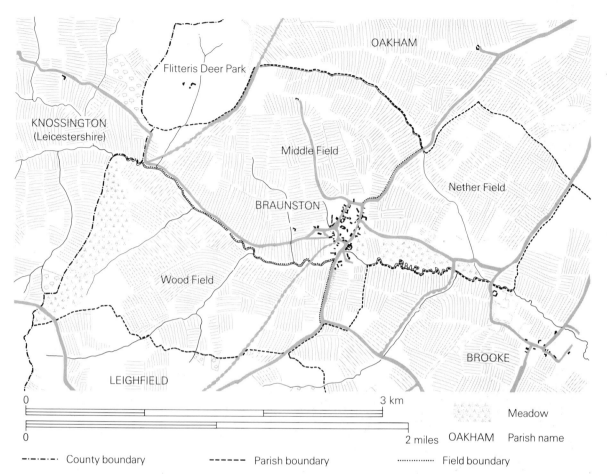

OAKHAM

Flitteris Deer Park

KNOSSINGTON
(Leicestershire)

Middle Field

Nether Field

BRAUNSTON

Wood Field

BROOKE

LEIGHFIELD

| 0 | | 3 km |

| 0 | | 2 miles |

Meadow

OAKHAM Parish name

–·–·– County boundary   ----- Parish boundary   ············· Field boundary

127 A reconstructed plan of a typical medieval village, Braunston (Leicestershire, formerly Rutland), based on aerial photographs and an eighteenth-century estate map. There was a chequerboard pattern of blocks of ridge and furrow and areas of meadow for grazing. Braunston is on the edge of uncultivated forest land and Flitteris Deer Park can be seen taking advantage of this border waste area between the two countries of Rutland and Leicestershire. After R.F. Hartley (Leicestershire Museums)

126 A plan of the village of Boarstall (Buckinghamshire) made in 1444, showing a regular layout. In the centre are the parish church and a moated manor, with a gatehouse, and a number of peasant houses. Beyond, blocks of ridge and furrow may be seen laid out in different directions. Round the edge is the waste forest land which was used for hunting.

The research project at Wharram has tried to demonstrate on one single village site as many different aspects of village life as possible, from the church to the lord and the peasant, how they built their buildings and how they spent their daily lives. It has been most valuable to see the picture as a whole from one site, but of particular importance have been the evidence for the medieval peasant house and way of life, and the record of constant change over the centuries.

Other post-Conquest settlements

The Wharram Research Project was gradually expanded in its scope as ideas developed on how medieval rural settlement should be studied. At the same time in other parts of the country the then Ministry of Works initiated a policy of excavating single houses on threatened deserted medieval village sites, which were at that time being increasingly destroyed for development. Local groups also carried out similar work, so that by 1960 a sample was achieved of peasant house types from many parts of England. Some of the work was still unsatisfactory, employing small-scale excavations and trenches, but the growing realisation of the necessity for open area excavation, initiated at Wharram

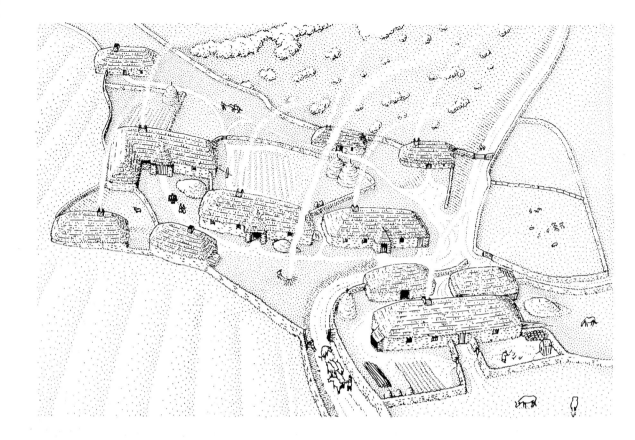

Percy and used on the official Ministry of Works excavations, led to the almost universal use of this method. When the first excavation of a peasant house was started at Wharram Percy an open area excavation was laid out, but this comprised only the area of the rectangular earthwork which was presumed to cover the remains of the medieval peasant house. As the excavation developed and it became clear that, not only had the house been constantly rebuilt over the centuries, but that this had been done in different positions, it was necessary to extend the area of excavation. It, therefore, became apparent that to get the full story it would be necessary to excavate a complete enclosure to its fullest extent.

The policy in the 1960s thus developed from the investigation of houses to the full excavation of the whole enclosures in which the peasant houses stood. This policy was adopted by the then Ministry of Public Building and Works on its rescue excavations and was followed on the important series of research excavations which were started in the 1960s in different parts of the country to look at different types of village. The three main projects were at Upton (Gloucestershire), Gomeldon (Wiltshire) and Hound Tor (Devon). At Upton a farm complex built of Cotswold stone was excavated over a period of ten years. At Gomeldon, on the Wessex chalk, work was extended to several enclosures; seven buildings with flint foundations were excavated, producing an important sequence: a twelfth-century long-house and a larger building in the thirteenth century were followed by the development of a court-yard farm with separate buildings for people and for farming activities.

128 Reconstruction of the hamlet of Hound Tor (Devon) in the thirteenth century, comprising a number of long-houses (see 125) built of granite and set in small irregular enclosures. In the background are three corn-drying kilns, with open moorland for grazing beyond and the ridge and furrow of the open field system on the left. After G.M.T. Beresford

At Hound Tor, between 1960 and 1968, almost all of this small hamlet on Dartmoor was excavated. This was an important upland site at 335 metres (1100 ft), with a sequence from early turf-built houses to later stone houses. This was significant in showing the change in building material: there was so much stone lying about that the granite would have had to have been cleared before the first houses could have been constructed; nevertheless, the granite was not used for building until the thirteenth century. The reconstruction (128) shows how the settlement may have looked in the thirteenth century, before its abandonment: with the worsening climate and the reduction of the pressure on land with the declining population in the fourteenth century, it ceased to be worthwhile to cultivate land at this altitude. Its high position, well above the present treeline, can be clearly seen in 129, which shows the ruined granite walls of one of the long-houses. The site comprised a number of long-houses, of a type which still survive on Dartmoor today, and a number of smaller buildings. The more substantial long-house in the right foreground of 128 had two associated outbuildings, suggesting a higher status. The three buildings just inside the boundary wall in the background were corn-drying kilns.

These research excavations, together with a wide range of sites all over the country excavated by the Ministry of Public Building and Works, enabled a series of three basic plan types to be established by 1970: a simple one- or two-roomed house, like the small buildings at Hound Tor, where the cottager or peasant without land would live; secondly, the long-house with living quarters and farm activities under

129　A thirteenth-century house at Hound Tor (Devon), showing the walls constructed of rough granite blocks. Its upland position is shown by the valley in the background.

one roof: this was the typical house type occupied by the peasant farmer over much of the country; thirdly, the courtyard farm in which the occupants and the farming activities were separated in different buildings, often at right angles to each other to form a courtyard. These were not chronological or regional variations, but depended on the prosperity and farming activities of the individual medieval peasant in different villages at various times. At Gomeldon there was a sequence from a twelfth-century long-house to a thirteenth-century farm; at Hangleton (Sussex) both long-houses and farms were in use together in the thirteenth century, while at Wharram Percy long-houses continued till the village was deserted in the late fifteenth century. Other sites on the Yorkshire Wolds which were deserted in the sixteenth and seventeenth centuries show that courtyard farms did not devolop until then in that area, while long-houses continued in use well into the nineteenth century side by side with farms.

All the excavations so far mentioned were on sites where building-stone was readily available, so that the ruined foundations showed up clearly as rectangular earthworks in the grass (see 109 and 117). Little excavation had taken place on the Midland clay sites, where the decayed timber buildings left only marks in the ground and no earth-

130 Oblique aerial photograph of a typical Midland clay deserted village, at Ingarsby (Leicestershire). Regular enclosures have a network of roads between, but these are not bounded by stone walls nor are any actual peasant house sites visible. The houses would have been built of timber, which has decayed, leaving no visible traces above ground. Compare 109 and 117.

works, so that the peasant house might be anywhere within an enclosure up to fifty metres across (131). Pioneer work took place in the 1960s in Norfolk and the Midlands, but it was not until a specific programme was initiated by the Ministry of Public Building and Works in the late 1960s and early 1970s at two Midland sites, Barton Blount (Derbyshire) and Goltho, that whole enclosures were stripped. These yielded very complex sequences of timber buildings: at Goltho they had been rebuilt successively on quite different sites in the enclosure. From this work a sequence of types of building construction was proposed by Guy Beresford. Initially, structures were either built entirely of clay, or they were primitive timber buildings constructed of rough timbers without any framing; the timbers were set up to 1 metre (2–3ft) apart in individual postholes or trenches, as in the Saxon period, then the walls were infilled with clay mixed with straw. These were followed by primitive framed buildings, where the timbers were only roughly fitted together; the posts were raised up on individual stones placed on the ground, and the panels were filled with wattle and daub. Finally in this sequence came fully timber-framed buildings, often on dwarf stone walls where sufficient stone was available.

In the 1970s it was increasingly realised that the whole settlement and not single houses or even enclosures should be investigated. At this stage the Medieval Village Research Group, which now, significantly, dropped the prefix 'Deserted', initiated its complete village and parish survey at Wharram Percy. In the 1950s there had been initial attempts to look at a larger area, but the first planned excavation of a complete medieval village, however, was undertaken between 1972 and 1977 at Caldecote (Hertfordshire). It was possible here, in a fairly small deserted village, as at Hound Tor, to investigate not only most of the enclosures but also the manor house and rectory – only the church could not be excavated. The drawing (131) of one of the Caldecote enclosures shows how it may have looked in the fifteenth century, when there was a large farm with a dwelling house and five farm buildings spread haphazardly over the enclosure. By the fourteenth century, and even more so in the fifteenth century, farms had become more frequent, as peasants became more prosperous in the easier conditions resulting from the decay of manorial lordship after the Black Death. Other examples of farms have been found at Barton Blount and Grenstein (Norfolk), though longhouses still continued in many areas.

Most medieval village excavations have taken place on sites which were deserted in the fourteenth or fifteenth centuries; as a result, few sixteenth-century peasant houses have been excavated. The first surviving houses of comparable status do not date back before the late sixteenth century; these have been studied by the Vernacular Architecture Group, which since the 1950s has tried to do for lesser standing buildings what the Medieval Village Research Group has attempted for the earlier period. Although traces of open central hearths, which were a feature of medieval buildings, have been found in many surviving buildings, where they were later replaced by chimneys set in the walls

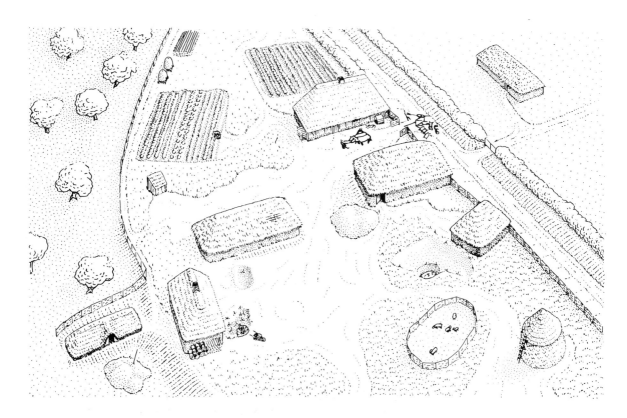

or in major partitions, this transition had not been found on excavated sites. At Caldecote, however, which was not deserted until the sixteenth century, the hiatus is filled and the process of change can be clearly seen in the excavated houses, with central hearths replaced by wall chimneys, demonstrating clearly this important development in living conditions. The only other excavation where this continuity into the post-medieval period had been studied was in the long-term rescue excavation in the 1950s and 1960s at West Whelpington (Northumberland), a site which was not abandoned until the early eighteenth century.

Standing medieval manor houses have been a major study since the middle of the nineteenth century, and quite a few attempts were made at excavation on the sites of others. Many of these were on a small scale, and the more extensive excavations were almost entirely confined to the hall and the main living quarters. No attention was paid to the associated farm buildings, which formed the economic base and which are a constant feature of manorial documents. Although the Ministry of Works carried out a programme of manor house excavations on threatened sites in the 1950s and 1960s, these were of limited extent: there was a shortage of funds and often the full site was not available for investigation. The first attempt at the complete excavation of a manor house was on a moated site at Northolt (Middlesex). The main buildings were examined, but the resources of this voluntary excavation were not sufficient to excavate entirely all the associated buildings, and in

131   A reconstruction of how a single enclosure in the deserted village at Caldecote (Hertfordshire) may have looked in the fifteenth century. Instead of a single long-house, there were several farm buildings set haphazardly in an irregular enclosure. The main living house was beyond the gate. The enclosure would have been used for various purposes by the peasant, particularly for cultivating his own crops and for grazing his animals. After G. M. T. Beresford

particular it became apparent that the farm buildings were likely to have been in a second enclosure, which was built over with a 1930s housing estate.

The situation changed in 1973 with the formation of the Moated Sites Research Group, which set out to record and collate work on the many thousands of moated sites, most of which contained medieval manor houses. During the last ten years an increasing effort has been put into surveys, and the group has also championed large-scale excavations with the aim of looking at the full economic unit. There have been several important recent excavations. One of the most valuable has been Faccombe Netherton (Hampshire), where the manorial complex developed from late Saxon times through to the medieval, as at Goltho and Portchester. The excavation of a moated site at Penhallam (Cornwall) produced a complete courtyard plan of a twelfth- and thirteenth-century manor house, which may be compared with surviving examples like Cotehele, also in Cornwall. Despite an extensive search, however, the farm buildings here, and at many other recent excavations, remained elusive.

Two major recent excavations have at last produced full evidence for a whole economic unit: Grove (Bedfordshire) and Chalgrove (Oxfordshire). Grove, in the valley of the Ouzel, was a Saxon royal manor, which was given to an alien priory in the twelfth century but later reverted to the Crown. A programme of rescue excavation first uncovered the main living accommodation and its associated buildings, in a sequence extending from late Saxon times through to the post-Conquest period. More recent work has uncovered a large outer court surrounded by a series of farm buildings more extensive than anything else found so far, not excepting the Knights Templars' site at South Witham (see p. 189). On a more modest scale, and of a type which might be expected on any manor site, were the buildings at Chalgrove (132). On the right are the main hall, living quarters and associated buildings: these may be compared with the earthworks of the north manor at Wharram Percy (121). To the left may be seen the farm buildings with, in the foreground, a large barn which sets the site much more in its economic context, showing its role as an estate centre and not simply a manorial living house.

In addition to excavation, field surveys of many kinds have contributed greatly to a fuller understanding of medieval rural settlement. While the primary documentary work by Hoskins, Beresford and others led to the identification of some fifteen hundred deserted medieval villages in the 1950s, fieldwork and aerial photography have doubled the number to about three thousand. Although many people have taken part in the programme of research encouraged and collated by the Medieval Village Research Group, this major achievement has been the result of nearly forty years flying by Kenneth St Joseph from Cambridge. While he ranged widely over all archaeological periods, his oblique aerial photographs, such as those he and Beresford published in 1958 in *Medieval England: An Aerial Survey*, have made a major impact

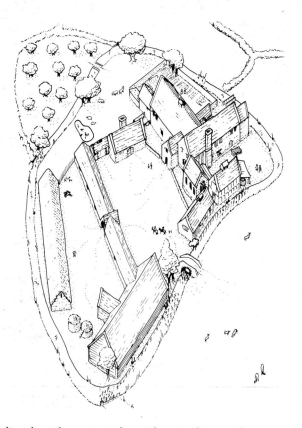

132 A reconstruction of a typical thirteenth-century manor house surrounded by a moat at Chalgrove (Oxfordshire). The main living accommodation was on the right and the various farm buildings, in two courtyards, to the left, forming the whole economic unit (compare with similar plan in 121). After Oxford Archaeological Unit

on medieval settlement studies. The six thousand prints of deserted villages in the Medieval Village Research Group files are a major source of information which could never be observed from the ground and which have transformed our understanding of village forms and types. In 117 and 130 the contrast between the earthwork remains of deserted villages on stone and clay sites can be seen; these photographs may be compared with the earlier vertical aerial photograph of the 1920s (109).

The medieval open fields also show up with remarkable clarity from the air and again St Joseph's oblique aerial photographs catch the full effect of the undulating ridge and furrow (133). Ground surveys of many field systems have also been carried out, particularly by David Hall, but these can often be plotted more simply and accurately from aerial photographs. The plan of a field system at Braunston, on the border of medieval Rutland and Leicestershire shows the chequerboard pattern of blocks of ridge and furrow, resulting from ploughing the various furlongs on different alignments (127); this pattern can still be seen on the RAF vertical aerial photographs from which this map has been constructed. Comparison with an eighteenth-century estate map enables the three fields, Wood, Middle and Nether, to be named, while the meadows are indentified as Lammas fields. Braunston is on the edge of uncultivated forest land. The open fields may be seen petering out at Leighfield, while Flitteris Deer Park took advantage of this border waste.

133 Oblique aerial photograph of Padbury (Buckinghamshire), showing the ridge and furrow of the medieval open fields, now under grass for grazing, preserving the rise and fall of the earthworks. The layout of the ridge and furrow follows exactly a map drawn in 1591. The open fields were enclosed in 1795. The straight hedges of the new fields run obliquely across the medieval field systems.

Such correlation between photographs and maps has been attempted for several areas.

It has traditionally been assumed that this patchwork open field pattern, which is so typical of the Midlands, was the universal type of open field system. Recent work by Mary Harvey in Yorkshire has shown that, outside the Midlands, large areas of open fields were laid out with long strips, up to one thousand metres in length, all going in the same direction. Even in the Midlands similar examples have been identified, and Hall has suggested that many of these were later subdivided by headlands to form smaller rectangular patterns of open fields. It is as yet uncertain whether the regular laying out of thousand-metre strips was done when villages became nucleated in late Saxon times, or whether it is to be equated with some later medieval replanning after the Norman Conquest. Either way, fieldwork has demonstrated that there is still much to be learnt about the medieval landscape.

New Directions

Future research, directed at whole landscapes rather than single villages, may be seen as the culmination of a study which has ranged from the initial excavations of single peasant houses, through the investigation of whole enclosures and the other elements of village anatomy, to an appraisal of the significance of the total landscape pattern, of the varying settlement forms in their settings of fields and crofts, wastes and woodlands. These new directions in research are epitomised by the recent amalgamation of the Medieval Village Research Group with the Moated Sites Research Group under the title of the Medieval Settlement Research Group. Much of the work of the last forty years has concentrated on villages, and especially those which became deserted. But there are deserted hamlets and farms, not only in the peripheral areas of Britain where little or no village nucleation ever took place, but also, interspersed between the nucleated villages, in the Midlands, where until lately it was thought that all settlements had been nucleated by medieval times. Surviving villages have not been immune from change: there must be ten thousand settlements which have shrunk, expanded, migrated along the routes which connect them to their neighbours, or otherwise changed their form in ways still to be analysed and explained. These are some of the issues to be looked at by the next generation, with new techniques and new approaches, but based on the work of the past and, above all, based on that unique document, the British landscape.

Glossary

Anneal — To toughen glass by exposure to slowly diminished heat.

Antonine Wall — A permanent frontier, with a turf wall and forts, laid out in the early 140s AD along the Glasgow–Edinburgh line. It was briefly abandoned, c. AD 155–8, and finally given up c. AD 163.

Ard — Light plough, lacking a mould board.

Bastion — The projecting part of a fortification.

Bloom — Rough metal produced by smelting iron ore, before being sent for forging.

Bloomery — The first forge in an iron works through which the metal passes after melting and in which it is made into blooms.

Crop mark — Area where underlying archaeological feature becomes visible, due either to greater growth of crop (over greater depth of soil, e.g. a ditch or pit) or parching of crop over shallow depth of soil (e.g. wall foundation).

Curtain wall — The part of a wall which connects two bastions or towers.

Dendrochronology — Dating timber by differences in the size of the annual growth rings of trees.

Diatom — A variety of *Algae*, only visible under the microscope, which can give an indication of local environmental conditions, particularly the salinity of the soil.

Frit — A calcined mixture of sand and fluxes ready to be melted into a crucible to form glass.

Full — To beat cloth for the purpose of cleansing and thickening it.

Hadrian's Wall — A permanent frontier on the Tyne–Solway line, built in the 120s AD, briefly given up in favour of the Antonine Wall in the mid-second century and retained until the late fourth century AD.

Henge — Ceremonial circular monument usually comprised of continuous circular ditch with external bank broken by one, or more often two, opposed entrances.

Leat — An open water course to conduct water for mills.

Lunula — Crescent-shaped flat gold ornament worn round the neck.

Mattock — Pickaxe-shaped digging implement with broad cutting edge.

Marching camp — A temporary fortified enclosure erected by the Roman army while on the march, whether on peacetime manoeuvres or on campaign.

Microlith — Small flint implement produced to provide cutting edge for composite tool or weapon.

Multivallate — Defences formed by multiple lines of ditches and ramparts.

Ogival — S-shaped curve.

Oolite — Type of limestone.

Otolith — Ear-bone.

Quern — Grinding stone.

Radiocarbon — Carbon 14 is a radioactive isotope found in all living matter. When the living matter dies no further carbon is taken in and the radioactive carbon begins to decay. By measuring the amount of radioactive carbon remaining, the age of the material can be assessed.

Revetment — A retaining structure of stone or timber supporting the face of an earthen structure or wall.

Ring work	An enclosure, often circular, whose primary defence is a bank and ditch.
Rolling	Damage received due to movement within a deposit.
Saithe	Coal-fish.
Samian ware	A red-gloss pottery, used mainly as tableware, which was manufactured in Gaul in the first and second centuries AD.
Sarmatians	A tribe that eventually settled in the Danube region, after migrating there in the late first millennium BC.
Sarsen	Sandstone blocks found in the chalk Downs.
Shieling	Shelter.
Spall	Small chip.
Spelt	Type of wheat.
Stalled cairn	Chambered tomb in which upright slabs of stone are used to subdivide the tomb into compartments.
Stanegate frontier	The first frontier line between the Tyne and the Solway consisted of a patrolled road, the Stanegate, laid out in the later first century AD.
Stratification	The arrangement of layers in an archaeological deposit.
Strip houses	A typical form of house in Roman Britain, which is rectangular in form and has a shop and/or workshop on the ground floor, with the living quarters above.
Thermoluminescence	Extra electrons are trapped by certain minerals over time but are freed by heating beyond a certain temperature. Materials such as fired clay or burnt flint will then accumulate new electrons from natural radioactivity in the ground. When reheated these will be driven off as light energy and the relative amount of this can be measured to give a date.
Vexillation fortress	A permanent base for a *vexillatio*, or detachment of legionary troops. The bases vary in size from 8–12 hectares (20–30 acres), about half the size of a normal legionary fortress, and were probably used as winter quarters.
Wheelhouse	A stone-built circular house whose internal partition walls project inwards like the spokes of a wheel.

Bibliography

1. Prehistoric Britain

General

V.G. Childe's culture-historical approach is well illustrated by *The Dawn of European Civilization* (1925). The most influential books of the geographical determinist school were those of C. Fox *The personality of Britain* (1932) and *The Archaeology of the Cambridge Region* (1923). The post-War economic–ecological approach was mapped out by J.G.D. Clark in his *Prehistoric Europe: the Economic Basis* (1952). The same author published the crucially important *Excavations at Star Carr* (1954) and the anti-invasionist case in 'The invasion hypothesis in British Archaeology', *Antiquity* 40 (1966) pp.172–189. A major contribution to the 'new archaeology' was D.L. Clarke's *Analytical Archaeology* (1968). Recent general surveys of British prehistory have been few. *British Prehistory, a new outline* edited by C. Renfrew (1974) offered the first overall view of the post-radiocarbon era and a more detailed catalogue of the accumulating evidence was provided by J.V.S. Megaw and D.D.A. Simpson in their *Introduction to British Prehistory* (1979). A useful general survey of the history of agriculture in Britain is P.J. Fowler's *The Farming of Prehistoric Britain* (1983), while a stimulating view of social prehistory is offered by R. Bradley in *The Social foundations of prehistoric Britain* (1984). A well illustrated general outline can also be found in I.H. Longworth *Prehistoric Britain* (1985).

Palaeolithic and Mesolithic

The geological background is well covered in D.Q. Bowen, *Quaternary Geology* (1978), which includes details of the more recent work. A detailed synthesis of the lower Palaeolithic can be found in D.A. Roe, *The Lower and Middle Palaeolithic periods in Britain* (1981), and useful gazetteers appear in J.J. Wymer's *Lower Palaeolithic Archaeology in Britain as represented by the Thames Valley* (1968) and *Palaeolithic sites of East-Anglia* (1985). The current excavations at Pont Newydd are reported in H.S. Green (ed.), *Pont Newydd Cave: A Lower Palaeolithic Hominid site in Wales. The first report* (1984), which includes work on the raw material and details of the dating. J. Campbell's *Upper Palaeolithic of Britain* (1977) is the most recent work on that period, though its prime use is as a gazetteer. There have been no full reports as yet on Hengistbury Head, although some of the experimental work by R.N.E. Barton and C.A. Bergman is published in *World Archaeology* (1982), pp.237–48. Handaxe experiments undertaken by M.Newcomer can be found in *World Archaeology* 3 (1971), pp.85–94 and *The Journal of Field Archaeology* 7 (1980), pp.345–52. The earlier groundwork in microwear was developed and published by V. Keeley in *Experimental Determination of stone tool uses: a microwear analysis* (1980), but the more recent re-evaluations have yet to be published. There is no recent synthesis of the British Mesolithic, but the relevant section in A. Morrison, *Early Man in Britain and Ireland* (1980) provides a useful summary. Star Carr itself has been fully published, J.G.D. Clark, *Excavations at Star Carr* (1954), and the most important published re-interpretation is by M.Pitts in *World Archaeology* 11 (1979), pp.32–42. Discussion of the seasonality of the sites on Oronsay can be found in *Proceedings of the Prehistoric Society* 46 (1980), pp.19–44 by P. Mellars. The most useful papers relating to the general economic and environmental background to the Mesolithic are P. Mellars in *Problems in Economic and Social Archaeology* (edited by G. de G. Sieveking *et al*, 1976) and R. Jacobi *et al* in the *Journal of Archaeological Science* 3 (1976), pp.307–20.

Neolithic

The only major synthesis to be published since the Second World War is that of S. Piggott, *The Neolithic Cultures of the British Isles* (1954). Full publication of the recent work at the Hambledon Hill and Crickley Hill enclosures is awaited, but a preliminary account of the former is given in R.J. Mercer, *Hambledon Hill, a Neolithic landscape* (1980) and the same author has published 'Excavations at Carn Brea, Illogan, Cornwall, 1970–73', *Cornish Archaeology* 20 (1981). A number of unchambered long barrows have been published, including P. Ashbee, 'The Fussell's Lodge long barrow excavations 1957', *Archaeologia*, 100 (1966), pp.1–80, and most recently B.E. Vyner, 'The excavation of a Neolithic cairn at Street House, Loftus, Cleveland', *Proceedings of the Prehistoric Society* 50 (1984), pp.151–95. Chambered tombs have been catalogued in G.E. Daniel, *The Prehistoric chambered tombs of England and Wales* (1950) and A.S. Henshall, *The chambered Tombs of Scotland*, vols 1 and 2 (1963, 1972). A change in approach to their study was heralded by a paper by I.A. Kinnes, 'Monumental function in British Neolithic burial practices' *World Archaeology*, 7 (1975), pp.16–29. Work in the Somerset Levels has been published in a series of papers by J.M. Coles and his collaborators in the *Proceedings of the Prehistoric Society*, beginning in 1968, and from 1975 in the *Somerset Levels Papers*. The products of the stone axe factories have been summarised in T.H.McK Clough and W.A. Cummins, *Stone Axe Studies*, Council for British Archaeology Research Report 23 (1979). The characterisation of flint has been explored in a number of papers, including G. de G. Sieveking *et al*, 'Prehistoric flint mines and their identification as sources of raw material' *Archaeometry* 14 (1972), pp.151–76.

Important recent work on Orkney in the later Neolithic, including excavations at Skara Brae and Knap of Howar, has been summarised by D.V. Clarke and A. Ritchie in C. Renfrew (ed), *The Prehistory of Orkney* (1985). The results of excavations in the main later Neolithic Wessex enclosures appeared in: G.J. Wainwright and I.H. Longworth, *Durrington Walls: Excavations 1966–8*, Research Report of the Society of Antiquaries of London 29 (1971); G.J. Wainwright *et al*, 'The excavation of a Later Neolithic enclosure at Marden, Wiltshire', *Antiquaries Journal* 51 (1971), pp.177–239; and G.J. Wainwright *Mount Pleasant, Dorset: Excavations 1970–71*, Research Report of the Society of Antiquaries of London 37 (1979). Recent excavations at the Grimes Graves Flint Mines have been summarised in G.de G. Sieveking, 'Grimes Graves and Prehistoric European Flint Mining' in H. Crawford (ed.), *Subterranean Britain*, (1979), pp.1–43, and R.J. Mercer, *Grimes Graves, Norfolk. Excavations 1971–2*, Department of the Environment Archaeological Report 11 (1981).

Beaker

British Beaker pottery was catalogued by D.L. Clarke in *Beaker pottery of Great Britain and Ireland* (1970), an alternative scheme for its classification being offered by J.N. Lanting and J.D. Van der Waals, 'British Beakers as seen from the Continent', *Helinium*, 12 (1972), pp.20–46. A totally new approach was offered by C. Burgess and S. Shennan in their *Beaker Phenomenon: some suggestions*, British Archaeological Report 33 (1976), pp.309–31 and a later balanced judgement appeared in H. Case, *The Beaker Culture in Britain and Ireland*, British Archaeological Reports, Supplementary Series 26 (1977), pp.71–101. Supplementary information on Beaker domestic sites has been published by A.M. Gibson, *Beaker Domestic Sites*, British Archaeological Reports, British Series 107 (1982), and H.M. Bamford, *Beaker Domestic sites in the Fen Edge and East Anglia*, East Anglian Archaeology Report 16 (1982).

Bronze Age

A recent survey of the earlier part of the period can be found in C. Burgess, *The Age of Stonehenge* (1980), and a novel interpretation in D.V. Clarke, T.G. Cowie and A. Foxon, *Symbols of power at the time of Stonehenge* (1985). The Kimpton cemetery was published by M. Dacre and A. Ellison 'A Bronze Age Urn Cemetery at Kimpton, Hampshire', *Proceedings of the Prehistoric Society* 47 (1981), pp.147–203, and a discussion of Deverel-Rimbury cemeteries in general appears in A. Ellison, *Deverel-Rimbury cemeteries: the evidence for social organisation*, British Archaeological Reports, British Series 83 (1980), pp.115–26. Recent work on Dartmoor has been published by A. Fleming in two papers: 'The Prehistoric Landscape of Dartmoor' Pts 1 & 2, *Proceedings of the Prehistoric Society* 44 (1978), pp.97–123, and 49 (1983), pp.195–241, and by N.D. Balaam *et al*, 'The Shaugh

Moor Project: Fourth Report (summarising conclusions of earlier reports), *Proceedings of the Prehistoric Society* 48 (1982), pp.203–78. The earlier work on round barrows was synthesised by P. Ashbee, *The Bronze Age Round Barrow in Britain* (1960), and amongst important recent reports are those of I.F. Smith and D.D.A. Simpson, 'Excavation of a round barrow on Overton Hill, N. Wiltshire', *Proceedings of the Prehistoric Society* 32 (1966), pp.122–55 and F.M. Lynch, 'Brenig Valley excavations 1973 and 1974', *Transactions of the Denbigh Historical Society* 23 (1974), pp.9–64 and 24 (1975), pp.13–37. A number of settlements have been excavated or are in the course of excavation, and several are summarised in J. Barrett and R. Bradley (eds), *Settlement and Society in the British Later Bronze Age*, British Archaeological Reports, British Series 83 (1980). A preliminary account of the Langdon Bay wreck can be found in K. Muckelroy, 'Middle Bronze Age trade between Britain and Europe, a maritime perspective' *Proceedings of the Prehistoric Society* 47 (1981), pp.275–97 and of the Dainton metalworking site in S. Needham, 'An assemblage of Late Bronze Age Metalworking debris from Dainton, Devon', *Proceedings of the Prehistoric Society* 46 (1980), pp.177–215.

Iron Age

C.F.C. Hawkes classified the British Iron Age material in a major paper, 'Hillforts', *Antiquity* 5 (1931), pp.60–97, and elaborated his ideas in 'The ABC of the British Iron Age', *Antiquity* 33 (1959), pp.170–82. This scheme was criticised, especially by F.R. Hodson, 'Cultural grouping within the British pre-Roman Iron Age', *Proceedings of the Prehistoric Society* 30 (1964), pp.99–110. Two major surveys, with full bibliographies, were published in 1974: B.W. Cunliffe, *Iron Age Communities in Britain* (2nd edn, 1978) and D.W. Harding, *The Iron Age in Lowland Britain*; T.C. Champion, J.V.S. Megaw and I.B.M. Ralston contributed the Iron Age section to J.V.S. Megaw and D.D.A. Simpson, *Introduction to British Prehistory* (1979); no general synthesis has been published in the 1980s. Important monographs on individual sites have been published by Mortimer Wheeler, *The Stanwick Fortifications, North Riding of Yorkshire*, Research Report of the Society of Antiquaries of London 17 (1954); T.C.M. Brewster, *The Excavation of Staple Howe* (1963); Ian Richmond, *Hod Hill* 2 (1968); S.C. Stanford, *Croft Ambrey* (1974) and *Midsummer Hill* (1981); P.J. Drury, *Excavations at Little Waltham 1970–71*, Council for British Archaeology Research Report 26 (1978); G.J. Wainwright, *Gussage All Saints*, Department of the Environment Archaeological Report 10 (1979); B.W. Cunliffe, *Danebury*, Council for British Archaeology Research Report 52, 1984. Several hillfort excavations are summarised in D.W. Harding's *Hillforts* (1976) and *oppida* are covered by J.R. Collis, *Oppida* (1984). The Butser experiments are recorded by P.J. Reynolds, *Iron-Age Farm* (1979). For the Yorkshire burials see I.M. Stead, *The Arras Culture* (1979) and for the cremation burials in south-eastern England, A.Birchall 'The Aylesford-Swarling Culture: the problem of the Belgae reconsidered', *Proceedings of the Prehistoric Society* 31 (1965), pp.241–367, and I.M. Stead, 'A La Tène III burial at Welwyn Garden City', *Archaeologia* 101 (1967), pp.1–62. Cyril Fox's *Pattern and Purpose* (1958) is the only major monograph devoted to Early Celtic Art in Britain, but the northern material is covered in more detail in Morna MacGregor's *Early Celtic Art in North Britain* (1976). The collection of moulds from Gussage All Saints has been thoroughly studied by Jennifer Foster, *The Iron Age Moulds from Gussage All Saints* (British Museum Occasional Paper 12 (1980). Celtic deities and rituals are discussed by Anne Ross, *Pagan Celtic Britain* (1967). D.F. Allen has published several papers on British coins, especially 'The origins of coinage in Britain: a reappraisal' in S.S. Frere (ed.) *Problems of the Iron Age in Southern Britain* (1960), pp.97–308; for more recent views see J.P.C. Kent, 'The origins of coinage in Britain' in B.W. Cunliffe (ed.) *Coinage and Society in Britain and Gaul: some current problems*, Council for British Archaeology Research Report 38 (1981), pp.40–2.

2. A Roman Province
General
There are many hundreds of volumes that are of direct relevance to the themes of this chapter, and it is possible here to include only a very limited selection. There are now many general works, written at different levels, of which S.S. Frere, *Britannia* (1978) and P. Salway, *Roman Britain* (1981) are fundamental. R.G. Collingwood and I.A. Richmond, *The Archaeology of Roman Britain* (1969) is now out of date in many respects, but still very useful, as are J.Liversidge, *Britain in the Roman Empire* (1968), M. Todd, *Roman Britain* (1981), and J.S. Wacher, *Roman Britain* (1978). A.L.F. Rivet, *Town and Country in Roman Britain* (1964) continues to be particularly valuable, as is A.R. Birley, *The People of Roman Britain* (1979), and S.S. Frere and J.K. St Joseph, *Roman Britain from the air* (1983).

The major modern source books are A.R. Birley, *The Fasti of Roman Britain* (1981), R.G. Collingwood and R.P. Wright, *The Roman inscriptions of Britain: I. Inscriptions on stone* (1965) and A.L.F. Rivet and C. Smith, *The place names of Roman Britain* (1979). Similarly invaluable are the Ordnance Survey maps, namely of *Roman Britain* (1979), *Hadrian's Wall* (1972), *The Antonine Wall* (1975), while there is an excellent guide, R.J.A. Wilson, *A guide to the Roman remains of Britain* (1980). For roads see I.D. Margary, *Roman roads in Britain* (1967).

The Army
See particularly P.A. Holder, *The Roman Army in Britain* (1982), A. Johnson, *Roman Forts* (1983) and S. Johnson, *The Roman forts of the Saxon Shore* (1976). Wales is still best covered by V.E. Nash-Williams, *The Roman Frontier in Wales* (2nd edn 1969, revised by M.G. Jarrett), while for the northern frontiers, amongst many very important works, are D.J. Breeze and B. Dobson, *Hadrian's Wall* (1978), D.J. Breeze, *The northern frontiers of Roman Britain* (1982), and W.S. Hanson and G.S. Maxwell, *Rome's north west frontier. The Antonine Wall* (1983). Later Roman military matters are usefully dealt with by S. Johnson, *Later Roman Britain* (1980), and by D.A. Welsby, *The Roman military defence of the British provinces in its later phases*, British Archaeological Reports, British Series 101 (1982). See also T.F.C. Blagg and A.C. King (eds), *Military and Civilian in Roman Britain*, British Archaeological Reports, British Series

136 (1984), and P.J. Casey (ed.), *The end of Roman Britain*, British Archaeological Reports, British Series 71 (1979).

Towns
For towns there are J.S. Wacher, *The towns of Roman Britain* (1975), W. Rodwell and T. Rowley (eds), *Small towns of Roman Britain*, British Archaeological Reports, British Series 15 (1975), and now F. Grew and B. Hobley (eds), *Roman urban topography in Britain and the western Empire*, Council for British Archaeology Research Report 59 (1985).

Villas and the countryside
For villas see A.L.F. Rivet (ed.), *The Roman Villa in Britain* (1969) and M. Todd (ed.), *Studies in the Romano-British villa* (1978). For the countryside D. Miles (ed.), *The Romano-British countryside*, British Archaeological Report, British series 103 (1982), and C.W. Phillips (ed.) *The Fenland in Roman Times*, Royal Geographical Society Research Memoir no.5 (1970).

Art and Religion
Art and religion are now well covered: see in particular E. and J.R. Harris, *The oriental cults in Roman Britain* (1965), M. Henig, *Religion in Roman Britain* (1984), J.Munby and M. Henig (eds) *Roman life and art in Britain*, British Archaeological Reports, British series 41 (1977), D.S. Neal, *Roman mosaics in Britain*, Britannia Monographs no.1 (1981), W. Rodwell (ed.) *Temples, churches and religion: recent research in Roman Britain*, British Archaeological Reports, British series 77 (1980), C. Thomas, *Christianity in Roman Britain* (1981) and J.M.C. Toynbee, *Art in Britain under the Romans* (1964). C.M. Johns and T.W. Potter, *The Thetford Treasure* (1983) is a very detailed study of an important late-Roman group of gold and silver objects, and the British Museum collections are summarised in the *Guide to the Antiquities of Roman Britain* (1958, 1964), and now in T.W. Potter, *Roman Britain* (1983). There has been a plethora of publications on pottery: J. Dore and K. Greene (eds), *Roman pottery studies in Britain and beyond*, British Archaeological Reports, International series 30 (1977), and A.C. and A.S. Anderson (eds) *Roman pottery research in Britain and north-west Europe*, British Archaeological Reports, International series 123 (1981) are Festschriften for two great pottery scholars, John Gillam and Graham Webster, and illustrate the range.

Excavations
Annual site reports, and much more, will be found in the *Journal of Roman Studies* until 1970, and thereafter in *Britannia*, and there are innumerable site monographs. Some of the most important include P.T. Bidwell, *The legionary bath-house and basilica and forum at Exeter* (1979); G.C. Boon, *Silchester, the Roman town of Calleva* (1974); A.K. Bowman and J.D. Thomas. *Vindolanda: the Latin writing-tablets*, Britannia Monograph no.4 (1983), G. Clarke, *The Roman cemetery at Lankhills* (1979); B.W. Cunliffe, *Excavations at Fishbourne* (1971); B.W. Cunliffe, *Excavations at Potchester* I (1975); S.S. Frere, *Verulamium Excavations* I (1972); II (1983), III (1984); M.G. Jarrett and S. Wrathmell, *Whitton, an Iron Age and Roman farmstead in South Glamorgan* (1981); W.H. Manning, *Report on the excavations at*

Usk, the fortress excavations (1981); G.W. Meates, *The Roman villa at Lullingstone, Kent* (1979); R. Merrifield, *London, city of the Romans* (1983); D.S. Neal, *The excavation of the Roman villa in Gadebridge Park, Hemel Hempstead* (1974); Ian Richmond, *Hod Hill* (1968); I.M. Stead, *Excavations at Winterton Roman villa* (1976).

3. Anglo-Saxon England

Suggested further reading

The notes to this chapter (pp. 157–9) refer to a wide range of recent articles and books on individual aspects of Anglo-Saxon archaeology. The short list below gives a number of essential basic recent works in the field which provide background and starting points for further reading:

Ahrens, C. (ed.), *Sachsen und Angelsachsen* (1978).
Campbell, J. (ed.), *The Anglo-Saxons* (1982).
British Academy Corpus of Anglo-Saxon Sculpture, regional volumes in progress (1984–).
Hill, D., *An Atlas of Anglo-Saxon England* (1981).
Meaney, A.L., *A Gazetteer of Early Anglo-Saxon Burial Sites* (1964)
Ordnance Survey, *Map of Britain in the Dark Ages*, 2nd edition (1966).
Ordnance Survey, *Map of Britain before the Norman Conquest* (1973).
Whitelock, D., *The Beginning of English Society* (1952).
Whitelock, D. (ed.), *English Historical Documents, 1, c.500–1042*, 2nd edition (1979).
Wilson, D.M. (ed.), *The Archaeology of Anglo-Saxon England* (1976).
Wilson, D.M., *The Anglo-Saxons*, 2nd edition (1981).
Wilson, D.M., *Anglo-Saxon Art* (1984).

The major national journals which publish articles in the field are: *Anglo-Saxon England*; *Anglo-Saxon Studies in Archaeology and History*; *Antiquaries Journal*; *Archaeological Journal*; *Journal of the British Archaeological Association*; *Medieval Archaeology*. The German periodical *Studien zür Sachsenforschung* also regularly contains articles on Anglo-Saxon archaeology.

The following monograph series also regularly publish specialist reports and surveys in this field: British Archaeological Reports; Council for British Archaeology Research Reports; East Anglian Archaeology Reports; English Heritage (Historic Buildings & Monuments Commission for England) Monograph Series; Society for Medieval Archaeology Monograph Series.

4. Technology, towns, castles and churches

General

The principal general surveys are Colin Platt, *Medieval England* (1978); Helen Clarke, *The Archaeology of Medieval England* (1984); and John M. Steane, *The Archaeology of Medieval England and Wales* (1985). For regional cultures see E.M. Jope, 'Regional cultures of medieval Britain' in *Culture and Environment, Studies presented to Sir Cyril Fox* (1963), pp. 327–50. The best initial survey of medieval objects is J. Ward Perkins (ed.), *London*

Museum *Medieval Catalogue* (1940), though this has now been supplemented by finds reports from many excavations, both urban and rural. J.P. Allan, *Medieval and post medieval finds from Exeter 1971–1980* (1984) is an example of the more recent treatment of finds. Annual reports of work in medieval archaeology are published in the Medieval Britain section of *Medieval Archaeology* (1957 onwards).

Industry

The best recent bibliography is in D.W. Crossley (ed.), *Medieval Industry* (1981), where there are papers on milling (pp. 1–16), iron smelting (pp. 29–42), blacksmithing (pp. 51–63), bronze-smithing (pp. 63–72), pottery (pp. 96–126) and glass (pp. 143–51). For ironworking see J.H. Money, 'Medieval iron workings in Minepit Wood Rotherfield Sussex', *Medieval Archaeology* xv (1971), p. 86, and D.W. Crossley, *The Bewl Valley Ironworks c. 1300–1730 AD* (1975). A comprehensive survey of ironmaking in the Weald is H. Cleere and D.W. Crossley, *The iron industry of the Weald* (1985).

Trade

For the road system see B.P. Hindle, 'Roads and Tracks', in L. Cantor (ed.), *English Medieval Landscape* (1982), pp. 193–217. Two studies of distribution are S. Moorhouse, 'Documentary evidence and its potential for understanding the inland movement of medieval pottery', *Medieval ceramics 7* (1983), pp. 45–87; and A. Vince, 'The Medieval and post medieval ceramic industry of the Malvern region: the study of a ware and its distribution' in D.P.S. Peacock (ed.), *Pottery and Early Commerce* (1977), pp. 275–305.

Towns

For the development of urban archaeology see M. Biddle, 'Archaeology and the history of British towns' *Antiquity, 42* (1968) and C.M. Heighway, *Erosion of History: Archaeology and Planning in Towns* (1972). General surveys are M.W. Barley (ed.), *Plans and Topography of Medieval Towns in England and Wales* (1975); M.W. Barley (ed.), *European Towns: their archaeology and early history* (1977); and C. Platt, *The English Medieval Town* (1979). For waterfronts and their implications for trade see G. Milne and B. Hobley, *Waterfront archaeology in Britain and Northern Europe* (1981). The best recent summary is J.A. Schofield, *Recent archaeological research in English towns* (1981). An important survey of new towns is M.W. Beresford *New Towns of the Middle Ages* (1967). For specific towns in England see M.O.H. Carver, 'Three Saxo-Norman tenements in Durham City', *Medieval Archaeology 33* (1979); R. Shoesmith, *Hereford City Excavations: excavations at Castle Green* (1980) and *Hereford City Excavations: excavations on and close to the defences* (1982); H. Clarke and A. Carter, *Excavations in Kings Lynn 1963–1970* (1977); R.H. Jones, *Medieval Houses at Flaxengate Lincoln* (1980); J. Schofield and J. Dyson, *Archaeology of the City of London* (1981) and G. and C. Milne, *Medieval waterfront development at Trig Lane, London* (1982); J.H. Williams, *St Peters St Northampton* (1979); C.P.S. Platt and R. Coleman Smith, *Excavations in Medieval Southampton* (1975); M. Biddle, *Winchester in the early Middle Ages* (1976) and the series of

interim reports in *Antiquaries Journal* 1964–72 (listed in
H. Clarke above); G. Andrews, 'Archaeology in York an
assessment', in P.V. Addyman and V.E. Black (eds), *Archaeological
Papers presented to M.W. Barley* (1984), pp. 173–208. For
Scotland see J.C. Murray (ed.), *Excavations in the medieval burgh
of Aberdeen 1973–81* (1982).

Castles
The main surveys and bibliographies are J.R. Kenyon, *Castles,
town defences, and artillery fortifications in Britain: a bibliography*,
1: 1947–74, with appendix to 1977 (1978), 2: 1977–82
(1983), and D.J.C. King, *Castellarium Anglicanum: an index and
bibliography of the Castles of England, Wales and the Islands* (1983).
For specific castles see B. Hope Taylor, 'The Excavation of a
motte at Abinger, Surrey' *Archaeological Journal* 107 (1950),
pp. 15–43; J.G. Coad and A.D.F. Streeten, 'Excavations at Castle
Acre, Norfolk 1972–77: country house and castle of the Norman
Earls of Surrey', *Archaeological Journal* 139 (1982), pp. 138–301;
P.A. Barker and R. Higham, *Hen Domen Montgomery a timber
castle on the English Welsh border* (1982); B.K. Davison, 'Castle
Neroche: an abandoned Norman fortress in South Somerset',
Somerset Archaeology and Natural History 116 (1972), pp. 16–58;
P. Mayes and L.A.S. Butler, *Sandal Castle Excavations 1964–73*
(1983). For Farnham see M.W. Thompson, 'Recent excavations
in the keep of Farnham Castle Surrey', *Medieval Archaeology* 4
(1960), pp. 81–94. For the reports on the Royal Archaeological
Institute's Research project into the origins of the castle in
England see A. Saunders (ed.), 'Five Castle Excavations',
Archaeological Journal 134 (1977), pp. 1–156.

Churches and Monasteries
The best bibliography for churches is contained in R. Morris,
The Church in British Archaeology (1983). A general survey is
W.J. Rodwell, *The archaeology of the English church* (1981). For
Asheldam see P.J. Drury and G.O. Pratt, 'Investigations at
Asheldam, Essex', *Antiquaries Journal* 58 (1978), pp. 133–51.
An overall survey of the recent results of monastic archaeology
is lacking, but for friaries see L. Butler, 'Houses of the Mendicant
Orders in Britain: recent archaeological work' in P.V. Addyman
and V.E. Black (eds), *Archaeological Papers from York presented to
M.W. Barley* (1984), pp. 124–36. For particular sites see J.E.
Mellar and T. Pearce, *The Austin Friars, Leicester* (1981); P.A.
Rahtz and S.M. Hirst, *Bordesley Abbey* (1976), and S.M. Hirst,
D.A. Walsh and S.M. Wright, *Bordesley Abbey 2* (1983);
P. Greene, *Norton Priory* (1972) and *Current Archaeology* 43
(1974), pp. 246–50; 70 (1980), pp. 343–9. For South Witham
see P. Mayes, *Current Archaeology* 9 (1968), pp. 232–7. The
excavations of York Minster are published in *Royal Commission
on Historical Monuments*, York, vol. II.

Post-medieval Britain
Annual surveys of post-medieval archaeological work are
published in *Post Medieval Archaeology* from 1967. For royal
palaces and castles of the Tudor period see H.M. Colvin (ed.),
History of the Kings Works IV, 1485–1660, Part II (1982); for
Nonsuch see pp. 179–205, for Camber Castle, pp. 415–47. A
useful appraisal of the development of artillery fortifications before

1539 is contained in J.R. Kenyon, 'Early artillery fortifications in
England and Wales', *Archaeological Journal* 138 (1981),
pp. 205–40. The report on Nonsuch is M. Biddle, 'Nonsuch
Palace 1959–60: an interim report', *Surrey Archaeological
Collections* 58 (1961), pp. 1–20, and the decoration is discussed
in M. Biddle, 'Nicolas Bellin of Modena', *Journal of the British
Archaeological Association* 29 (1966), pp. 106–21.

Environmental Evidence
An indication of the state of this study in an urban context is
A.R. Hall and H.K. Kenward, *Environmental Archaeology in the
urban context* (1982). Specific studies are T. O'Connor, '*Animal
bones from Flaxengate Lincoln c. 870–1500* (1982) and M. Maltby,
Animal bones from Exeter (1979).

5. The Medieval Countryside

Landscape
The pioneer work is W.G. Hoskins, *The Making of the English
Landscape* (1955). This was followed by a series of *Landscape*
volumes for many counties. M. Beresford, *History on the Ground*
(1957) describes six journeys into the medieval landscape. For
more recent work see the volumes of *Landscape History* published
since 1979. For a personal account of forty years in the field see
M.W. Beresford, 'Mapping the Medieval Landscape', in
S.J. Woodell (ed.), *The English Landscape* (1985), pp. 106–28.

Sources
For documents, M.W. Beresford, *The Lost Villages of England*
(1954, reprinted 1984) is the pioneer survey of the historical
evidence for changing medieval settlement; C. Dyer, *Lords and
Peasants in a Changing Society: The Estates of the Bishopric of
Worcester 680–1540* (1980) is a regional survey of the long-
term social and economic changes in the medieval countryside;
P.D.A. Harvey, *A Medieval Oxfordshire Village: Cuxham
1240–1400* (1965) shows how documents can throw
considerable light on aspects of medieval life in a classic Midland
manor. For aerial photography, M.W. Beresford and
J.K.S. St Joseph, *Medieval England: An Aerial Survey* (1958,
2nd edn 1979) compares aerial photographs with maps and
documents to give a fresh understanding of medieval settlement.
For fieldwork, C. Taylor, *Fieldwork in Medieval Archaeology*
(1974) and M. Aston and T. Rowley, *Landscape Archaeology: An
Introduction to Fieldwork Techniques on Post-Roman Landscapes*
(1974) show the importance of fieldwork in our understanding
of the medieval landscape.

Settlement development
C. Taylor, *Village and Farmstead: A History of Rural Settlement in
England* (1983) puts the development of medieval settlement in a
wide chronological setting; P. Sawyer (ed.), *English Medieval
Settlement* (1979) gives more detailed evidence for various aspects
of medieval settlement. The results of the latest research are in
the papers of two Oxford Conferences, Margaret L. Faull (ed.),
Studies in Late Anglo-Saxon Settlement (1984) and Della Hooke,
Medieval Villages (1985). For regional studies see P. Wade-Martins,
Village Sites in Launditch Hundred, East Anglian Archaeology 10

(1980), and M.L. Faull and S.A. Moorhouse (eds), *West Yorkshire: an Archaeological Survey to AD. 1500* (1981).

For medieval settlement plans, B.K. Roberts, *Rural Settlement in Britain* (1977) gives a general survey of the many forms of settlement plans; *Royal Commission on Historical Monuments (England), Northamptonshire* 1–4 (1975–82) demonstrates the wide range of village plans and changes to them in a single county. Ann Ellison, *Medieval Villages in South-east Somerset* (1983) surveys the archaeological implications of development within ninety-three surviving medieval villages in the Yeovil District.

For changing medieval settlements, M. Beresford and J.G. Hurst (eds). *Deserted Medieval Villages: Studies* (1971) links the historical and documentary evidence and includes a bibliography and gazetteer of excavations; P. Wade-Martins, *Excavations in North Elmham Park, 1967–1972*, East Anglian Archaeology 9, 2 vols (1980) is a detailed excavation report on the major changes in settlement layout over time. For current work see the *Annual Reports of the Medieval Village Research Group.*

Archaeological Evidence for Saxon settlements

P.A. Rahtz, 'Buildings and Rural Settlement', in D.M. Wilson (ed.), *The Archaeology of Anglo-Saxon England* (1976) gives a general survey and gazetteer of excavated Anglo-Saxon buildings. For palaces, B. Hope-Taylor, *Yeavering, an Anglo-British Centre of Early Northumbria* (1977) and P. Rahtz, *The Saxon and Medieval Palaces at Cheddar* (1979) are detailed archaeological reports on major Anglo-Saxon palaces in Northumbria and Wessex. For peasant settlements, M. Millett with S. James, 'Excavations at Cowdery's Down, Basingstoke, Hampshire, 1978–81, *Archaeological Journal* 140 (1983), pp. 151–279, and S.E. West, *West Stow: The Anglo-Saxon Village*, East Anglian Archaeology 24 (1985) are detailed archaeological reports on two of the large excavations of Anglo-Saxon settlements in recent years.

Medieval village excavations

J.G. Hurst, 'The Wharram Research Project: Results to 1983'.

Medieval Archaeology 28 (1984), pp. 77–111, is a summary of thirty years' multi-disciplinary work on all aspects of a medieval village and its development. G. Beresford, 'Three Deserted Medieval Settlements on Dartmoor: A Report on the late E. Marie Minter's Excavations', *Medieval Archaeology* 23 (1979), pp. 98–158: an important upland settlement (Hound Tor) with change from turf to stone-built houses; G. Beresford, *The Medieval Clay Land Village: Excavations at Goltho and Barton Blount*, Society for Medieval Archaeology Monograph 6 (1975) gives results from the Midland clay area where building-stone was not readily available. J. Chapelot and R. Fossier, *The Village and House in the Middle Ages* (1985) puts work in Britain in its wider setting in a most important study. For manors see the annual publications of the Moated Sites Research Group for current work. For a general survey, A. Aberg (ed.), *Medieval Moated Sites*, Council for British Archaeology Research Report 17 (1977); for a detailed county survey, H.E. Jean Le Patourel, *The Moated Sites of Yorkshire*, Society for Medieval Archaeology Monograph 5 (1973); for excavation reports on two manors with a long and complex development from Saxon to medieval times, G. Beresford, *Goltho: The Development of an Early Medieval Manor c. 850–1150* (forthcoming) and G.E. Cadman, 'Raunds 1977–1983: An Excavation Summary', *Medieval Archaeology* 27 (1983), pp. 107–22.

Daily life

I.H. Goodall, 'The Medieval Blacksmith and his Products' and Alison R. Goodall, 'The Medieval Bronzesmith and his Products', in D.W. Crossley (ed.), *Medieval Industry*, Council for British Archaeology Research Report 40 (1981), pp. 51–62 and 63–71, show how archaeological objects can fill out many aspects of daily activities, dress and house furniture and constructional details. For agriculture see T. Rowley (ed.), *The Origins of Open Field Agriculture* (1981), a series of papers on the complex problems of the open fields; D. Hall, *Medieval Fields* (1982), a general survey concentrating on the archaeological evidence linked with documents.

Index